AF566806

Energy Management

Editors

Dr. Parag Diwan
Mohammed Yaqoot

Energy Management / Dr. Parag Diwan, Md. Yaqoot

ISBN 978-81-8274-477-6

First Published in 2010

Published by

PENTAGON ENERGY EARTH
An Imprint of
PENTAGON PRESS
206, Peacock Lane, Shahpur Jat,
New Delhi-110049
Phones: 011-64706243, 26491568
Telefax: 011-26490600
email: rajan@pentagonpress.in
website: www.pentagon-press.com

Printed at

Simran Print House, New Delhi.

Preface

Energy has played a unique role in the development of economy and history of modern times. No other resource has been so critical in shaping destiny of nations, the development of global trade strategies and relationship among countries. No other resources has offered such great promises for improving the well being of entire nations, many of these promises have sadly remain unrealized and which often have turned into curses looming over their future. No other resource had such a huge impact on the geography of our world and the way our society is organized.

Energy fulfils an endless list of expectations that are necessary for our modern way of life to continue for another day. All this depends on energy; electricity for the lights, refrigerator, computer and communications; natural gas or electricity for the stove; gasoline or diesel fuel for the car, bus and train; jet fuel for the airplane; heating oil or natural gas to heat at a home or a building. Electricity itself is derived for the most part from burning coal, natural gas, and oil, and to a lesser extent, nuclear and hydropower. A rather miniscule, but growing, contribution is made from alternative sources such as wind, solar, geothermal, biomass. However contribution from renewable energy is at least estimates about 10% of entire energy needs. This still leaves the bulk of energy demand for electricity generation to be fulfilled by conventional means. Despite all the hoopla, the hydrogen economy, the green answer to the World's burgeoning energy needs, has far to go technology-wise before it is commercially feasible.

Having divergent and perhaps mutually exclusive energy management policies prevents integration into a single, coherent, and consistent policy toward energy management; the world will have to live with a portfolio of energy management policies that fit each nation, not one that applies globally. While it may be possible to develop regional energy policies, such as the European Union or North America, even here there is a great deal of divergence among the individual nations as to their dependence on various types of energy.

We have tried to present a balanced view on energy management without succumbing to the temptation to tell one side of the story. In preparing ENERGY MANAGEMENT we discovered to our amazement divergence of opinion rather than consensus on simple matters such as where does oil come from, the relationship between global warming and the rising concentration of carbon dioxide in the atmosphere, and whether we are running out of oil. Our approach has been to try to represent both sides of a point.

However, we would like to warn the reader that there is a wide range of opinion on energy management issues. Some are far from settled or other are more like questions begging for answers. We would like to thank University of Petroleum and Energy Studies and the resources provided to us to conduct the background research. The material present here is an adaptation and compilation in a structured format of the literature available in the public domain.

12th Feb. 2010 Dr. Parag Diwan
New Delhi Mohammed Yaqoot

Contents

Chapter I

National and International Energy Policy

ENERGY POLICY

Introduction

Energy policy is the manner in which a given entity (often governmental) has decided to address issues of energy development including energy production, distribution and consumption. The attributes of energy policy may include legislation, international treaties, incentives to investment, guidelines for energy conservation, taxation and other public policy techniques.

NATIONAL ENERGY POLICY

Measures Used to Produce an Energy Policy

A national energy policy comprises a set of measures involving that country's laws, treaties and agency directives. The energy policy of a sovereign nation may include one or more of the following measures:

- statement of national policy regarding energy planning, energy generation, transmission and usage
- legislation on commercial energy activities (trading, transport, storage, etc.)

- legislation affecting energy use, such as efficiency standards, emission standards
- instructions for state owned energy sector assets and organizations
- active participation in, co-ordination of and incentives for mineral fuels exploration and other energy-related research and development
- fiscal policies related to energy products and services (taxes, exemptions, subsidies, etc.)
- Energy security and international policy measures such as: international energy sector treaties and alliances, general international trade agreements, special relations with energy-rich countries, including military presence and/or domination.

Frequently the dominant issue of energy policy is the risk of supply-demand mismatch energy crisis). Current energy policies also address environmental issues. Some governments state explicit energy policy, but, declared or not, each government practices some type of energy policy.

Factors within an Energy Policy

There are a number of elements that are naturally contained in a national energy policy, regardless of which of the above measures was used to arrive at the resultant policy. The chief elements intrinsic to an energy policy are:

- What is the extent of energy self-sufficiency for this nation
- Where future energy sources will derive
- How future energy will be consumed (e.g. among sectors)
- What fraction of the population will be acceptable to endure energy poverty
- What are the goals for future energy intensity, ratio of energy consumed to GDP
- What is the reliability standard for distribution reliability
- What environmental externalities are acceptable and are forecast
- What form of "portable energy" is forecast (e.g. sources of fuel for motor vehicles)
- How will energy efficient hardware (e.g. hybrid vehicles,

household appliances) be encouraged

- How can the national policy drive province, state and municipal functions
- What specific mechanisms (e.g. taxes, incentives, manufacturing standards) are in place to implement the total policy

State, Province or Municipal Energy Policy

Even within a state it is proper to talk about energy policies in plural. Influential entities, such as municipal or regional governments and energy industries, will each exercise policy. Policy measures available to these entities are lesser in sovereignty, but may be equally important to national measures. In fact, there are certain activities vital to energy policy which realistically cannot be administered at the national level, such as monitoring energy conservation practices in the process of building construction, which is normally controlled by state-regional and municipal building codes (although can appear basic federal legislation).

European Union

Although the European Union has legislated, set targets, and negotiated internationally in the area of energy policy for many years, and evolved out of the European Coal and Steel Community, the concept of introducing a mandatory common European Union energy policy was only approved at the meeting of the European Council on October 27, 2005 in London. Following this the first policy proposals, Energy for a Changing World, were published by the European Commission, on January 10, 2007.

United Kingdom

The energy policy of the United Kingdom has achieved success in (a) reducing energy intensity (but still really high), (b) reducing energy poverty and (c) maintaining energy supply reliability to date. The United Kingdom has an ambitious goal to reduce carbon dioxide emissions for future years, but it is unclear whether the programs in place are sufficient to achieve this objective (the way to be so efficient as France is still hard). Regarding energy self sufficiency, the United Kingdom policy does not address this issue, other than to concede historic energy self sufficiency is currently ceasing to exist (due to the decline of the North Sea oil production). With regard to transport, the United Kingdom has a historically good policy record encouraging public transport into the cities, but with a huge defeat in the case of train transport, and with the high speed train, which has the potential to reduce to near zero the use of the aero plane into the domestic sector, and with the near Europe); however, the policy does not significantly encourage hybrid vehicle use or ethanol fuel use, which programs represent the most viable near term means to gain control over rising transport fuel consumption. Regarding renewable energy, the United Kingdom has goals for wind and tidal energy, but it has acted inconsistently to stimulate these sectors.

Russia

Russia, one of the world's energy superpowers, is rich in natural energy resources, the world's leading net energy exporter, and a major supplier to the European Union. The main document defining the energy policy of Russia is the Energy Strategy, which sets out policy for the period up to 2020. Russia has also signed and ratified the Kyoto Protocol.

Energy policy of India

India is keen to decrease its reliance on fossil fuels to meet its energy demand. The energy policy of India is characterized by trade-offs between four major drivers:

- Rapidly growing economy, with a need for dependable and reliable supply of electricity, gas, and petroleum products;
- Increasing household incomes, with a need for affordable and adequate supply of electricity, and clean cooking fuels;
- Limited domestic reserves of fossil fuels, and the need to import a vast fraction of the gas, crude oil, and petroleum product requirements, and recently the need to import coal as well; and
- Indoor, urban and regional environmental impacts, necessitating the need for the adoption of cleaner fuels and cleaner technologies.

These trade-offs are often difficult to achieve. For example, the supply of adequate, yet affordable electricity generated and used cleanly is a continuing challenge because expansion of supply, and adoption of cleaner technologies, especially renewable energy, often means that this electricity is too expensive for many Indians, particularly in rural areas. In recent years, these challenges have led to a major set of continuing reforms and restructuring.

ENERGY CONSERVATION

Energy conservation has emerged as a major policy objective, and the Energy Conservation Act 2001, was passed by the Indian Parliament in September 2001. This Act requires large energy consumers to adhere to energy consumption norms; new buildings to follow the Energy Conservation Building Code; and appliances to meet energy performance standards and to display energy consumption labels. The Act also created the Bureau of Energy Efficiency to implement the provisions of the Act.

Rural Electrification

The key development objective of the power sector is supply of electricity to all areas including rural areas as mandated in section 6 of the Electricity Act. Both the central government and state governments would jointly endeavour to achieve this objective at the earliest. Consumers, particularly those who are ready to pay a tariff which reflects efficient costs have the right to get uninterrupted twenty four hours supply of quality power. About 56% of rural households have not yet been electrified even though many of these households are willing to pay for electricity. Determined efforts should be made to ensure that the task of rural electrification for securing electricity access to all households and also ensuring that electricity reaches poor and marginal sections of the society at reasonable rates is completed within the next five years. India is using Renewable Sources of Energy like Hydel Energy, Wind Energy, and Solar Energy to electrify villages. Reliable rural electrification system will aim at creating the following: (a) Rural Electrification Distribution Backbone (REDB) with at least one 33/11 kv (or 66/11 kv) substation in every Block and more if required as per load, networked and connected appropriately to the state transmission system (b) Emanating from

REDB would be supply feeders and one distribution transformer at least in every village settlement. (c) Household Electrification from distribution transformer to connect every household on demand. (d) Wherever above is not feasible (it is neither cost effective nor the optimal solution to provide grid connectivity) decentralized distributed generation facilities together with local distribution network would be provided so that every household gets access to electricity. This would be done either through conventional or non-conventional methods of electricity generation whichever is more suitable and economical. Non-conventional sources of energy could be utilized even where grid connectivity exists provided it is found to be cost effective. (e) Development of infrastructure would also cater for requirement of agriculture & other economic activities including irrigation pump sets, small and medium industries, khadi and village industries, cold chain and social services like health and education. Particular attention would be given in household electrification to dalit bastis, tribal areas and other weaker sections. Rural Electrification Corporation of India, a Government of India enterprise will be the nodal agency at Central Government level to implement the programme for achieving the goal set by National Common Minimum Programme of giving access to electricity to all the households in next five years. Its role is being suitably enlarged to ensure timely implementation of rural electrification projects. Targeted expansion in access to electricity for rural households in the desired timeframe can be achieved if the distribution licensees recover at least the cost of electricity and related O&M expenses from consumers, except for lifeline support to households below the poverty line who would need to be adequately subsidized. Subsidies should be properly targeted at the intended beneficiaries in the most efficient manner. Government recognizes the need for providing necessary capital subsidy and soft long-term debt finances for investment in rural electrification as this would reduce the cost of supply in rural areas. Adequate funds would need to be made available for the same through the Plan process. Also commensurate organizational support would need to be created for timely implementation. The Central Government would assist the State Governments in achieving this. Necessary institutional framework would need to be put in place not only to ensure creation of rural electrification infrastructure but also to operate and maintain supply system for securing reliable power supply to consumers. Responsibility of operation & maintenance and cost recovery could be discharged by utilities through appropriate arrangements with Panchayats, local authorities, NGOs and other franchisees etc. The gigantic task of rural electrification requires appropriate cooperation among various agencies of the State Governments, Central Government and participation of the community. Education and awareness programmes would be essential for creating demand for electricity and for achieving the objective of effective community participation.

Electricity Industry

Several new capacity additions have been facing various problems, resulting in severe power shortage in India. The electricity industry has been restructured by the Electricity Act 2003, which unbundles the vertically integrated electricity supply utilities in each state of India into a transmission utility, and a number of generating and distribution utilities. Electricity Regulatory Commissions in each state set tariffs for electricity sales. The Act also enables open access on the transmission system, allowing any consumer (with a load of greater than 1 MW) to buy electricity from any generator. Significantly, it also requires each Regulatory Commission to specify the minimum percentage of electricity that each distribution utility must source from renewable energy sources. The introduction of Availability based tariff has brought about stability to a great extent in the Indian transmission grids.

Alternative Bio-Diesel Sources

The former President of India, Dr. Abdul Kalam, is one of the strong advocaters of Jatropha cultivation for production of bio-diesel. In his recent speech, the President said that out of the 600,000 km^2 of waste land that is available in India over 300,000 km^2 is suitable for Jatropha cultivation. Once this plant is grown the plant has a useful lifespan of several decades. During it life Jatropha requires very little water when compared to other cash crops. For plan for supplying incentives to encourage the use of Jatropha has been implemented.

Wind Power

The once-impoverished village of Muppandal benefited from the building of the nearby Muppandal wind farm, a renewable energy source, which supplies the villagers with electricity for work. The village had been selected as the showcase for India's $2 billion clean energy program which provides foreign companies with tax breaks for establishing fields of wind turbines in the area. Now huge power-producing windmills tower over the palm trees. The village has attracted wind energy producing companies creating thousands of new jobs, dramatically raising the incomes of villagers. The suitability of Muppandal as a site for wind farms stems from its geographical location as it has access to the seasonal monsoon winds.

Oil

The state-owned Oil and Natural Gas Corporation (ONGC) acquired shares in oil fields in countries like Sudan, Syria, Iran, and Nigeria—investments that have led to diplomatic tensions with the United States. Because of political instability in the Middle East and increasing domestic demand for energy, India is keen on decreasing its dependency on OPEC to meet its oil demand, and increasing its energy security. Several Indian oil companies, primarily lead by ONGC and Reliance Industries, have started a massive hunt for oil in several regions in India including Rajasthan, Krishna-Godavari and north-eastern Himalayas. The proposed Iran-Pakistan-India pipeline is a part of India's plan to meet its increasing energy demand.

Nuclear Power

India boasts a quickly advancing and active nuclear power program. It is expected to have 20 GW of nuclear capacity by 2020, though they currently stand as the 9th in the world in terms of nuclear capacity. An achilles heel of the Indian nuclear power program, however, is the fact that they are not signatories of the Nuclear Non-Proliferation Treaty. This has many times in their history prevented them from obtaining nuclear technology vital to expanding their use of nuclear industry. Another consequence of this is that much of their program has been domestically developed, much like their nuclear weapons program. United

States-India Peaceful Atomic Energy Cooperation Act seems to be a way to get access to advanced nuclear technologies for India. The 2000s saw progress in co-operation with other countries. The United States-India Peaceful Atomic Energy Cooperation Act, along with other bilateral agreements, should allow US technology to be exported to India, but the issue remains hotly debated in American politics. India been using imported enriched uranium and are under International Atomic Energy Agency (IAEA) safeguards, but it has developed various aspects of the nuclear fuel cycle to support its reactors. Development of select technologies has been strongly affected by limited imports. Use of heavy water reactors has been particularly attractive for the nation because it allows Uranium to be burnt with little to no enrichment capabilities. India has also done a great amount of work in the development of a Thorium centered fuel cycle. While Uranium deposits in the nation are extremely limited, there are much greater reserves of Thorium and it could provide hundreds of times the energy with the same mass of fuel. The fact that Thorium can theoretically be utilized in heavy water reactors has tied the development of the two. A prototype reactor that would burn Uranium-Plutonium fuel while irradiating a Thorium blanket is under construction at the Madras/Kalpakkam Atomic Power Station. Uranium used for the weapons program has been separate from the power program, using Uranium from scant indigenous reserves.

Solar Energy

India's theoretical solar potential is about 5000 T kWh per year (i.e. ~ 600 TW), far more than its current total consumption. Currently solar power is prohibitive due to high initial costs of deployment. However India's long-term solar potential could be unparalleled in the world because it has the ideal combination of both high solar insolation and a big potential consumer base density. With a major section of its citizens still surviving off-grid, India's grid system is considerably under-developed. Availability of cheap solar can bring electricity to people, and bypass the need of installation of expensive grid lines. Also a major factor influencing a regions energy intensity is the cost of energy consumed for temperature control. Since cooling load requirements are roughly in phase with the sun's intensity, cooling from intense solar radiation could make perfect energy-economic sense in the subcontinent, whenever the required technology becomes competitively cheaper.

Policy Framework

In general, India's strategy is the encouragement of the development of renewable sources of energy by the use of incentives by the federal and state governments. Other examples of encouragement by incentive include the use of nuclear energy (India Nuclear Cooperation Promotion Act), promoting windfarms such as Muppandal, and solar energy (Ralegaon Siddhi). A long-term energy policy perspective is provided by the Integrated Energy Policy Report 2006 which provides policy guidance on energy-sector growth.

JAPAN ENERGY POLICY

National Energy Policy and Energy Overview

According to the Japanese government, the "underlying goal of Japan's energy policy is to attain the 3Es, **energy security, economic growth and environmental protection** simultaneously." Japan's most recent comprehensive national energy policy goes on to say,

Japan stands at a major crossroads in terms of energy. The hurdles we must surmount are by no means low, and, unless we change our lifestyles and the socio-economic system, we will not be able to overcome them. Japan may be required to make some painful energy choices in the future. An assessment of the underlying policy measures that bolster these intertwined "3E"energy goals is therefore warranted. Figure below provides a quantitative overview of the Japanese energy situation in 1996.

Energy Security

Since Japan is dependent upon imports for more than 80% of its primary energy supply and 99.7% of its petroleum, energy security is the preeminent energy policy goal for Japan. Measures taken to enhance Japan's energy security will include:

- **Diversifying sources of petroleum** away from heavy reliance on Middle East oil (in 1995 78.6% of Japan's crude oil came from the Middle East).
- **Expanding the use of nuclear power and other "oil alternative" energy supply** sources (i.e., coal, natural gas, renewables) to reduce oil imports. As a result of the policy goal of shifting Japan's energy mix away from imported oil, Japan's nuclear power output nearly doubled between 1985 and 1996, and the portion of Japan's total energy supply accounted for by oil has fallen from over 80% after the first "oil crisis" to 55% today.
- **Implementing strict new energy efficiency measures** for the industrial, buildings and transportation sectors.

Economic Growth

Japan has some of the highest energy costs of any industrialized nation, i.e., it has the highest electricity prices and the second highest gasoline prices in the OECD. These high energy costs were easier to bear during previous periods of high economic growth. With concern mounting over the current economic malaise, the Japanese government seems intent on deregulating major aspects of its energy economy as a way to increase economic efficiency, lower energy prices, stimulate economic growth, and improve the competitiveness of energy-intensive export industries. Over the past three years, Japan has taken steps to deregulate all aspects of its energy sector:

- **Deregulation of the Petroleum Sector**—Japan has enacted a series of laws and administrative measures within the past few years designed to spur competition and lower prices in the petroleum and gasoline markets. In March of 1996, the Japanese government repealed laws that virtually prohibited the importation of refined petroleum products.
- **Deregulation of the Natural Gas Sector**—In March 1995, the revised Gas Utility Industry Law went into effect. This law is designed to spur competition in the natural gas sector. The principal change has been to allow natural gas distribution companies to supply large industrial

customers outside of their service areas. The government has also relaxed other restrictions, enabling industrial firms to purchase natural gas from firms other than designated natural gas distributors.

- **Deregulation of the Electric Utility Sector**—Japan has the highest electricity costs of any OECD nation. The Government of Japan and in particular the Ministry of Industry and International Trade has decided that the only way to reduce electricity prices in Japan is to deregulate the industry and expose the nation's 11 regional integrated utility monopolies to more competition. The Japanese government believes that a more competitive electricity market has the potential to reduce Japanese electricity rates by 20%, thereby bringing these rates more in line with the average for the OECD. A government-chartered advisory body, the **Electric Utility Council**, suggested that the market for large customers should be partially liberalized. The government's efforts to liberalize the utility sector are somewhat at odds with its concerns over energy security.

Environmental Protection

In the 1990s, global environmental problems, among others, came to be highlighted worldwide. Regarding the **global warming issue**, since nearly 60 percent of carbon dioxide emissions that account for the great portion of greenhouse gases are originating from energy consumption, concern about energy has been growing from the perspective of environmental preservation. Environmental constraints have constituted a major factor in working out any energy policy.

- At the 3rd Conference of Parties to the Framework Convention on Climate Change (COP3), held in 1997, express restrictions in the form of quantitative targets were imposed on greenhouse gas emissions by advanced countries. Such limitations were prescribed for the first time from the outside. Given that we will have to continue relying on fossil fuels in years ahead, we are needed to explore possible solutions in formulating and implementing an energy policy within the context of these environmental constraints. In September 1998, the Japanese electric power industry released a report which claimed higher energy consumption in Japan over the course of the next decade.

- A set of detailed and specific measures designed to reduce, Japan's growth in energy usage to a real rate of 0% was adopted. These measures spell out specific actions to be taken in the industrial, residential and commercial, and transport sectors to increase energy efficiency.
- Industrial Sector Energy Efficiency Measures include the introduction of "quantitative targets" to reduce energy consumption at all Japanese factories. The targets calls for an average annual reduction in energy intensity of more than 10%. At present, these targets are to be met through voluntary actions. Firms that are unable to meet these more stringent energy conservation standards can conceivably face punishments, including fines and having the government publicly label them as being in non-compliance. The government will offer **"energy audits"** for these factories to help them identify energy saving opportunities. There are some 70,000 government-certified energy auditors in Japan.
- **Residential and Commercial Sector.** The government is advancing a broad energy codes and standards program for buildings and appliances to increase energy efficiency requirements. This program will, among other things, establish new home insulation standards, "energy conservation labels" for homes and buildings, establish stricter energy.

Japan's Initiatives

Japan is forging ahead with the following initiatives, focusing on the Asian region, in order to realize the basic energy policy philosophy of achieving the 3 E's simultaneously beyond the framework of a single nation and on the regional and global levels.

1. Discussion about Regional Energy Policy

2. Asia Pacific Energy Research Center (APERC)

Conclusion

For Japan, energy conservation is the highest priority in its work to achieve the 3 E's—economic development, energy security, and environmental protection—simultaneously as the basic philosophy of the nation's energy policy. To hold down energy consumption, however, efforts will have to be made not only to improve the energy consumption rate through **conventional measures**, such as an increase in the energy utilization efficiency of equipment and improvements on the thermal efficiency of production facilities, but also to make a drastic reform in all aspects of society, including a change **in the people's lifestyles**.

A basic consideration on the supply side should be to secure an adequate **supply of fossil fuels**. At the same time, however, policy wise support is needed to stimulate the introduction of **non-fossil energy** sources, that have a number of advantages in terms of energy of security and environmental protection. An attempt is also required to form a consensus of public opinion that could boost the demand for these non-fossil energy sources to be introduced on the community level. Moreover, positive policy measures are needed to achieve technological innovation viewed from a wider span of time.

An energy policy should essentially be pursued by each and every country on its own. Still, efforts are needed to infuse more elements of competition and enhance efficiency through a free and dynamic functioning of the market mechanism in order to meet the tendencies toward the interdependence of national economies and the globalization of the energy market. Regarding the energy security issue and environmental problems, the **3 E's should be achieved simultaneously** on the transnational, regional and global basis through a set of measures for supplementing national policy efforts. To this end, multilateral and bilateral policy connection and technological cooperation will have to be pushed ahead in a positive manner. For energy policy-makers, therefore, a major task to tackle in years ahead will be to make the most of the market's **supply-demand adjustment function** while minimizing negative impacts on environment and long-term energy security through supplementing inefficient functioning and externalities of the market mechanism.

U.S.A. ENERGY POLICY

1. Energy Challenges Facing the united States
2. The Impacts of High Energy Prices on Families, Communities, and Businesses
3. Sustaining the Nation's Health and Environment
4. Increasing Energy Conservation and Efficiency
5. Increasing Domestic Energy Supplies
6. Increasing America's Use of Renewable and Alternative Energy
7. A Comprehensive Delivery System
8. Enhancing National Energy Security and International Relationships.

Introduction

In his second week in office, President George W. Bush established the National Energy Policy Development Group, directing it to "develop a national energy policy designed to help the private sector, and as necessary and appropriate, State and local governments, promote dependable, affordable, and environmentally sound production and distribution of energy for the future." This Overview sets forth the **National Energy Policy Development (NEPD)** Group's findings and key recommendations for a National Energy Policy.

America in the year 2001 faced the most serious energy shortage since the oil embargoes of the 1970s. A fundamental imbalance between supply and demand defines their nation's energy crisis. This imbalance, if allowed to continue, would inevitably undermine America's economy, standard of living, and national security. The principal energy challenges America faces are **promoting energy conservation**, repairing and **modernizing energy infrastructure**, and increasing energy supplies in ways that protect and improve the environment.

The recommendations of this report address the energy challenges facing America. Taken together, they offer the thorough and responsible energy plan long needed.

Components of the National Energy Policy

- The National Energy Policy proposes and follows **three basic principles**:
- The Policy is a long-term **comprehensive** strategy.
- The policy will advance new, **environmentally** friendly technologies to increase energy supplies and encourage cleaner, more efficient energy use.
- The Policy seeks to raise **the living standards** of the American people.

Applying these principles, America urges action to meet five **specific national goals**. America must modernize conservation, modernize energy infrastructure, increase energy supplies, accelerate the protection and improvement of the environment, and increase the nation's energy security.

Energy Challenges Facing the United States

The national energy policy must be comprehensive in scope. America's failure over the past several years is a result of the lack of careful planning and lack of a comprehensive national energy plan. These challenges have developed from years of neglect and can only be addressed with the implementation of sound policy.

The NEPD Group recommends that the President issues an Executive Order to direct all federal agencies to include in any regulatory action that could significantly and adversely affect energy supplies, distribution or use.

The NEPD Group recommends that the President directs the executive agencies to work closely with Congress to implement the legislative components of a national energy policy.

The Impacts of High Energy Prices on Families, Communities, and Business

American families, communities, and business all depend on reliable and affordable energy for their health, safety and livelihood. To cope with the impacts of high energy prices on these people, NEPD gives the following recommendations:

Recommendation

The NEPD Group recommends that he President direct the Secretary of Energy to explore potential opportunities to develop educational programs related to energy development and use.

The NEPD Group recommends that the President take steps to mitigate impacts of high energy costs on low-income consumers. These steps would include:

Strengthening the Low Income Home Energy Assistance Program.

Directing the Secretaries of Interior and Health and Human Services to propose legislation for using a portion of oil and gas royalty payments.

The NEPD Group recommends that he President increase funding for the weatherization Assistance program. The Department of Energy will have the option of using a portion of those funds to test improved implementation approaches for the weatherization program.

The NEPD Group recommends the President direct FEMA to prepare for potential energy emergencies.

Sustaining the Nation's Health and Environment

Energy development initiatives will be successful only if they adequately address their impacts on natural resource values. Federal, state, tribal and local governments have the responsibility of protecting unique natural resources and environmental values.

Recommendation

The NEPD Group recommends that the President direct the EPA Administrator to work with Congress to propose legislation that would establish a flexible, market-based program to significantly reduce and **cap emissions of sulfur dioxide, nitrogen oxides, and mercury** from electric power generators.

Establish mandatory reduction targets for emissions of three main pollutants; sulfur dioxide, nitrogen oxides, and mercury.

Phase in reductions over a reasonable period of time, similar to the successful **acid rain reduction program** established by the 1990 amendments to the Clean Air Act.

Provide regulatory certainty to allow utilities to make modifications to their plants without fear of net litigation.

Environmental Protection Agency's (EPA) Acid Rain Program, enacted as part of the 1990 Clean Air Act Amendments, is the only program directed primarily at reducing air emissions from electric utilities.

The NEPD Group recommends that the President direct the Secretary of the Interior to work with Congress to create the **"Royalties Conservation Fund"** which will earmark potentially billions of dollars in royalties from new oil and gas production in ANWR to fund land conservation efforts and eliminate the maintenance and improvements backlog on federal lands.

The NEPD Group recommends that the President issue an Executive Order to rationalize permitting for energy production in an environmentally sound manner by directing federal agencies to expedite permits and other federal actions necessary for energy-related project approvals on a national basis.

Increasing Energy Conservation and Efficiency

Energy efficiency is the ability to use less energy to produce the same amount of lighting, heating transportation, and other energy service. **Conservation and energy efficiency** are important elements of a sound energy policy. The federal government can also promote energy efficiency and conservation through programs like the **Energy Star program**, which is a joint program run by the Department of Energy and the EPA. Energy Star is only awarded to appliances that significantly exceed minimum energy efficiency standards. It does not extend to all products. Energy efficiency would be further promoted if the Energy Star program were expanded to a broader range of products.

Recommendations

The NEPD Group recommends that the President directs the Office of Science and Technology Policy and the President's Council of Advisors on Science and Technology to review and make recommendations on using the nation's energy resources more efficiently.

The NEPD Group recommends that the President directs the Secretary of Energy to conduct a review of current funding of energy efficiency **research and development programs** in light of the recommendations of this report.

The NEPD Group recommends that the President directs the Secretary of Energy to promote greater energy efficiency.

Expand the Energy Star program beyond office buildings to include schools, retail buildings, health care facilities, and homes.

Extend the Energy Star labeling program to additional products, applications, and services.

Strengthen Department of Energy public education programs relating to energy efficiency.

The NEPD Group recommends that the President direct the Secretary of Energy to improve the energy efficiency of appliances by supporting **expanding scope of the appliance standards program**.

The NEPD Group recommends that the President direct heads of executive departments and agencies to take appropriate actions to conserve energy use at their facilities to the maximum extent consistent with the effective discharge of public responsibilities. Agencies located in regions where electricity shortages are possible should **conserve especially during periods of peak demand**.

The NEPD Group recommends that the President and the Secretary of the Treasury to work with Congress to encourage increased energy efficiency through **combined heat and power (CHP) projects** by shortening the depreciation life for CHP projects or providing an **investment tax credit**.

The NEPD Group recommends that the President direct the Secretary of Transportation to review and provide recommendations on establishing **Corporate Average Fuel Economy (CAFÉ)** standards.

The NEPD Group recommends that the President direct the Secretary of Transportation to review and promote technologies and strategies and work with Congress on legislation to increase energy efficiency with a **tax credit for fuel efficient vehicles**.

The NEPD Group recommends that the President direct the EPA and DOT to develop ways to reduce demand for petroleum transportation fuels by establishing a program of **reduce emissions and fuel consumption**.

The NEPD Group recommends that the President direct the Secretary of Energy to establish a national priority for improving energy efficiency pursued though the **combined efforts of industry, consumers,** and federal, state, and local governments.

The NEPD Group recommends that the President direct the

EPA Administrator to develop and implement a strategy to increase public awareness about energy efficiency.

Increasing Domestic Energy Supplies

America's energy strength lies in abundance and diversity of its energy resources, and in it its technological leadership in develcping and efficiently using these resources. One of the most important energy issues facing the Administration and Congress is electricity to provide ample **electricity supplies at reasonable prices**, states are opening their retail markets to competition. This is the most recent step in a long **transition from reliance on regulation to reliance on competitive forces**. This transition began in 1978 with enactment of the Public Utility Regulatory Policies Act, which promoted independent electricity generation. Open-access transmission policies adopted by the Federal Energy Regulatory Commission (FERC) in the late 1980s further promoted competition in wholesale power markets. Congress largely ratified these policies with enactment of the **Energy Policy Act of 1992**, which further promoted non-utility generation. FERC took another large step to promote competition with its open access rule in 1996, which provided **greater access to the transmission grid**, the highway for interstate commerce in electricity.

Recommendations

The NEPD Group recommends that the President direct the Secretaries of Energy and the Interior to promote **enhanced oil and gas** recovery from existing wells through new technology and continued partnership with public and private entries.

The NEPD Group recommends that the President direct the Secretary of the Interior to consider **economic incentives** for environmentally sound offshore oil and gas development where warranted by specific circumstances.

The NEPD Group recommends that the President direct the Secretaries of Commerce and Interior to re-examine the current federal **legal and policy regime (statutes, regulations, and Executive Orders).**

The NEPD Group recommends that the President direct the Secretary of the Interior work with Congress to authorize exploration and, if resources are discovered, **development of the 1002** Area of ANWR.

The NEPD Group recommends that the President direct the Secretary of Energy to propose **comprehensive electricity legislation** that promotes competition, protects consumers, enhances reliability, promotes renewable energy, improves efficiency repeals the Public Utility Holding Company Act, and reforms that Public Utility Regulatory Policies Act.

The NEPD Group recommends that the President encourage FERC to **use its existing statutory authority to promote competition** and encourage investment in transmission facilities.

The NEPD Group recommends that the President support the expansion **of nuclear energy in the United States** as a major component of our national energy policy. Following are specific components of the recommendation:

- Encourage **the Nuclear Regulatory Commission (NRC) to ensure** that safety and environment protection are high priorities as they prepare to evaluate and expedite applications floor licensing new advanced-technology nuclear reactors.
- Encourage the NRC to facilitate efforts by utilities to expand nuclear energy generation in the United States by updating existing nuclear plants safely.
- Encourage the NRC to relicense existing nuclear plants that meet or **exceed safety standards.**
- Direct the Secretary of Energy and the Administrator of the Environmental Protection Agency to assess the potential of nuclear energy to **improve air quality**.
- Use the **best science to provide a deep geologic repository** for nuclear waste.

The NEPD Group recognizes there is a need to reduce the time and cost of the hydropower licensing process. The NEPD Group recommends that the President encourage the federal Energy Regulatory Commission (FERC) and direct federal resource agencies to make the licensing **process more clear and efficient**, while preserving environmental goals.

Support **administrative and legislative reform of the hydropower** licensing process.

Direct federal resource agencies to **reach interagency agreement** on conflicting mandatory license conditions before they submit their conditions to FERC for inclusion in a license.

Encourage FERC to adopt **appropriate deadlines** for its own actions during the licensing process.

Increasing America's Use of Renewable and Alternative Energy

A sound national energy policy should encourage a clean and diverse portfolio of domestic energy supplies, which will help to ensure that future generations of Americans will have access to the energy they needs by harnessing abundant, naturally occurring sources of energy, such as the **sun, the wind, geothermal heat, and biomass**.

Recommendations

The NEPD Group recommends that the President direct the Secretaries of the Interior and energy to re-evaluate access limitations to federal lands in order to increase **renewable energy production**.

The NEPD Group recommends that the President direct the Secretary of the Treasury to work with Congress on legislation to expand the section 29 tax **credit to make it available for new landfill methane projects**.

The NEPD Group recommends that the President direct the Secretary of the Interior to determine ways to reduce the delays in **geothermal lease processing** as part of the permitting review process.

The NEPD Group recommends that the President direct the Administrator of the EPA to develop a new renewable energy **partnership program** to help companies more easily buy renewable energy.

He NEPD Group recommends that the President direct the Secretary of the Treasury to work with Congress on legislation to extend and **tax credits for electricity produced using wind and biomass**.

The NEPD Group recommends that the President direct the Secretary of the Treasury to work with Congress to new legislation to provide a new **15% tax credit for residential solar energy property**, up to a maximum credit of **$2000**.

The NEPD Group recommends that the President direct the Secretary of the Treasury to work with Congress to continue the **ethanol** excise tax exemption.

The NEPD Group recommends that the President direct the Secretary of Energy to develop **next-generation technology**—including hydrogen and fusion and support legislation reauthorizing the Hydrogen Energy Act.

The NEPD Group recommends that the President direct the Administrator of the Environmental Protection Agency to issue guidance to encourage the development of well-designed combined heat and power **(CHP) units that are both highly efficient and have low emissions.**

A Comprehensive Delivery System

America's energy infrastructure is comprised of many components such as the physical network of pipes for oil and natural gas, electricity transmission lines and other means for transporting energy to consumers. **The electricity infrastructure includes a nationwide power grid** of long-distance transmission lines that move electricity from region to region, as well as local distribution lines that carry electricity to homes and business. **Major industry restructuring has separated electric** utilities that supplied generation, transmission, and distribution services into distinct entities. To facilitate competition at the wholesale level, in 1996, the Federal Energy Regulatory Commission (FERC) required transmission—owning utilities to **"unbundle" their transmission and power marketing functions**, and provide nondiscriminatory, open access to their transmission systems by other utilities plants, which are primarily fueled by local, nuclear, natural gas, water and, to a lesser utilities and independent power producers.

Recommendations

The NEPD Group recommends that the President direct the Secretary of Energy to work with the Federal Energy Regulatory Commission (FERC) **to improve the reliability** of the interstate transmission system and to develop legislation providing for enforcement by a self-regulatory organization subject to FERC oversight.

The NEPD Group recommends that the President direct the Secretary of Energy to **expand the Department's research** and development on transmission reliability and superconductivity.

The NEPD Group Recommends that the President direct the appropriate federal agencies to take actions to remove constraints on the transmission grid and allow the nation's electricity supply to meet the growing needs of the economy.

Direct the Secretary of Energy, to examine the benefits of **establishing a national grid, identify transmission bottlenecks,** and identify measures to remove transmission bottlenecks.

Direct the Secretary of Energy to work with FERC to relieve transmission constraints by encouraging the use of incentive rate-making proposals.

The NEPD Group recommends that the President direct the Secretaries of Energy and State, coordinating with the Secretary of the Interior and the Federal Energy Regulatory Commission to expedite the **construction of a pipeline to deliver natural gas to** the lower 48 states.

The NEPD Group recommends that the President support legislation to improve **the safety of natural gas pipelines**, protect the environment, strengthen emergency preparedness and inspections and bolster enforcement.

The NEPD Group recommends that the President direct the Administrator of the EPA to study opportunities to maintain or improve the environmental benefits of state and local clean fuel programs.

The NEPD Group recommends that the President direct the Administrator of the EPA and the Secretary of Energy to take steps to ensure America has **adequate refining capacity** to meet the needs to consumers.

Provide more **regulatory certainty to refinery** owners and streamline the permitting process where possible to ensure that regulatory overlap is limited.

Adopt Comprehensive Regulations

The NEPD Group recommends that the President direct the Administrator of the EPA, in consultation with the Secretary of Energy and other relevant agencies, to review New Source Review regulations on investment in new utility and refinery generation capacity, energy efficiency, and environment protection.

The NEPD Group recommends that the President direct the Attorney General to review existing enforcement actions regarding New Source Review to ensure that the enforcement actions are consistent with the Clean Air Act and its regulations.

Enhancing National Energy Security and International Relationship

U.S national energy security depends on sufficient energy supplies to support U.S and global economic growth. Major improvements in exploration production technology, as well as the trend toward opening new areas around the globe for exploration and development, have yielded significant dividends.

Recommendations

The NEPD Group recommends that the President make energy security **a priority of trade and foreign** policy.

The NEPD Group recommends the President support initiatives by Saudi Arabia, Kuwait, Algeria, Qatar, the UAE, and other supplies to open up areas of their energy sectors to foreign investment.

The NEPD Group recommends that the President direct the Secretaries of State, Energy and Commerce work to improve dialogue among energy producing and consuming nations.

The NEPD Group recommends that the President direct the Secretaries of State, Commerce and Energy to use their membership in multilateral organizations, such as the Asia-Pacific Economic Cooperation (OECD), the World Trade Organization (WTO) Energy Services Negotiations, the Free Trade Area of the Americas (FTAA) and to reduce barriers to trade and investment.

The NEPD Group recommends that the President direct the Secretaries of State, Treasury, and Commerce to initiate a comprehensive review of sanctions. Energy security should be one of the factors considered in such a review.

The NEPD recommends that the President direct the Secretaries of Energy and State, in consultation with the FERC, to review their respective oil, natural gas, and electricity authorities, and to propose reforms as necessary.

The NEPD Group recommends that the President direct the Secretaries of State, Energy, and Commerce to reinvigorate the U.S.-Africa Trade and Economic Cooperation Forum and the U.S. African Energy Ministerial process.

The NEPD Group recommends that the President direct the Secretaries of Commerce, State and Energy to continue working with relevant companies and countries to establish the commercial conditions that will allow oil companies operating in Kazakhastan the option of exporting their oil.

The NEPD Group recommends that the President direct appropriate federal agencies to complete the current cycle of oil spill response readiness workshops.

The NEPD Group recommends that the President direct the Secretaries of State, Commerce, and Energy to deepen the focus of the discussions with Russia on energy and the investment climate.

The NEPD Group recommends that the President direct the Secretaries of State, Commerce, and Energy to continue to work in the APEC Energy Working Group to examine oil market data transparency issues and the variety of ways petroleum stock scan be used as an option to address oil market disruptions.

The NEPD Group recommends that the President direct the Secretaries of State and Energy to work with India's Ministry of Petroleum and Natural Gas to help India maximize its domestic oil and gas production.

The NEPD Group recommends that the President seek to increase international cooperation on finding alternatives to oil, especially for the transportation sector.

The NEPD Group recommends that the President direct the Secretary of State to reinvigorate its dialogue with the European Union on energy issues.

The NEPD Group recommends that the President promote a coordinated approach to energy security by calling for an annual meeting of G-8 Energy Ministers or their equivalents.

The NEPD Group recommends that the President direct the Secretary of Energy to work within the International Energy Agency (EIA) to ensue that member states fulfill their stockholding.

The NEPD Group recommends that the President direct the

Secretary of Energy to encourage major oil-consuming countries that are not IEA members consider **strategic stocks as an option** for addressing potential supply disruptions.

The NEPD Group recommends that the President direct the Secretary of Energy **offer to lease excess SPR storage facilities** to counties (both IEA and non-IEA members) that might not otherwise build storage facilities or hold sufficient strategic stocks, consistent with statutory authorities.

The NEPD Group recommends that the President direct the Secretary of Energy to **work closely with Congress to** ensure that our SPR protection is maintained.

EUROPE'S ENERGY POLICY

Energy Policy of European Union

European Union consists of countries like Austria, Belgium, Denmark, Finland, France, Germany, Greece, Ireland, Italy, Luxemburg, Netherlands, Portugal, Spain, Sweden, united kingdom, etc.

Present Scenario

European Union has a 44% share of energy consumption and oil continues to dominate the fuel mix. Some 80% of the energy the EU consumes is from fossil fuel. The share of imported oil is about 70% and is expected to increase in the coming years. Most of the oil consumption is for transportation and natural gas is the fastest grouping component. However, coal has lost substantial market. Cheaper, less capital intensive and possibly less risky fuel sources like natural gas could undermine future investments in nuclear plants. Renewable energy plays a small but growing role in the energy mix.

Some of the facts related to EU are :

- Energy Import Dependence : 52%.
- Energy related carbon emissions : 878 million metric tons.
- Energy consumption per capita : 164 million BTU.
- Carbon emissions per &1000 GDP : 0.12 metric tons.
- Energy consumption per $ 1 GDP : 8100 BTU
- Carbon Emission per capita : 2.3 metric tons.

- Kyoto commitment : 8% reduction in greenhouse gas emissions from 1990 levels by 2008-12.

Developments

In December 1995, the European commission issued the white paper. **"An energy policy for the European Union".** Even though two of the three treaties that form the legal foundation of the EU (the European Coal and Steel Community Treaty of 1951 and the European Atomic Energy Community Treaty of 1957) are based on the cooperation in the energy sector, the European commission has not, until recently, moved to create a common EU energy policy.

Some of the objectives of Common Energy Policy are :

1. Strengthening of Economic Integration.
2. Realization of a single European Market.
3. Focus on market integration and deregulation, aiming to minimize its policy intervention.
4. To enhance economic competitiveness.
5. To ensure energy security.
6. More and more job creation.
7. Environmental Protection.

Pillars of European Union Energy Policy

The pillars, which represent the most significant pillars of EU energy policy are:

1. *Utility Deregulation:* One of the most important energy and economic policy goals of the European commission is the creation of a single, integrated European energy market. A key action facilitating the development of these networks will be community wide reduction of existing regulatory barriers and **introduction of competition**.

   Other important developments include:

   - Adoption of a Directive for the Internal Market for electricity in 1996. It marks the first major legislative step towards the creation of an open and competitive European electricity market. Under this law, all members states were required to open at least 25.37%

of their electricity supply to competition. Now more than 60% of the European consumers are able to select their power supplier.

- The council of Minister's adoption, in February 1998, of the European Union **common position on rules** for the internal market in natural gas.
- Fully liberalizing and integrating the EU's energy market will be an exceptionally difficult task because of the major differences in attitudes and existing institutions among member states. However, due to some specific economic and legal reasons, **liberalization of energy industries is now a priority policy** issue in EU.

2. *Energy Security:* Increasing dependence on imports is a rising concern. While, member states have participated in the cooperative crisis management institutions, such as the International Energy Agency, since 1970s.

   The development of the common market and the expansion of the EU provide Europe with greater potential flexibility in responding to external supply interruptions.

   Thus, objections of EU policy with regard to energy security are to ensure **sufficient community coordination during crisis**, to reduce the cost associated with such security measures and to develop an effective EU—wide fuel stock management system. For this, first a revision of member states' compulsory oil stock obligations to improve readiness for future oil stocks and then the coordination of stock management measures ensuring their compatibility with the internal market, is required. The EU is also seeking to enhance energy security through variety of policy actions aimed at diversifying internal fuel mix external sources of energy supply (a broad portfolio), renewable energy and energy efficiency.
3. *Protection of Environment and Climate:* The commission believes that the goals of greater economic competitiveness and environmental protection are not necessarily in conflict and that policies that move industry to invest in new, cleaner, less energy intensive

technologies will prove an advantage rather than a penalty to European firms in the long-term.

On January 25, 1999, the European council adopted to promote development and deployment of new energy efficiency and renewable energy technologies. European union is also a party to the UNFCCC and a signatory of the Kyoto Protocol. As a result of which, Eu may be the only industrialized region to live up to its carbon reduction commitment, aided in this to a large extent by the closing of inefficient coal fired power plants in eastern Germany and intensive fuel switching (from coal to natural gas) in the UK's electricity sector.

In committing to an 8% emissions reduction from 1990 levels within the period 2008-12 the Eu adopted the most ambitious target in the industrialized world. European council issued a community strategy on climate change, specifying member state's individual greenhouse gas reduction responsibilities.

In 1996, the commission proposed a Community-level carbon tax that would provide an EU-wide incentive for higher levels of energy efficiency and low and no carbon energy sources.

Chapter 2

Energy Conservation Aspects

INTRODUCTION TO ENERGY CONSERVATION

Meaning of Energy

"The word 'energy' comes from the Greek word *energia*, vigor of expression, activity. The word was coined by philosopher Aristotle from the word elements en (in) + *ergon* (work). A century or so after Aristotle the term *hai energiai*, expressing the concept in Alexandria, Egypt. The psychological meaning of energy, 'vigor or intensity of action', was introduced in English early in the 19th century by the poet Samuel Taylor Coleridge; the scientific meaning of the word have sprung up over the past 150 years."

In India the concept of energy as "*shakti*" has been the focus of philosophic, scientific and metaphysical thoughts since *vedic* times. Many verses can be found in the Vedas and other ancient books which eulogies, commend and pray *'shakti'*. *'Shakti'* causes the great movements of the stars, planets and the earth. It causes wind and rain. *'shakti'* is also the origin of fire, heat and light and the power to enable man plants to grow and work.

The term energy presently connotes the 'capacity for doing work'. Every work by body, mind or by machine requires energy and as soon as the energy is exhausted it stops working. Let us take the example of a human body. A human being takes food and water, which are a source of energy for him. This energy is stored in his body and through the muscle system it is transmitted to his limbs, which perform work. The performing of work consumes energy stored and as soon as it is exhausted the limbs will not be able to perform work. When energy is replenished by food, water etc., and the body again attains capacity for doing work and can perform a given task.

However, it is not the human energy, which we are concerned with. The present energy crisis or shortage of energy, which are external to man. The need for external (to man) sources of energy arose when mankind progressed from a primitive to a civilized state. In the ancient times human needs were limited and all of them could be fulfilled with the exertion of their own body. Whether it was hunting, collecting the food or carrying of loads, a human body was sufficient to perform the required tasks. However, the human beings were constantly engaged in a struggle against nature and in this endeavor the first external source of energy which human being discovered was fire. The fire they got was either from the wood or, later on, from animal tallow, which was used both for heating and lighting. Similarly, in course of time, as agriculture replaced hunting as the occupation, human body was not considered sufficient for doing mechanical work and animals were used for performing certain tasks.

For thousands of years, these three source— firewood for heating, animal tallow and other vegetable oils for lighting and draught animal power for other mechanical functions fulfilled the energy needs of the mankind. Apart from these, there is evidence of the use of wind energy in shipping since ancient times. It was probably only through wind energy (which propelled the sails) that large ships transported goods and passengers over long distances. Later on windmills were used in the medieval period to perform certain work on the land. Water mills were also used for the same purpose, which used the hydropower as a source of energy.

As mankind progressed, the wants increased and human needs required greater capacity to do work, which could not be fulfilled by the above-mentioned sources. At this time, fossil fuels were found which fulfilled the increased energy needs of the mankind mostly for heating purposes. The first fossil fuels to be exploited were surface deposits of asphalt, peat and coal; oil from surface seepage and gas venting from underground reservoir. The invention of steam engine by James Watt in the late eighteenth century was landmark for mankind in the use of energy. It was for the first that heat energy (of coal) was converted into mechanical energy through the steam engine. The steam engine greatly enhanced the human capacity to work and marked the beginning of the industrial revolution. Steam engines were initially used for driving a water pump, but later on for such diversified functions such as driving of ships, moving the textile mills and to drive locomotives, which transported goods and human beings on the land over long distances at a scale and speed, which could never be achieved through draught animal power, used earlier. The invention of the internal combustion engine in the late nineteenth century greatly reduced the size of an engine and increased its efficiency which meant a high degree of convenience and high productivity. The internal combustion engine which used petroleum oil (which was previously used for heating and lighting purposes only) as its source of energy greatly facilitated road transportation. In fact, individual automobile transportation became possible only because of the internal combustion engine. Since then the use of petroleum has been constantly increasing and it is fulfilling our major energy needs. As a matter of fact it is the shortage of petroleum oil that has brought about the realization of the energy crisis.

One major use of steam engine and internal combustion engine is in the generation of electricity. Although mankind knows the electricity since long, the controlled generation of electricity was made possible only during the end of last century. The development of controlled electricity generation revolutionized the work processes and has affected the society in a way; very few inventions have done so far. It has several advantages over other energy forms:

(a) It is convenient and has greatly simplified the design and operation of electric driven machines.
(b) It is clean at the point if its use.
(c) It can be easily transmitted over long distances and above all.
(d) It can be very conveniently and easily converted to any other form of energy.

In fact electricity is not a primary source of energy and a

dynamo merely converts the mechanical energy into electrical energy.

Classification of Energy

Various classification systems of energy commodities are in use. Energy is classified by:

(a) Material form (Solid—liquid—gas—electricity—OR coal—oil—gas—electricity)
(b) Technology (Conventional Vs Non-conventional)
(c) Market (Commercial and non-commercial)
(d) Level of energy flow (Primary—secondary—final—use energy)

The above forms can be explained as follows:

Primary Energy: The energy available from energy sources extracted from a stock of reserves under the ground (e.g. coal, crude oil, natural gas) or captured from a flow of resources on or above the (e.g. water, wind or solar power), before such energy sources have undergone any process other than separation and cleaning.

Secondary Energy: The energy available after transformation of primary energy source (e.g. petroleum products, electricity)

Final Energy: The energy made available to the consumer before its final utilization, or energy consumed by the final user for all energy purposes. Final energy excludes all energy lost in the transformation of primary to secondary energy, nergy used within the transformation industries, and energy lost in the distribution process e.g., electricity used in generating electricity in conventional thermal power plants, is not included.

Useful Energy: The act of heat, light or work actually made available to a final user of energy (industry, transport, household etc.) on the output side of the user's equipment and appliances.

Primary Energy Requirement: Primary energy requirement is equivalent to the gross inland consumption of the geographical region concerned. It is equal to the sum of the indigenous primary energy sources together with net trade and stock changes in both Primary and Secondary energy sources. Net trade and stock changes are treated as "Primary energy equivalents" needed in order to meet energy requirements of the economy.

Market, Technology and Renewability: Energy sources are all sources from which useful energy can be recovered directly or by means of a conversion or transformation process. Energy is commonly classified according to "commerciality', conventionality' or "Renewability" which are terms not always used consistently or appropriately.

Commercial Energy: Energy sources that pass wholly or almost entirely through the marketplace. Non-commercial energy is all other energy sources not covered under commercial energy.

Non-Commercial Energy: Cow—dung, firewood, etc.

Conventional Energy: A term that may cause confusion, as it is sensitive to time and space. For instance, nuclear power was "non-conventional" in developed countries 20 to 30 years ago. The "new renewable" (high-technology solar, wind and water energy) will become conventional in 20 to 30 years time. Traditional solar drying, wind and water mills, and animate energy are very conventional in developing countries, but are regarded as "non-conventional" in developing countries. Biogas has been conventional in the People's Republic of china for decades, but not in other developing countries

Renewable Energy: A convenient term for the energy obtainable from biomass, solar radiation, temperature differences that pushes currents in deep oceans or that are found in rocks beneath the earth's surface, are pressure differences that produce winds, neural or man-made difference in water levels.

"Conventionality" and "renewability" are too sensitive to time and circumstances to be regarded as satisfactory descriptions of energy The renewable sources are perennial and non-exhaustible.

K.L.E.M. Model

K.E. Bounding has criticized the traditional model as being similar to the medieval elements of earth, air, fire and water. He suggests that know-how; energy and materials might be a more appropriate set of inputs. However, the more popular model is called the K, L, E, M model, which recognizes capital (K), Labour (L), Energy (E) and Materials (M) as the factors of production, which are indispensable to any productive activity.

Energy Characteristic of Developing Countries

The developing countries of the world differ in their nature and economic characteristics. The same thing can be said about the energy characteristics of these countries. However, some characteristics are common to most of the countries of the developing world. We may enumerate them as under:

Low but rapidly increasing commercial energy consumption: So far as the absolute levels of commercial energy consumption are concerned they are very low as compared with the developed countries of the world. This may be accounted for several reasons i.e. lack of industrialization, lower incomes, lower mobility of manpower, lower percentage of urban population etc. However, the rate of increase of commercial energy consumption is higher as compared to the developed world. This may be traced two reasons. Firstly, an increase in absolute level of energy consumption initiated by the development process and secondly, by increasing substitution of non-commercial sources by commercial sources of energy.

Non-Commercial Energy still the major source: Non-commercial sources of energy are still the dominant portion of the total energy supplies in the developing countries. This is due to the fact that over three-fourth of the population still lives in the rural areas, where even electricity has not reached. Another reason that we may give, is that the income levels of the people are so low that they can not afford to purchase the commercial energy non-commercial energy is freely available for collection and in the urban areas, have no choice but to rely on non-commercial energy, for meeting their energy needs.

Unequal Distribution of Energy: Not only that energy consumption levels are low, they are unevenly distributed. This unevenness of distribution is with respect to rich-poor; urban and regional distribution, with the result that energy consumption levels of some groups and some people are abysmally low and people are not able to meet even their basic requirements. While the energy consumption of poor is only for coking purposes, the rich are able to afford it for comport, transportation and entertainment.

Inefficient use of energy: Apart from lower levels of consumption of developing countries are further afflicted by inefficiency in the use of energy resources. This further reduces the benefits emerging out of the energy consumption to the people. The inefficiency in the use of energy resources pervades in household as well as industrial and transport sectors of the economy. The wooden stove used in most of only 5-7 urban households have energy goes waste. In the industrial and transport sectors also the output per unit of energy input is low. This is on account of both technological backwardness as well as ignorance about the opportunities for wasteful consumption by those who do not have to bear the burden of energy costs.

Energy Dependence Upon Outsiders: Several developing countries of world have virtually no or very low reserves of either coal or petroleum oil—the two major sources of energy these days-with the result that they have to depend upon energy imports to satisfy the needs of commercial energy. No doubt, several developed countries are also dependent on energy imports, yet the economic impact of energy imports is very high on the developing countries as compared to developed ones. The developed countries have adequate economic resources to bear the cost of energy imports but the developing countries always short of foreign exchange, have to face serious difficulties.

Great Potential for Renewable Sources of Energy: On account of geographical reasons, there is great scope for the use of renewable sources of energy in the developing countries. The developing countries are mostly located in that part of the earth where intensive sunshine is available almost throughout the year. There is, therefore, tremendous scope for the use of solar energy. Wind energy, biomass and hydro-energy are also available in substantial amount in the developing countries. In spite of its high scope the actual utilization of lack of technological development and several other factors.

Availability of cheap energy in the past has led to an indiscriminate increase in its use all over the world. As a result the future development process is most likely to be threatened. The phenomenon is similar to the role of land exhaustion that the classical economists had perceived and it will definitely act as a limit to growth, not only in the developed countries alone but also in the developing countries. Although, the classical economist's prediction has not come true so far, there is no guarantee that it will not happen in future. In fact, the threshold level has been brought too near to us. The rapid rise in population and income has resulted in an unprecedented increase in energy consumption and the exhaustion of oil reserves (which is the significant source of energy supply at present) is predicted to be no within a couple of decades. It is probably true what Adlie Stevenson once remarked; "we never seem to see the handwriting on the wall until our back is up against it".

Comparison of Conventional and Non-conventional Energy Sources

Sl. No.	Parameters	Conventional Energy supplies	Non-conventional Energy supplies
01.	Source	Static and stored in earth	Natural Flows
02.	Examples	Coal, oil and Gas	Wind, Solar, Biomass, Tidal
03	Availability	Remain in bound concentrated form	Diffused Form
04	Location for use	Anywhere transferable	Location specific, Non-transportable
05	Cost at sources	Increasingly expensive	Free
06	Conversion process/utilization device/transmission and distribution media	Established/ Commercialized	Under R&D Stage, certain items are established.
08	Cost of equipment	Moderate	Quite high in present context.
09	Scale of production	Large scale	Small scale
110	Skills for production	Available and developed	Interdisplinary, varied and non-developed
111.	Skills for utilization	Developed	Learning Stage
112.	Dependence	System is dependent on outside supplies	Self-sufficient but nature dependent
113.	Safety	Dangerous when faulty	Usually safe
114.	Economics	Availability is costly but harnessing cheap	Availability is free but harnessing is costly.

Energy Conversion Factors

Sl.No.	Energy Type	Energy Unit	Conversion into (Kilo Calorie)
1.	Agro aste	Tones	1598929.9704
2.	Baggage	Tones	1598929.9704
3.	Baggage/Fire-wood/ Paddy/tusic	000 Liters	1598929.9704
4.	Charcoal	Tones	7395051.1130
5.	Coal	Kgs	6195.8536
6.	Coal	Kwh	859.8450
7.	Coal	Million Cal	1,00,000.0000
8.	Coal	Tone	6195853.6352
9.	Coal & lignite	MKCal	1,00,000.0000
10.	Coal & lignite	Tones	6195853.6352
11.	Coconut Shell	Tones	1848762.7700
12.	Coke	Tones	6195853.6352
13.	Diesel	Liters	9244.8860
14.	Diesel	Tones	10093245.4380
15.	Dissolved Acety lene	000 liters	6541033.7250
16.	Electricity	Kwh	859.8452
17.	Fire wood	Tone	3797458.6797
18.	Fuel	Kls	9109.8050
19.	Furnace Oil	000 liters	9819819.8198
20.	Furnace Oil	Tones	10900000.0000
21.	Furnace oil & HSD	kls	9244885.5696
22.	Furnace oil & LSHS	Tones	10093245.4380
23.	Gas	000 cu.mts.	238845.8960
24.	Gas	Tones	14106238654.7906
25.	Hard & Coke	Tones	6195853.6352
26.	HSD	Kls	9244885.5696
27.	Husk	Tones	975000.0000
28.	Kerosene	Kls	8972309.0909
29.	LDO & LSHS	Kls	9244885.5696
30.	LDO & LSHS	Tones	10093245.4380
31.	LPG & Natural Gas	Tones	10792777.3001
32.	Lignite	Tones	3665090.2837
33.	LPG	Kls	637457.5943
34.	LPG	Therms	26142.0177
35.	Liquid oxygen	000Cumeters	579854.1600
36.	Low sulphur heavy stock	Kls	166215960.0000
37.	Low sulphur heavy stock	Tones	10533104.0413
38.	Lubricants	Kls	162447840.0000
39.	Lubricants	Tones	10365911.9136
40.	Naphtha	Kls	13145520.0000

41.	Naphtha	Tones	11488487.6278
42.	Natural Gas	000 Cu meters	9509.8882
43.	Nitrogen	000 Cu meters	59472.6283
44.	Non-Coking Coal	Tones	6448839.2889
45.	Oxygen	000 Cu meters	57985416.0000
46.	Petrol	Kls	143188560.0000
47.	Petroleum Coke	Tones	6448839.2089
48.	Propane	Tones	10792777.3001
49.	Rice Husk	kgs	90075.0000
50.	Saw Dust	Tones	2600000.0000

ENERGY CONSERVATION CONCEPTS

Concept of Energy Conservation

Energy conservation is another name for more efficient utilization of energy resources. If resources are not unlimited and short of our needs, then it is most natural and rational that they are utilized in a way that uses less rather than more energy for performing a given task. Putting another way 'Energy Conservation' would mean that a given amount of energy inputs would produce larger amounts of output than what it did previously. In a macro setting it would imply that nation's energy consumption would be reduced without hampering the process of economic growth. The demand for energy is a derived demand. Energy itself is not that which is of value. It is what is accomplished with energy inputs like controlling the temperature, of a room, providing light, producing heat to melt metals, or providing motive power to do a mechanical work inside a factory or drive an automobile or locomotive, which is important for determining the demand for energy. It is, therefore, the task accomplished rather than energy consumed which provides the economic welfare. Therefore, assigning a value directly to the rate at which energy is consumed will be a wrong proposition. An example will illustrate the point. There are suppose two air-conditioned houses, one is well built and insulated with materials which do not permits heat losses and second one is poorly constructed and permits heat to escape from the house. Naturally, energy consumption in the first house will be lesser than in the second house for maintaining the given level of temperature. By no stretch of imagination people in the second house can be said to be achieving a higher economic welfare than those living in the first house. Energy conservation is, therefore, rationalization of use and reduction of losses.

Energy conservation should be clearly distinguished from energy curtailment, which means using lesser amount of energy per se. on the other hand, energy conservation is not a reduction per se but a better utilization so that a given task be achieved with lesser energy. Curtailment may reduce economic output and well being, energy conservation on the other hand generally increase economic productivity and improve well being.

Objectives of Energy Conservation

Energy conservation may be resorted to on account of several factors. One objective of energy conservation may be to avoid wastages and achieve a higher economic efficiency. The second objective may be to preserve resources to be used by future generations. Preventing environmental deterioration may be another objective of energy conservation. Since all non-renewable energy sources take their toll of the environment, the reduction in energy consumption through conservation will slow down environmental deterioration. Another objective may be to reduce energy dependence on foreign countries. This is especially true of petroleum oil. Since most of the countries import oil, any dislocation in imports may cause serious disruptions in the economy of a country. This may also have serious security implications. Some energy sources have several non-energy uses. Therefore, if the demand for these sources for energy purposes can be reduced greater supply of that material will be available for non-energy uses. This may be an important objective of energy conservation. Lastly, it is said that since, ultimately we will have to depend upon renewable sources for meeting our energy needs, energy conservation should be used for postponing the depletion date of non-renewable sources, so that enough time is available for developing technologies for the economical utilization of renewable sources of energy.

Approaches to Energy Conservation

Energy conservation may be achieved by any or all of the following approaches:

1. Technical measures.
2. Structural measures.
3. Social and behavioral measures.

Technical measures imply a change in the type of machinery tools or implements with which energy is being used. "Two basic kinds of technical approaches are leak plugging and machine switching. Leak plugging eliminates the waste in existing technologies, while machine switching involves the replacement of existing devices with more efficient ones. To insulate a house is to plug a leak; to replace an electrical resistance furnace with a heat pump is to switch machine. To tune up a car is to plug a leak; to trade it for more fuel efficient model is to switch machine". Structural measures represent those measures, which require a change in the structure of the economy so that a lesser amount of energy is required for producing a given level of national income. Social and behavioral measures mean a change in the behavior pattern of the people. The life style of the people should be altered to require lesser amount of direct and indirect energy imbibed in goods and services consumed by the people. Each measure of conservation has its own scope, problems, requirements and limitations.

Technical Measures: Their Scope and Limitations

Technical measures of energy conservation mean using energy with some alteration in the capital equipment. In this the effort is to increase the thermodynamic efficiency level of a machine. Although, achieving cent per cent efficiency level is impossibility, technical improvements over time result in a higher amount of work done by a given amount of energy. Altering the energy using equipment means a certain amount of investment and, therefore, this approach means a substitution of energy by capital. Since, both energy and capital are factors of production, from a techno-economic point of view it is a simple case of substitution of one factor by another. Economically, therefore, energy saving investment is not justified unless the cost of energy saved is more than the cost of additional capital investment. The yearly cost of a capital investment consists of annual interest, depreciation and operating cost, if any. Symbolically, therefore, an energy-conserving project may be taken up only when:

$$E_C > I_i + I_d + OC$$

Where Ii = Interest on investment
Id = Depreciation
OC = Operation cost
Ec = Cost of energy saved

A major component of the total cost of new capital equipment is the interest cost. Therefore, the rate of interest will have an important bearing on the conservation process. High interest rates tend to discourage investment and therefore the higher interest rates, instituted as an instrument of countering inflation has the undesirable side effect of discouraging energy saving investment. It is only a high level of interest rate that is harmful but an atmosphere of uncertainty in the capital market also tends to discourage people from undertaking energy saving investments.

The relationship between energy saving capital investment and energy saved is not linear. At low levels of efficiency (of a machine) small investments will result in high savings of energy. As the efficiency levels increase returns on investment-in terms of energy saved-show a declining trend. This indicates that for every machine (and that can be true for the economy as a whole also) there is an optimum level after which cost of energy saving investment will tend to be higher than the cost of energy saved. If investment is pursued beyond that level it may save energy on a technical scale but on an economic scale it will not be worthwhile.

Apart from rate of interest, price of energy also has an important bearing on energy conservation. If there is a rise in the price of energy then, the value of energy saved will increase. This will make profitable several investment proposals, which were not economical at the earlier low price. Therefore, we can say that arise in the price of energy has a favorable impact on energy conservation and vice versa.

This positive relationship between cost of energy and energy conservation implies an upward supply curve of energy conservation. The supply curve above the marginal cost level has great significance in determining the supply of energy through conservation. This supply can be easily compared with the supply of energy through production. "If our aim in the society is to provide maximal amenities for a given investment of capital, labor and materials, and if the costs are less to save a unit of energy than to provide that same unit of energy, then the investment should be made in saving rather than providing".

The scope for technical approach to energy conservation is limited. Every energy consuming capital-equipment has a life of several years and in some cases several decades and that it is not economical to dispose it of. Refrigerator has a life of 15 years, Automobile 15-20 years and houses 50 years or more, industrial plants also last for nearly half a century. This time constancy of capital stock severely limits the introduction of energy conservation methods. It is always easy and economical to introduce energy consuming efficiency at the time of installation, rather than making modifications later on. The profitable level of energy conservation investment, therefore, would be limited to the annual turnover of capital stock i.e. annual depreciation plus additions to it. It is here that economic growth rate has an important role to play. "Because faster economic growth implies faster turnover of the capital stock, whenever new capital stock is more efficient than the old, faster growth in economic activity implies more repaid adjustment and therefore declines in energy use per unit of economic activity. This phenomenon explains Japan's impressively rapid adjustment to higher energy prices".

Conservation, therefore, is not a quick remedy to face the energy crisis. It is a long drawn process, which becomes effective only over a long period of time. "We, therefore, need to make decisions now to significantly influence the system 10, 20 or 30 years hence".

The scope for technical approach to energy conservation is tremendous, both with respect to leak plugging and machine switching. Leak plugging often requires only a bit of energy consciousness, effort and ingenuity on the part of energy using human beings. A thermodynamic efficiency level of 100 per cent is as ideal as impossible; still the present efficiency levels are far below this to warrant a substantial improvement in it. The developing countries are believed to be less efficient with respect to use of energy as compared to developed ones and hence the scope for technical energy conservation is much higher in the developing countries than in the developed ones.

The scope of energy conservation exists in all sectors of national economy viz. industry, transportation, household and commerce. In industry huge savings can be made particularly in those industries, which use energy at a massive scale e.g., steel, non-ferrous metals, cement, chemicals etc. The developing countries on account of their poor technical know-how, consume many times more energy per unit of output as compared to the developed countries.

Petroleum is used in the industry as a fuel oil. The PCRA has identified the following main areas of saving fuel oil.

(a) Proper storage and handling of furnace oil by avoiding spillage, leaks, improvements in heating and pumping system, draining of water and sludge etc.
(b) Preparation of furnace oil by ensuring proper preheats temperature to maintain the correct viscosity at the burner tip, provision of filters.
(c) Studying the flame profiles and advising on the choice of burners, operation of burners for optimum excess air, studying the draft requirements and instructing operators on the finer aspects of draft control.
(d) Advice on the correct instrumentation and control practices suited to the needs of the unit concerned.
(e) Evaluating the performance of the boilers and furnaces installed and recommending measures for economic loading and steps to reduce blow down losses, radiation losses etc.

Having a steam distribution system, with proper layouts, correct size of pipelines, lagging, steam trapping and air venting, as well as returning the condensate to the process or to the hot wells. Installing flash vessels to use the flash steam.

Improving the design of existing furnaces to ensure that the industrial furnaces especially forging units are built with chimneys, providing insulation bricks, ceramic fibres to keep down radiation losses.

Installation of waste heat recovery devices like recuperators, regenerators and waste heat boilers and furnaces to recover waste heat from the hot flue gases.

Replacement of old, obsolete and inefficient equipment by modern, thermally efficient and less energy consuming units.

Out of these several measures 'Waste heat recovery systems' have been identified as the most productive. Analysis done by PCRA in 413 industrial units equipped with furnaces has indicated that installation of waste heat recovery system would lead to a saving of about 10 per cent of the fuel oil, amounting to Rs.25 crores and the investment potential for waste heat recovery system will amount to Rs.30 crores. Projecting this on a national level, it is possible to save 1,40,000 kilolitres fuel oil annually by installation of waste heat recovery system on furnaces. The savings potential in terms of money would be over Rs.38 crores. The investment needs for waste heat recovery systems are estimated at Rs.60 crores.

In agriculture also savings can by made by improving the efficiency levels of pump sets and tractors. However, here the real problem is not to identify the areas of conservation but more importantly to make the knowledge available to the farmers. A National Productivity Council study has identified "the miss-matching of the capacity of pump sets to the irrigation needs" as the areas where enormous savings can be made.

In transportation also there is enormous scope for energy conservation by increasing the technical levels of efficiency of the motor vehicles. The need for energy conservation is highest in the transport sector because here no other substitute fuel is available at least in the near future. A PCRA study has shown that 'India can save at least six per cent of the total oil consumed in the transport sector through efficient driving practices and better maintenance of vehicles. The introduction of conservation devices can be faster in the transport sector than in the industry because of a shorter life span of the vehicles as compared to industrial plants.

Similarly in the household and the commercial sectors the conservation measures can be introduced to save energy. The majority of the households living in rural areas use their fuels very inefficiently with a thermal efficiency level below 10 per cent. This involves a huge wastage of precious firewood. An improved form of village 'Chula' with an efficiency level of 20 per cent can reduce the fire wood needs to one half.

In the commercial sector, energy is required mainly for lighting and air conditioning. Here better designing of buildings with insulated walls will reduce energy consumptions to a significant extent. The present designing of office buildings and commercial complexes requires continuous lighting, which not only produce light but heat also (the best of florescent lamps produce only 20 per cent of energy as light; the rest 80 per cent is converted into heat). The heat so produced again requires energy for air conditioning. A better designing of buildings to provide for better natural lighting without heat losses will tremendously improve energy efficiency. Technology needs to be directed to develop a glass, which, while permitting light to pass through it, reflects back the heat.

The essence of conservation is to prevent wastages either through leak-plugging, designing or altering the energy using equipment in such a way that the output increases. However, it is to be kept in mind that wastage is not a thing in itself. It is only in a relative sense that this word is significant. "If energy is free, there is no waste. On the other hand, if cost goes up things that are not wasteful today may be wasteful tomorrow. Waste is an economic term and it changes with the situation". Therefore, any programme to conserve energy must incorporate in it the cost effectiveness and the cost includes energy and non-energy costs. Energy conservation is not using less energy per se because other resources, after all, are not of zero value. If in an effort to reduce our energy cost, the total cost increases then although in a physical sense we are using lesser amount of energy to perform a task but economically this sort of an approach leads to reduce economic welfare. It has been aptly commented by Joel Darmstadt, "It is important to emphasize that to achieve conservation it is not sufficient to point to reduced energy use per unit of output or activity. It is necessary to show how such a change conforms to overall cost effectiveness-a calculation depending on the joint use of all input factors (energy and non-energy) and they're cost in a given year".

Structural Measures

The technical measures of energy conservation that we have discussed so far try to increase the efficiency of a machine or equipment. The machine or equipment should be taken as a unit or a sub-system of a bigger economic system. No doubt, technical measures will increase the efficiency of the economic system as a whole through aggregation; there can be measures, which through structural adjustments increase the efficiency of the system as a whole without increasing the efficiency of its sub-systems. They can be called structural measures of energy conservation.

A task can be performed by different modes and the amount of energy required by different modes differs. Therefore, using the more energy efficient mode in place of less efficient one will naturally increase the efficiency of the system as a whole.

For example, goods and passengers can be transported from one place to another by railways, roads, airways, waterways or pipe lines wherever possible. Now the energy consumed per tone mile is different for all these modes of transportation.

Table 2.1: Energy Costs of Transportation

A

Mode of passenger	Mode of passenger	Movement passenger mile per U.S. Gallon
Bus	1,090	125
Railroad	1,700	80
Automobile	4,250	32
Airplane	9,200	14

B

Mode of freight movement	Energy used per tone mile Btu	Tone miles per U.S. Gallon
Pipeline	450	300
Water	540	250
Railroad	680	200
Truck	2340	58
Airplane	37000	3.7

Source: Transfer of Technology, Its implications for Development and Environment. A Study by UNCTAD Secretariat, United Nations, New York, 1978, p. 45.

These tables show how much savings can be made not by any technological invention or modification but by changing the modal-mix of the transport. For the same amount of energy the pipeline will carry about six-times as much goods, waterways about five time, and railways about four times the goods as compared to road transport. No doubt there are advantages and disadvantages of each mode e.g. trucks give a door-to-door service which is not possible by any other mode. However, this in no ways reduces the importance of the potential for energy conservation by changing the modal-mix. At least the long distance goods can be very economically transported by more efficient modes.

Even within the railways the goods can be hauled by coal, diesel or electricity. Here electricity is the most effective and cheapest mode of haulage. No doubt, electricity, which hauls the locomotive, is produced from coal but the efficiency of coal used through electricity is more than when it is used directly in a steam locomotive. Because power plants are able to burn coal more thoroughly than in a steam locomotive. "It is estimated that coal used through electric traction is nearly five times more efficient than its direct use on steam locomotive."

No doubt electrification of railways is capital intensive but since its operation costs are low it can be profitably introduced on routes with high density of traffic. Similarly we know that personalized transportation is much more energy intensive than public transport. An efficient, convenient and fast public transportation system would greatly reduce the need for personal transport and this will go a long way in reducing the energy intensity of the system as a whole. (Even the abolition of control, which will permit a smooth flow of traffic, has been identified as a potential source of conservation by the Sixth Plan document).

Progressive electrification of economy will also be an important means of energy conservation. The big power plants use coal, which is relatively more abundant, and save oil. Moreover, they burn fuel (coal or oil) more thoroughly than when small size motors produce power independently. Similarly, a gallon of oil burnt in a power plant gives more light from an electric lamp than a gallon burned directly in an oil lamp. Another advantage of progressive electrification of economy will be that it will ensure a better utilization of capital equipment than when power is produced independently by several independent units. For example, the diesel engine might run only 40 hours a week at an average 30% of its maximum rating to give an overall utilization factor of 7% only. The power plant by providing electricity to a number of users whose demand occur at different and partly overlapping times, might give an overall efficiency factor of 65%. Thereby, giving a much better utilization of invested capital.

Social and Behavioral Measures

The third type of measures of energy conservation is called social or behavioral measures. These are related to the behavioral patterns of the people and reduce the consumption of energy sources without significantly reducing economic welfare. These types of measures are simplest and virtually without cost because they are behavioral adaptations that save energy without any negative effect. These measures, therefore, do not require investment except in educating the people. As Kenneth Building once remarked, "Conservation is just thinking before using energy". The people may be persuaded to change their lifestyles for reducing the energy consumption. Air-conditioning at a lower level, Car-pools, switching of lights when not in use etc. may be some of the measures coming under this category. An important behavioral method is driving a car at the optimum speed. The speed is known to affect fuel consumption of vehicles significantly. The low speed as well as high speed results in a high rate of energy consumption. In between there is an optimum speed at which energy consumption is minimum. There is need to educate and motivate people to dive their vehicles at the optimum speed.

The demolition of a perceived prestige associated with owning a big car may also serve the purpose. The steps for this may be educating the people and making them aware of the potential advantages of energy conservation. One reason for slow progress of conservation is insufficient awareness of the opportunities.

The scope foı conservation of energy exists right from the stage of extraction to the point where it changes into work-heat, light or motive power. The scope with structural and social measures is perhaps more than the technological measures, indicating an important role of economists in this field. The scope for conservation is greater in non-electric energy using sectors than in electric using sectors because electric use is already relatively more efficient.

Barriers to Energy Conservation

In spite of the tremendous scope, the barriers to energy conservation are many. The first and foremost barrier may be identified as the high cost of energy saving devices and equipments. The buyer is more aware of the purchase price of a device rather than its annual cost. Therefore, he becomes disinclined to spend additional money on better equipment even though it may mean a net saving on annual cost basis. Some purchasers may not purchase the energy conserving equipment, even when they understand its usefulness, because they may not have sufficient funds at their disposal.

If a high price of energy conserving equipment is a barrier then low price of energy is also a barrier to the introduction of energy conservation. The low energy prices do not create enough motivation for introducing energy conserving methods. It is, therefore, often suggested by leading economists that energy prices should not be controlled; the prices should reflect their true economic value. It has been often commented that, 'Low price of power and sheltered markets have fostered a climate in which the need for energy economy is not sufficiently appreciated".

Another barrier to speedy introduction of energy conservation is the lead-time required for switching over from energy consuming equipment to a more efficient one. As has already been pointed out, introduction of more energy efficient equipment is limited to the annual wastage of the capital stock plus accretion to it.

The environmental and safety standards may also come in the way of a speedy implementation of energy conservation programme. We cannot adopt those methods, which are energy efficient but have other harmful ecological and health impacts. For example, reduced ventilation will reduce the heat losses of space conditioning but they cannot be adopted for health reasons.

The unwillingness or inability of the people to change their life styles more commensurate with the energy reduction may also inhibit the energy conservation programme. J.De.Larosieere,

Managing Director of IMF in his address to International Monetary Conference on "Energy and the World Economy" aptly commented, "There are of course some limitations imposed by the characteristics of capital equipment and technology presently used by the existing stock of vehicles and other energy using devices, and by the deeply ingrained habits of consumption".

The lack of knowledge about the scope of energy consumption is also a significant barrier. People often think that the opportunity for conservation is complicated, costly and inconvenient. Adoption of cost effective conservation measures can take place only when decision makers have accurate site-specific information concerning the costs and benefits of energy conservation measures.

The high level investment required for the production of energy conserving equipments may also be identified as a barrier to energy conservation. The equipments are complicated and the required technology is sophisticated. Uncertainties about the future also tend to discourage investment in energy conservation industry.

Another viewpoint holds that conservation by definition being a negative concept is not exciting. Increase in production is more glorious. Managing Directors and Chairmen are more often than not non-technical men. They tend to attach greater value to an increase in production than a decrease in energy consumption.

Similarly, effectiveness of an energy conservation policy is severally restricted because "Conservation requires decisions by innumerable consumers; by contrast increased supply requires far fewer decisions. Thus the prediction of how much conservation is actually achieved-as contrast to how much is theoretically achievable-is intrinsically more uncertain than is the prediction of how much supply can be increased. To be more accurate, since energy supply and demand must balance, what is at issue is the relative freedom of choice afforded by policies that depend upon conservation rather than on increased supply.

It is most essential that the barriers to energy conservation are overcome and energy conservation policies are implemented effectively for the speedy development of an economy. The role of Government in this connection is very significant. Government can create conditions whereby the barriers to conservation are overcome to the benefit of the economy. "Government planning and guidance can be of importance in encouraging economies in energy use both in the public and private sector.

The first and foremost task is to give up artificial control of prices. Even when prices cannot be left free on account of other economic considerations, they should be regulated in such a way that sufficient financial incentive exists to motivate people to switch over to more energy efficient devices and methods. It has been suggested that a tax should be imposed on energy and the money so collected should be used for subsidizing the energy conserving equipment as well as financing investment in energy conserving industries. This will have a two-proned impact. On the one hand it will reduce energy consumption and on the other, make energy conserving equipment cheaper.

The control over or reduction in market rate of interest will also go a long way in reducing the annual cost of an energy-conserving project. The inflation is a contributory factor in pushing up the rates of interest and therefore inflation should also be controlled to promote energy conservation. As the Managing Director of I.M.F. J. de. Larisiere commented, "The fight against inflation is thus at the root of an effective energy policy."

The Government at the social cost should do the cost-benefit analysis of an energy conservation project and social benefits basis rather than private cost benefit basis. The social benefits of an energy conservation programme are apt to be more than the private benefits because an individual will take into account only the savings made on account of reduced energy consumption. The social benefits will include, apart from this, the benefit on account of a physical saving of the resources. A high extraction rate means that future generations will be deprived of resources. If the extraction rates are reduced then future generations are made available a given resource and therefore it can be said to have added to present social benefits. Environmental considerations are also important in this context.

There is need for technical research in energy conserving methods. Since the investments are high and the returns uncertain, the private individuals are unlikely to undertake such a research on an effective scale. However, before such a research is undertaken an audit of the energy consumption process is most essential. Such an energy audit will identify the leaks and the points of wastages. The research can, and then be directed to plug the leaks and eliminate wastages.

Developing a Conservation Culture

The most powerful instrument of energy conservation is probably developing 'Conservation Culture'. The people should be made aware not only of the financial benefits of conservation but also, perhaps more importantly, the environmental and social advantages of energy conservation. They should be educated that they have no right to consume in one generation the energy which has been accumulated in million of years. They must be educated that 'the earth does not belong to the present generation alone'. As Carl Sagan has said. Such awareness, about what they owe to their future generations may perhaps motivate people to adopt a modified life style and use the energy more efficiently. The 'conservation culture' perhaps has a greater role to play than all other measures combined together. It is rather a catalytic agent for an all round improvement in the use of scarce energy resources.

It can therefore be stated that social, institutional and cultural factors are more important than technological ones. We conclude with the remarks of Mr. S. Narisetti, the President of the Institute of Energy Management, Bombay. While addressing the 'Save Electricity'83' conference organized by the Institute of Energy Management in cooperation with certain electricity boards, he stated, "the barriers to achieving savings through conservation are many but most of them are not technological. The barriers are mostly economical, institutional, political or social in nature". He further stated that each programme of electricity conservation is a "co-operative effort where each industry, each consumer and the Government have their own role to play".

A study conducted by World-watch Institute shows that Developing countries could reap huge benefits from investing in more efficient use of energy. The Institute study "Empowering Development: The New Energy Equations" brought out says that by investing $ 10,000 million a year, the developing countries could not future growth of their energy demand by half, lighter the burden of population on their environment and health and staunch the flow of export earnings into fuel purchases. Gross savings from achieving the efficiencies that are currently possible in developing world industry, agriculture, buildings and transportation could total an average of $ 53,000 million a year for 35 years. As against this potential the actual effort and achievement has been low in most of the countries of the World. As an example, only less than 1 per cent of the $ 67,000 million loaned for energy by all development banks in the 1980s went into improving energy efficiency.

In India energy conservation has been made a major thrust area in the Eighth Five Year Plan. In order to give a boost to the energy conservation efforts, a comprehensive 'National Energy Efficiency Programme' is proposed to be launched during the Eighth Plan. This Programme would endeavor to coordinate and organize existing and new efforts and activities on energy conservation in the different sectors of the economy for achieving targeted energy savings of about 5000 M.W. in the electricity sector and 6 million tones in the petroleum sector during the Plan period.

It has been estimated that there exists a very high potential for energy conservation in different sectors of the economy as can be seen from the following table:

Table 2.2

Sector	Energy Conservation Potential (%)
Industry	25-30
Agriculture	30
Transport	20
Household and others	Not given but estimated To be substantial

Source: Eighth Plan, pp. 204-05.

In order to tap this high potential for energy conservation the National Energy Efficiency Programme has been allocated a sum of Rs. 1000 crores during the plan period. The NEEP is proposed to have the following components.

Policy Package would include-guidelines, inter alia on of energy pricing, and fiscal incentive and disincentives.

Financial Arrangements would include provision of adequate funds through financial institutions for energy efficient equipments for the users.

Technical Assistance: Capabilities for technical assistance and Training would be developed and strengthened in the energy supply and user sectors.

Technology Development: R&D efforts though CSIR and other Academic/engineering/technical institution would be encouraged for developing energy efficient equipments and method.

Energy legislation: A new package of selective legislation would be developed incorporating consumption standards, trained manpower, mandatory energy audits etc.

Institutional Set-Up: The institutional set up for strengthening existing agencies at the National, State, district and grass-root levels involved in energy conservation activities will prove this programme. Instead of proliferating administrative agencies, responsibilities would be fixed on the different existing agencies in the energy supply and user department in the matter of energy conservation.

Energy Conservation and Sustainable Development

Energy Conservation has deep and broad relationship with each of the three pillars of Sustainable Development—the economy, the environment and social welfare. It remains a strategic issue that social and economic development can be attained only so long as a secure, reliable and affordable supply of energy is ensured.

Sustainable Development is dependent upon balancing the interplay of policies and their effective implementation to achieve economic, environmental and social needs. Economic growth requires a secure and reliable energy supply, but is sustainable only if it does not threaten the environment; this requirement can be fulfilled by energy conservation.

Energy Conservation ensures sustainable development because sustainable development means meeting the present needs without compromising the needs of the future generations. Since, Energy Conservation refers to the less energy use with more results. It means that Energy Conservation is a way through which less energy sources are used for getting the same output.

Energy Conservation can take place in many ways like: using the inexhaustible energy sources in place of exhaustible energy sources like: coal oil etc., by substituting dearer energy source with cheaper energy source etc.

Energy Conservation not only save the energy sources, it also ensures the sustainable development because by the use of inexhaustible energy sources like wind, solar etc. the reserves of exhaustible energy sources can be sustained for a longer period.

Apart from above analysis, energy conservation has certain advantages which are as follows:

Energy conservation safeguards the energy supplies.

It promotes further improvements in energy efficiency along with further technologies, including renewable energies.

It encourages the systematic introduction of the best technological solutions where energy investments are made.

It ensures high safety standards in the operation and maintenance of energy equipment, plants and infrastructure and putting in place appropriate mechanisms.

Energy conservation reduces the energy consumption, thereby adding directly o the profits or bottom-line of the company.

Lowering the vulnerability to energy prices for unit/ corporate that has made energy conservation measures.

Energy conservation also reduces the need for investment in newer power plants and import of energy.

It reduces the dependence on conventional energy sources like, oil, and natural gas.

It helps in reducing the emissions of air pollutants in most cases.

Thus, it can see that every energy conservation measure will lead to sustainable development. Each measure affects positively the three pillars of sustainable development like the economy, the environment and the social welfare. Energy substitution will affect the economy of the country as well as the economy of the industries; use of non-conventional energy source will help in safeguarding the environment and also will reduce the health hazards and increase the employment opportunities in the society. In this way, energy conservation has multidimensional impact on sustainable development.

MEASUREMENT OF ENERGY CONSERVATION

General Principles

Although, there is a very great diversity in energy end-use technology, it appears that there are certain basic approaches or general principles which apply in a wide variety. Fundamental principles for energy management are an attractive concept because the principles suggest an initial approach to the problem. These principles alone will not improve use efficiency, but they can provide a basis for a rational approach for developing more specific technological responses.

Table 2.3

S. No.	Principle	Relative Cost	Relative Time to Implement	Relative Complexity	Relative Benefit (Typical)
1.	Review historical energy use	Low	1 year	Low	5-10%
2.	Energy audits (review current practices)	,,		,,	,, ,,
3.	Housekeeping and Maintenance		,,	,,	,, ,,
4.	Analysis of Energy use	Low to Moderate	1-2 years	Moderate to high	10-20%
5.	More efficient equipment	Moderate to high	,,	,,	10-30%
6.	More efficient process	,,	,,	,,	,,
7.	Energy containment (heat recovers & waste reduce)	Low to moderate	,,	Moderate to high	10-50%
8.	Substitute material	Low to moderate	1 Year	Low	10-20%
9.	Material economy (Scrap, recovery, selvage & recycle	Low	1-2 years	Low to high	10-50%
10.	Material quality selection (material purities & properties)	,,	1 years	Low	5-15%
11.	Aggregation of Energy uses	Moderate to high	,,	Moderate to high	20-50%
12.	Cascade to energy uses	Moderate to high	,,	,,	,,
13.	Alternative energy sources (energy form & full seeb)	,,	,,	,,	,,
14.	Energy conversion	Moderate to high	,,	,,	,,
15.	Economic Storage	,,	,,	,,	,,
16.	Economic Evaluation — Cost benefit, rate of return, life-cycle costing.	Low	1year	Low	5-15%

The Economics of Efficient Energy Use

The lowest ordinary rate of return on investment must be something more than sufficient to compensate the occasional losses to which lending, even with tolerable prudence, is exposed. Adam smith, 1776 the wealth of nations.

An economy study may be defined as a comparison between alternatives in which differences are expressed so far as practicable in monetary terms where technical considerations are involved. Such a comparison may be called an engineering studies which lays stress on the importance of clearly identifying the alternatives to numerical data that can be compared on a monetary basis. Engineering-economic studies finally reduced to the question "Does it seem likely that a proposed investment will ultimately be recovered, plus a return that seems attractive considering prospective returns obtainable in investments of like risk?"

Ultimately, the decision to go a head with we energy management project such as company policy availability of funds, the priorities of contending projects, the availability of fuel' prediction about future cost etc.

Although it is common to have procedures for the budgeting of investment funds, it often happens that there are no established criteria for comparing proposals. There are several different methods of performing economic analysis, some have advantages over the others depending on the type of problem being considered. Some are simple to apply, but may not give proper results for comply situation. The main types of economic analysis, which commonly used are: (a) Life-cycle, (b) Break Even, (c) Benefit/cost, (d) Payback Period, (e) Present worth, (f) Equivalent annual cost, (g) Capitalized cost, (h) Prospective (interval) rate of return, (i) Advanced methods.

In most of these methods, it is necessary to project future costs to obtain accurate and meaningful results. Historically, labor and material have been increasing by 6 per cent and 10 per cent or more per year. Recently, energy cost has been increasing at the rate of 8 to 15 per cent or more per year.

Basic Concepts of Economy Studies

At this point, it is appropriate to mention some of the main concepts that form the basis for energy management Economy Studies

The study is made from the view of the owners (or investor) of an enterprise or facility i.e., the ultimate pay or benefactor of the savings.

Suggested Checklist of Data for Energy Management Economic Studies

- Investment cost
- Expected economic life in years (or capital recovery period specified by management to be used for energy management economy studies)
- Estimated salvage at the end of life (if appropriate)
- Annual cost of materials
- Annual cost of direct labor
- Annual cost of indirect labor
- Annual cost of maintenance & repairs.
- Annual cost of power & fuels.
- Annual cost of supplies & lubricants

The study is a comparison of energy management alternatives and deals with prospective differences between the alternatives.

- The effects of the decision are in the future and begin at the time of the decision.
- Insofar as possible, the differences between alternatives should be reduced to difference in money receipts and disbursements.
- If there are no economic differences between alternatives, then intangible and subjective differences may be relied up on to choose between the competing alternatives.

Each economic analysis method can be used to compare the relative benefits of several energy management alternatives. However, each method has advantages and disadvantages. Some methods may yield different results for differing conditions, so one should be a familiar with the limitations of each approach as well as the valid conditions of applicability. For example, if computerized economic analysis cooperating several of these standard techniques in addition to including such items as taxes, cost escalation with time (for labor, material and energy) and non-uniform annual payback.

Examples of Economic Analysis Methods

In order to illustrate the various economic analysis techniques a standard energy management comparison problem will be analyzed using each of the main economic analysis methods. The problem chosen is to determine which of two 7.5 Kw (10hp) electric motors should be selected based on the given economic data and operating efficiencies.

Based on the data given for the two motors, the annual operating cost of each motor can be calculated. The yearly operating time of the motors, (8 hrs/day) (22 days/month) (12month/year) = 2,112 hrs/yr. The electricity used by each motor during one year is:

Motor A: 7.5 kw/80% (2,112hr/yr) = 19,800 kWh.

Motor B: 7.5 kw/90% (2,112hrs/yr) = 17,600 kWh.

The annual operating cost of each motor is therefore, given by the following:

> Annual maintenance and over head costs Electricity cost. Thus, the annual cost savings (excluding replacement cost) of purchasing; the initially more expensive motor B is 8,800 per year. But, motor B used 2,200 kWh less per year with the same output of useful work. Therefore, Motor B provides direct savings to the operator of the electric motors, the full used to generate the 2,200 kWh. of electricity has been conserved (this converts to approximately four barrels per year of crude oil in equivalent energy) considering conversion efficiencies.

Electricity Lost: 4/kWh.

Operating Schedule: 8hrs/day, 22-days/ month.

Life-Cycle Costing

As a first approximate to a detailed economic analysis, total life-cycles costs can be used to assist in making a division between competing energy management options. Life-Cycle Costing is based as a consideration of all the costs associated with an alternative during its entire lifetime. If one were to make a decision on motors A versus motor B based on initial cost only (which is often done by most individuals purchasing competing merchandise if the "functions" are essentially the same) there motor A would be selected this type of decision given no thought to future costs and possible future savings of one alternative over another—

	Motor A	Motor B
1. Out put Rating:	7.5kw (10hp)	7.5kw (10hp)
2. Conversion Efficiency	80%	90%
3. Initial cost:	$ 150.00	$ 300.00
4. Replacement cost:	20 yrs. (10,560hrs)	20 yrs (42,240hrs)
5. Salvage Value:	$ 10.00	$ 5.00
6. Annual Maintenance	50.00	50.00
7. O.H. Costs	$792	$704

Life-Cycle Costing is said to be "a first approximation" since no consideration is given to cost of money (interest). It is a better method than only considering initial costs as will be shown. Future costs to be considered are maintenance costs (labors and material), operating costs (electricity), and replacement costs (labor, equipment and salvage, if only)

Table. 4.2: Life-Cycle Costing

Item Descript	Motor A		Motor B	
	Per year	Total	Per year	Total
Annual Maintenance cost	$ 50.00	1,000	50.00	1,000
Operating cost	792.00	15,840	704.00	14,080
Replacement cost	30.00	600	15.00	300
Salvage Values	10.00	-200	5.00	-100
Total Life Cycle Cost		17,240		15,280.00

The above life-cycle costing analysis shows that over the 20 year life that motor A will cost the cover $1,960 more than motor B, ignoring escalation in replacement and electricity prices and not considering the interest rate money used in the investment.

Break—Even Analysis

It is often necessary to choose between two alternatives, Such as motor A &B where one alternative may be more economical in a selection and the other may be more effective for another set of conditions. By holding all but of the points of difference between the two alternatives constant and allowing the value of one to vary, it is possible to determine the value of the variable which results in the two alternatives to be equally economical. The value of the variable is defending as the "B.E.P." for that particular variable. This terminology is derived from business ventures when the investors want to defense the critical variable in the profit & loss functions for their business.

For the motor example, one may want to know (1) How many hours of full load operation are necessary before motor B will be more economical than motor A, or (2) What future cost of electricity will result in motor B being more economical than motor A for 3 years equivalence cooperating works) of full load operation.

How many hours of full load operation are necessary before motor B and as economical as motor A?

Sol: Let X represent the number g hours of full load operation for the two motors BE. Analysis is a useful tool for insolating a particular variable to study the differences between two alternatives so that the decision may be made relative to the anticipated value of the variable and w. r. t. the break-even pt.

The first principle is to review historical energy use. Often the question "why do we do this"? And answer "that's the way we have always do it" flag an area for immediate savings. Sometimes, seasonal variation or scheduling discontinuities are present but unrecognized; the review process brings them to and many suggest ways of combining operations or otherwise effective saving. Historical data are never sufficient, however, since they provide the total picture but not detects

Energy audits are means for investigating energy use by specific processes and marines, and provide sight into inefficient operation.

Improving housekeeping and maintenance in the plant will generally save energy. Well-lubricated equipment has reduced frictional losses. Cleaned light pictures transmit more light. Changing filters reduces pressure drop.

More efficient equipment curve often be substituted to fulfill the same function, e.g. sodium or metal halide lamps rather than incandescent lamps for area lighting. Many types of industrial and residential commercial equipment are now rated in terms of their efficiency. There are wide variations among manufacturers depending on price, quality, capacity and initial cost.

More efficient processes come often be substituted without detrimental effect on product quality. A classic example is a continuance steel rolling mill, which uses a continuous process to produce steel products, avoiding the energy loss involved in cooling.

Energy containment seeks to confine energy, reduce losses, and recover heat example includes repair of stem leaks; better insulation on boilers or piping and installation of recuperates or power recovery devices. Compressed air system leaks.

Substitute materials can sometimes be used to advantage e.g. in low temperature application, low melting-pt alloys temperature materials. A material which is easier to machine or which involves less energy to manufacture, can be substituted for an energy intensive material.

Material economy implies recovery of scrap, reduction of waste and "design for salvage". The powder metallurgy example noted above also illustrates this principle. Product design, which permits salvage or recovery of reusable pasts, motors and components, is another example. Structures, in fact, can be designed for reuse and relocation.

Output Elasticity of Energy Consumption

Output elasticity of energy consumption (Eo) =

Percentage Change in Energy consumption / Percentage Change in Output

The + (Plus) and – (minus) algebraic signs represent the relationship between the two variables. In this case, there are two variables one is energy consumption and other one is output. And energy consumption is dependent variable and output is independent variable.

In other words, output elasticity of energy consumption Eo, refers to the producers responsiveness of energy consumption with respect to change in output.

It is observed that in energy intensive industries Eo is higher. If there is positive relationship between energy consumption and output which means that with the increase in output, energy consumption also increases while negative relationship between these two variables shows energy consumption decreases with the increase in output.

The degree of output elasticity of energy consumption can be classified into:

1. Perfectly Inelastic Output Elasticity of Energy Consumption Eo = 0
2. Less elastic Output Elasticity of Energy Consumption Eo <1
3. Unitary elastic Output Elasticity of Energy Consumption Eo = 0
4. More elastic Output Elasticity of Energy Consumption Eo >1
5. Perfectly elastic Output Elasticity of Energy Consumption Eo= ¥

Output elasticity of energy consumption Output Elasticity of Energy Consumption will lie in between zero to infinite.

Perfectly inelastic: Output Elasticity of Energy Consumption (Eo) = 0 means that there is no change in energy consumption with the change in output.

Less Elastic: Output Elasticity of Energy Consumption refers to the less change in Eo <1 energy consumption with respect to change in output e.g. y output changes by 10%, energy consumption changes, but less than 10%. In this less Eo <1.

Unitary elastic: Output Elasticity of Energy Consumption (Eo) refers to the equal percentage change in energy consumption with the percentage change output. In this case Eo =1.

More elastic: Eo means energy consumptions changes with greater rate than the change in output. In this Eo >1.

Perfectly elastic: Eo means ultimate responsiveness in energy consumption with reference to change in output.

The above contents are analyzing in different ways, the energy efficiency and impact on control of cost structure. Now the further details are focused on analyzing the ways through which the additional revenue can be earned. It will be covering Green House gases, its inventories, keeling curve, Kyoto Mechanism, Carbon Credit Trading etc.

Greenhouse Gases

Greenhouse gases (GHG) are components of the atmosphere that contribute to the Greenhouse effect. Some greenhouse gases occur naturally in the atmosphere, while others result from human activities such as burning of fossil fuel and coal. Greenhouse gases include water vapor, carbon dioxide, methane, nitrous oxide, and ozone.

When sunlight reaches the surface of the Earth, some of it is absorbed and warms the Earth. Because the Earth's surface is much cooler than the sun, it radiates energy at much longer wavelengths than does the sun. The atmosphere absorbs these longer wavelengths more effectively than it does the shorter wavelengths from the sun. The absorption of this longwave radiant energy warms the atmosphere; the atmosphere also is warmed by transfer of sensible and latent heat from the surface. Greenhouse gases also emit long-wave radiation both upward to space and downward to the surface. The downward part of this long-wave radiation emitted by the atmosphere is the "greenhouse effect." The term is a misnomer, as this process is not the mechanism that warms greenhouses.

The major natural greenhouse gases are water vapor, which causes about 36-70% of the greenhouse effect on Earth (not including clouds); carbon dioxide, which causes 9-26%; methane, which causes 4-9%, and ozone, which causes 3-7%. It is not possible to state that a certain gas causes a certain percentage of the greenhouse effect, because the influences of the various gases are not additive. (The higher ends of the ranges quoted are for the gas alone; the lower ends, for the gas counting overlaps.) Other greenhouse gases include, but are not limited to, nitrous oxide, sulfur hexafluoride, hydrofluorocarbons, perfluorocarbons and chlorofluorocarbons (see IPCC list of greenhouse gases).

The major atmospheric constituents (nitrogen, N_2 and oxygen, O_2) are not greenhouse gases. This is because homonuclear diatomic molecules such as N_2 and O_2 neither absorb nor emit infrared radiation, as there is no net change in the dipole moment of these molecules when they vibrate. Molecular vibrations occur at energies that are of the same magnitude as the energy of the photons on infrared light.

It is worth noting that late 19th century scientists experimentally discovered that N_2 and O_2 did not absorb infrared radiation (called, at that time, "dark radiation") and that CO_2 and many other gases did absorb such radiation. It was recognized in the early 20th century that the known major greenhouse gases in the atmosphere did cause the earth's temperature to be higher than it would have been without the greenhouse gases.

Greenhouse Gas Inventories

Greenhouse gas inventories are a type of emission inventory that are developed for a variety of reasons. Scientists use inventories of natural and anthropogenic (human-caused) emissions as tools when developing atmospheric models. Policy makers use inventories to develop strategies and policies for emissions reductions and to track the progress of those policies. And, regulatory agencies and corporations rely on inventories to establish compliance records with allowable emission rates. Businesses, the public, and other interest groups use inventories to better understand the sources and trends in emissions.

Unlike some other air emission inventories, greenhouse gas inventories include not only emissions from source categories, but also removals by sinks. These removals are typically referred to as carbon sequestration.

Greenhouse gas inventories, typically use Global warming potential (GWP) values to combine emissions of various greenhouse gases into a single weighted value of emissions.

Some of the key examples of greenhouse gas inventories include:

- All Annex I countries are required to report annual emissions and sinks of greenhouse gases under the United Nations Framework Convention on Climate Change (UNFCCC)
- National governments that are Parties to the UNFCCC and/or the Kyoto Protocol are required to submit annual inventories of all anthropogenic greenhouse gas emissions from sources and removals from sinks.
- The Kyoto Protocol includes additional requirements for national inventory systems, inventory reporting, and annual inventory review for determining compliance with Articles 5 and 8 of the Protocol.
- Project developers under the Clean Development Mechanism of the Kyoto Protocol prepare inventories as

part of their project baselines.

- Corporation and other entities can prepare greenhouse gas inventories to track progress towards meeting an emission reduction goal.

Keeling Curve

The Keeling curve is a graph showing the variation in concentration of atmospheric carbon dioxide since 1958. It shows that some factors (possibly human activities) are increasing the greenhouse effect with implications for global warming.

Charles David Keeling of the Scripps Institution of Oceanography was the first person to make frequent regular measurements of the atmospheric carbon dioxide (CO_2) concentration, taking readings atop Mauna Loa in Hawaii from 1958 onwards.

These measurements show a steady increase in mean atmospheric CO_2 concentration from about 315 parts per million by volume (ppmv) in 1958 to over 380 ppmv by the year 2006. This increase in atmospheric CO_2 is considered to be largely due to the combustion of fossil fuels, and has been accelerating in recent years, most likely due to increased fossil fuel combustion and the release of frozen CO_2 from melting ice caps and permafrost. This is supported by measurements of carbon dioxide concentration in ancient air bubbles trapped in polar ice cores, which show that mean atmospheric CO_2 concentration was between 275 and 280 ppmv for several thousand years but started rising sharply at the beginning of the nineteenth century. Since carbon dioxide is a greenhouse gas, this has implications for global warming.

The Keeling curve also shows a cyclic variation of about 5 ppmv in each year corresponding to the seasonal change in uptake of CO_2 by the world's land vegetation. Most of this vegetation is in the Northern hemisphere, since this is where the majority of the land is located. The level decreases from northern spring onwards as new plant growth takes carbon dioxide out of the atmosphere through photosynthesis and rises again in the northern fall as plants and leaves die off and decay to release the gas back into the atmosphere.

Kyoto Mechanism

The Protocol broke new grounds with three innovative mechanisms: Joint Implementation (JI), Clean Development Mechanism (CDM) and Emissions trading/ carbon trading which have designed to boost the cost effectiveness of climate change mitigation by opening ways for parties to cut emissions or enhance carbon sinks more cheaply abroad than at home.

Under Joint Implementation mechanism, a developed country with relatively higher cost of domestic green house gas reduction activities, would take up greenhouse gas reduction project activities in another developed country.

The Clean Development Mechanism provides that a developed country would take up green house gas reduction activities in a developing country where the cost is much lower.

Carbon Credit Trading

The concept of carbon credit trading seeks to encourage countries to reduce their GHG emissions, as it rearwards those countries which meet their targets and provides financial incentives to the others to do so as quickly as possible. Surplus credit can be sold in the global market. One credit is equal to one tone of carbon di oxide emission reduced. Carbon Credits are available for companies engaged in developing renewable energy projects that offset the use of fossil fuels. Developed countries have to spend nearly $ 300 to $500 for every tone reduction carbon di oxide in contrast to $10-$25 to be spent by developing countries.

In countries like India, GHG emission is much below the target fixed by Kyoto Protocol and so, they are excluded from reduction of GHG emissions. On the contrary, they are entitled to sell surplus credits to developed countries. Thus, Carbon Credit trading takes place.

The foreign companies those who cannot fulfill the protocol norms can buy the surplus credit from companies in other countries through trading. Carbon credit trading is done in terms of Certified Emission Reductions (CERs). The CER unit I equal to one ton of carbon di-oxide.

Procedure for Carbon Trading

I. **Who is eligible:** Any project which reduces the emissions of green house gases is eligible for carbon credits. These projects can be broadly classified into the following categories. Energy Efficiency, renewable energy, Fuel Switching, waste to energy and industrial process.

II. **Preparation of Project Design Document:** Participants must prepare a Project Design Document (PDD) including a description of the baseline, i.e. the technology to be used and the monitoring methodology to be used, an analysis of the environmental impacts, Comments received from the Carbon Credit Purchaser from the project and description of new and additional environmental benefits that the project is intended to generate.

III. **Submission of Project Design Document (PDD):** It is submitted to National Clean Development Mechanism Authority for validation. Then, Project Design Document (PDD) is submitted to UNFCC for review and validation.

After a Project is running, it will be monitored by the host country, throughout project cycle. The CDM project cycle comprise seven steps:

(1) Submission of Project Design Document to National Clean Development Mechanism Authority.
(2) Project validation by the National Clean Development Mechanism Authority.
(3) Project registration in the host county.
(4) Project validation and registration by the executive board of the UNFCC.
(5) Project monitoring by the host country.
(6) Verification and Certification.
(7) Issuance of Certified Emissions Reductions (CERs).

The CER can be allotted in two different ways. One is a fixed crediting period of 10 years or first crediting period of seven year which can be extended twice for a period of further seven years, however, subject to undergoing the Project validation process again. Consultants for validation of CDM Project are: Price Water House Coopers, Ernst and Young and TERI.

Ministry of Non-conventional Energy Sources has been renamed as Ministry of New and Renewable Energy from 2006.

Demand Side Management (DSM)

DSM can be looked upon either traditionally as a tool, to be used to change the demand for energy or more generally as a tool for the society for better use and distribution of scarce resources. There are two types of DSM projects:

- **Energy Efficiency (EE):** It focuses on modifications in end-use technology (e.g. lighting).
- **Energy Conservation:** It is synonymous with energy generation. Conservation is cheaper than incremental cost of energy production. This concept receives more prominence in today's Indian scenario, where building one MW of power generation costs as much as Rs. 3 to 4 crore whereas the same power can be saved with less investment. If the consequent benefits of rise in productivity are included, the net cost of energy conservation to the economy is much less.

Unfortunately, Indian industry has not paid much attention to energy savings in the past. The high-energy consumption in Indian industries is due to three main reasons:

- Most manufacturing units are still dependent on old machinery
- Relatively high cost of capital as compared to European/ USA standards.
- There is uncertainty about the long-term growth of particular industrial sectors.

A recent World Bank report shows that Indian Industry has the potential to save 20 to 30 per cent of total energy consumption The following table indicates the average energy conservation potential in various sectors and in various energy intensive industries.

Energy Saving Potential

Sector/Industry	Energy Saving Potential
Domestic & Commercial	20%
Transport	20%
Agriculture	30%
Industries	25%
Iron & Steel	10%
Fertilizers	15%
Textiles	25%
Cement	15%
Chlor-alkali	15%
Pulp & Paper	25%
Aluminum	10%
Ferrous Foundry	20%
Petrochemicals	15%
Glass & Ceramics	20%
Refineries	10%

Source: CII Newsletter, Dec. 2000.

Energy, conservation and efficiency improvement in the Indian power sector requires special attention since the sector has been suffering from a chronic supply shortage, lack of capital investment for new capacity addition and environmental problems associated with coal-based power plants. High auxiliary consumption and T&D loss further aggravate the problem. Macroeconomic policies sometimes discourage the undertaking of energy efficiency measures. Environmentally harmful subsidies reduce the private costs of producers and consumers resulting in over-utilization of natural resources. Energy subsidies in India, for example, lead to energy intensive economic structures and technologies, and wasteful management practices. It has been estimated that the elimination of energy subsidies worldwide would reduce global carbon emission by 9.5%. In the electricity sector, there is no incentive to encourage conservation, as a minimum charge is required to be paid by the consumers. Government should review the minimum charge concept levied by SEBs and other power utilities and consumer should be charged the actual costs for the consumption of power. The energy audit program under the United Nations Department of Technical Cooperation for Development conducted by the Energy

Management Center reveals that it is possible to save about 37,008 kiloliter of fuel oil, about 1,320,845 tones of coal and about 69.2 million kWh of electricity, which is in monetary terms equivalent to Rs. 424.2 million per annum. This constitutes 16 per cent of the energy bill of audited units. Many DSM projects involve a combination of both energy efficiency and energy conservation measures that can result in low and no cost air pollution mitigation options. The level (and cost) of reduction is dependent on the source of electricity. If the electricity is generated by fossil fuels (e.g., coal, oil, natural gas), then the reduced demand shall translate into less generation and reduced level of emissions.

Therefore, the energy conservation measurement methods can derive the reduced value in cost structure and also provide the mechanism to generate additional funds through energy efficient measurements. These measures help the industry in reducing the cost and generating additional funds on the one hand and also contribute to the sustainable economic development of the country.

Chapter 3

Energy Management

INTRODUCTION TO ENERGY MANAGEMENT

Any activity (human, social or economic) consumes energy. Energy consumption involves fuel and infrastructure cost and it also leads to harmful emissions. Rising fuel prices, increasing environmental concern and cut-throat market competition necessitates minimum usage of energy for the same activity. Minimization of energy usage for the same amount of production or activity will ensure more profits or reduced cost, increased competitive edge in the market and reduced polluting and harmful emissions. The process of minimization of energy usage for any activity is called Energy Management. More precisely, Energy management is the judicious and effective use of energy to maximize profits (minimize costs) and enhance competitive positions.

Energy Management Includes

(a) Operating at optimum levels
(b) Minimizing wastage
(c) Repairing or maintaining equipments
(d) Replacing with more efficient equipments
(e) Utilizing waste

Presently, many businesses and industries are adopting a Total Quality Management (TQM) strategy for improving their operations. Any TQM approach should include an energy management component to reduce energy costs.

The primary objective of energy management is to maximize profits or minimize costs. Some desirable sub-objectives of energy management programs include:

(a) Improving energy efficiency and reducing energy use, thereby reducing emissions.
(b) Cultivating good communications on energy matters.
(c) Developing and maintaining effective monitoring, reporting, and management strategies for wise energy usage.
(d) Finding new and better ways to increase returns from energy investments through research and development.
(e) Developing interest in and dedication to the energy management program from all employees.
(f) Reducing the impacts of curtailments or any interruption in energy supplies.

Although energy conservation is certainly an important part of energy management, it is not the only consideration. Curtailment-contingency planning is certainly not conservation, and neither is load shedding.

Need for Energy Management

Economics

Profit maximization is the most important goal of any business body. Thus, any new activity can be justified only if it is cost effective: that is, the net result must show a profit improvement or cost reduction greater than the cost of the activity. Energy management has proven time and time again that it is cost effective.

An energy cost savings of 5-15% is usually obtained quickly with little or no required capital expenditure when an aggressive energy management progràm is launched. An eventual savings of 30% is common, and savings up to 70% have been obtained. These savings all result from retrofit activities. New buildings designed to be energy efficient often operate on 20% of the energy (with a corresponding 80% savings) normally required by existing buildings. In fact, for most manufacturing and other commercial organizations, energy management is one of the most promising profit improvements—cost reduction programs available today.

National good

Energy management programs are vitally needed today. One important reason is that energy management helps the nation to face some of its biggest problems. These problems are:

(a) ***Energy import bills:*** India spent US$ 15 billion (3% of its GDP) on oil imports during 2003. India imports most of its oil from Middle-East countries but they don't import from India in the same magnitude. This leaves a huge foreign exchange outflow and wide trade deficit for India which is not good for its economy.

(b) ***Energy security:*** India imports 75% of its oil and gas requirements. Indian economy, being heavily dependent on imported oil and gas, is very susceptible to any fuel embargo or fluctuating oil prices. With embargo and rising oil prices being a reality in contemporary world, Indian economy and consequently India is not secure.

(c) ***Foreign policy's dependence on fuel:*** Recent political developments around the world indicate that energy security is driving foreign policy decisions to a large extent. At times rogue states threaten fuel supply stoppage or decreased production to prevent international community from taking any punitive action against them. They also try to gain maximum out of bilateral or multilateral talks without conceding much. To have a strong and independent foreign policy, India needs to be self sufficient in energy.

(d) ***Lack of funds for basic necessities:*** India spent US$ 15 billion (3% of its GDP) on oil imports during 2003.

Important sectors like Education and Healthcare received only 3% and 0.9% of GDP respectively. Thus, heavy reliance on imported oil leaves India with very little funds to take care of basic necessities like education and healthcare.

(e) In addition to these, there are a host of major environmental problems related to energy usage like global warming, acid rain, ozone depletion, etc.

Minimizing energy usage through energy conservation techniques without sacrificing economic growth provides the answer for all the above energy related problems. Renewable energy technologies also offer the solution but its high capital cost and intermittent nature makes energy conservation option the clear winner.

Designing an Energy Management program

Management Commitment

The most important single ingredient for successful implementation and operation of an energy management program is commitment to the program by the top management. Without this commitment, the program will likely fail to reach its objectives. Thus the role of energy manager is crucial in ensuring that management is committed to the program.

Two situations are likely to occur with equal probability when designing an energy management program. In the first, management has decided that energy management is necessary and wants a program implemented. This puts the energy manager in the response mode. In the second, an employee has decided to convince management of the need for the program. So the employee is in aggressive mode. Obviously, the most desirable situation is the response mode. However, a large number of energy management programs have been started through the aggressive mode.

In a typical scenario of the response mode, management has seen rapidly rising prices and/or curtailments, has heard of other energy management programs, and has then initiated action to start the program. In this case, the management commitment already exists, and all that to be done is to cultivate that commitment periodically and to make sure the commitment is evident to all people affected by the program.

In the aggressive mode, an employee knows that energy costs are rising dramatically and that sources are less secure. He may have taken a course in energy management, attended professional conferences, and/or read papers on the subject. At any rate, he is now convinced that the company needs an energy management program. All that remains is to convince management and obtain their commitment.

The best way to convince management is with facts and statistics. We must have accurate data. Past figures can use actual utility bills, but future figures call for forecasting. Local utilities and various state energy agencies can help in providing management with accurate data. Follow this data with quotes on programs from other companies showing these goals are realistic.

Other company's experiences are widely published in literature; results can also be obtained through direct contacts with the energy manager in each company. However, as time progresses and the technology advanced, these figures tend to change. For example, a short time ago only a few people believed that an office building could reduce energy consumption by 70% or that manufacturing plants could operate on half the energy previously required, yet both are now occurring on a regular basis.

As the proponent of an energy management program, one could then talk about the likelihood of energy curtailments or brownouts and what they would mean to the company. It must be discussed what the energy management can do to minimize the impacts of curtailment and brownouts.

Finally, the energy manager should discuss the competition and what they are doing. Accurate statistics on this can be obtained from trade and professional organizations. The savings obtained by competitors can also be used in developing the goals for the facility.

Energy Management Coordinator/Energy Manager

To develop and maintain vitality for the energy management program, a company must designate a single person who has responsibility for coordinating the program. If none has energy management as a specific part of his or her job assignment, management is likely to find that the energy management efforts are given a lower priority than other job responsibilities. Consequently, little or nothing may get done.

The energy management coordinator should be strong, dynamic, goal oriented, and a good manager. Most important, management should support that person with resources including a staff. A multiplant or multidivisional corporation may need several such coordinators—one for each plant and one for each level of organization.

Back-up Talent

Unfortunately, not all the talent necessary for a successful energy management program resides in one person or discipline. For example, several engineering disciplines may be necessary to accomplish a full-scale study of the plant steam production, distribution, usage and condensate return system. For this reason, most successful energy management programs have an energy management committee. Two subcommittees that are often desirable are the technical and steering subcommittees.

The technical committee is usually composed of several persons with strong technical background in their discipline. Chemical, industrial, electrical, civil, and mechanical engineers as well as others may all be represented on this committee. Their responsibility is to provide technical assistance for the coordinator and plant-level people. For example, the committee can keep up with developing technology and research into potential applications company-wide. The results can then be filtered down. While the energy management coordinator may be a full-time position, the technical committee is likely to operate part –time, being called upon as necessary. In a multiplant or multidivisional organization, the technical committee may also be full time.

The steering committee has an entirely different purpose from the technical committee. It helps guide the activities of the energy management program and aids in communications through all organizational levels. The steering committee also helps ensure that all plant personnel are aware of the program. The steering committee members are usually chosen so that all major areas of the company are represented. Steering committee members should be selected because of their widespread interests and a sincere desire to aid in solving the energy problems. Such a committee should be able to develop a good composite picture of plant energy consumption which will help the energy management coordinator to choose and manage his/her activities.

Cost Allocation

One of the most difficult problems for the energy manager is to try to reduce energy costs for a facility when the energy costs are accounted for as part of the general overhead. In that case, the individual managers and supervisors don't consider themselves responsible for controlling the energy costs. This is because they don't see any direct benefit from reducing costs that are part of the total company overhead. The best solution to this problem is for top management to allocate energy costs down to "cost centers" in the company or facility. Once energy costs are charged to production centers in the same way that materials and labour are charged, then the managers have a direct incentive to control those energy costs because this will improve the overall cost-effectiveness of the production center.

For a building, this allocation of energy costs means that each of the tenants are given information on their energy consumption, and that they individually pay for that energy consumption. Even if a large building is "master metered" to reduce utility fixed charges, there should be a division of the utility cost down to the individual customers.

Reporting and Monitoring

It is critical for the energy management coordinator and the steering committee to timely and accurate knowledge of the energy consumption in the plant. This is best achieved through an effective and efficient system of energy reporting.

The objective of an energy reporting system is to measure energy consumption and compare it either to company goals or to some standard of energy consumption. Ideally, this should be done for each operation or production cost center in the plant, but most facilities simply do not have the required metering devices. Many plants only meter energy consumption at one place—where the various sources enter the plant. Systems that should be metered include steam, compressed air, and chilled and hot water.

As always, the reporting scheme needs to be reviewed periodically to ensure that only necessary material is being generated, that all needed data is available, and that the system is efficient and effective.

Training

Most energy management coordinators find that substantial training is necessary. Training basically involves sensitizing employees to energy management and enhancing their technical skills. Training can't be accomplished overnight, nor is it ever "completed". Changes occur in energy management staff and employees at all levels, as well as new technology and production methods. The energy management coordinator must assume responsibility for this training.

Starting an Energy Management Program

Several items contribute to the successful start of an energy management program. They include:

- Visibility of the program start-up.
- Demonstration of management commitment to the program
- Selection of a good initial energy management project

To be successful, an energy management program must have the backing of the people involved. Obtaining this support is often not an easy task, so careful planning is necessary. The people must:

- Understand why the program exists and what its goals are
- See how the program will affect their jobs and income
- Know that the program has full management support
- Know what is expected of them

Communicating this information to the employees is a joint task of management and the energy management coordinator. Some methods of communication in companies are:

- Memos:
- News releases
- Meetings
- Film, video tapes

Demonstration of Management Commitment

Management commitment to the program is essential, and this commitment must be obvious to all employees if the program is to reach its full potential. Management participation in the program start-up demonstrates this commitment, but it should also be emphasized in other ways. For example:

- Recognizing and rewarding individuals whose ideas and/or efforts have helped in energy savings
- Showing management's commitment through newsletters, bulletins, circulars, etc
- Funding cost-effective energy management proposals

Early Project Selection

The energy management program is on a treacherous footing

in the beginning. Most employees fear that their heating, lighting and air-conditioning comfort/extravagance may face a cut. If any of these occur, the employees won't support the program. So, it would be smarter to have less controversial actions as the early projects.

An early failure can be harmful, if not disastrous, to the program. An astute energy management coordinator will gain the support and trust of all concerned in the first set of projects. These projects should have a rapid payback, a high probability of success, and very few negative consequences. These ideal projects are not very difficult to find. Every plant has a few good opportunities, and the energy management coordinator should be looking for them.

One good example involved a rather dimly lit refrigerator warehouse area. Mercury vapour lamps were used in this area. The local energy management coordinator did a relamping project. He switched from mercury vapour lamps to high pressure sodium lamps (a significantly more efficient source) and carefully designed the system to improve the lighting levels. Savings were quite large; less energy was needed for lighting; less "heat of light" had to be refrigerated; and, most important, the employees liked it. Their environment was improved since light levels were higher than before.

Management of the Program

Establishing Objectives in an Energy Management Program

Management by objectives (MBO) is often utilized in most of the commercial establishments and industries. For a program to be effective, goals need to be set. These goals should be tough but achievable, measurable, and specific. They must also include a deadline for accomplishment. Once management and the energy management coordinator have agreed on the goals and established a good monitoring and reporting system, the coordinator should take over the responsibility and lead the program.

The goals could be one or more. The following list provides some examples of such goals:

- Total energy per unit of production will drop by 10% the

first year and an additional 5% the second year.
- Within 2 years, all energy consumers of 5 GJ per hour or larger will be separately metered for monitoring purposes.
- Each plant in the division will have an active energy management program by the end of the first year.
- All boilers of 50,000 lb/hour or larger will be examined for waste heat recovery potential during the first year.

The energy management coordinator must quickly establish the reporting systems to measure progress toward the goals and must develop the strategy plans to ensure progress. Gantt or CPM charting is often used to aid in planning and assignment of responsibilities.

A Model Energy Management Program

An excellent example of a longtime successful energy management program in a large corporation is that of the 3M Company, headquartered in St. Paul, Minnesota. 3M is a large, diversified manufacturing company with more than 50 major product lines; it makes some fifty thousand products at over fifty different locations around the country. The corporate energy management objective is to use energy as efficiently as possible in all operations; the management believes that all companies have an obligation to conserve energy and all other natural resources.

Energy productivity at 3M improved over 60% from 1973 to 1996. They saved over $70 million in 1996 because of their energy management programs, and saved a total of over $1.2 billion in energy expenses from 1973 to 1996. Their program is staffed by six people who educate and motivate all levels of personnel on the benefits of energy management. The categories of programs implemented by 3M include: conservation, maintenance procedures, utility operation optimization, efficient new designs, retrofits through energy surveys, and process changes.

Energy efficiency goals at 3M are set and then the results are measured against a set standard in order to determine the success of the programs. The technologies that have resulted in the most dramatic improvements in energy efficiency include: heat recovery systems, high efficiency motors, variable speed drives, computerized facility management systems, combustion improvements, thermal insulation, cogeneration, waste steam utilization, and process improvements.

The energy management program at 3M has worked very well, but management is not yet satisfied. They have set a goal of further improving energy efficiency at a rate of 3% per year for the next five years. They expect to substantially reduce their emissions of waste gases and liquids, to increase the energy recovered from wastes, and to constantly increase the profitability of their operations. 3M continues to stress the extreme importance that efficient use of energy can have on their industrial productivity.

Energy Accounting

Energy accounting is a system used to keep track of energy consumption and costs. A basic energy accounting system has three parts:

- Energy use monitoring
- Energy use record
- Performance measure

The performance measure may range from a simple index of Btu/ft^2 or Btu/unit of production to a complex standard cost system complete with variance reports. In all cases, energy accounting requires metering. Monitoring the energy flow through a cost centre, no matter how large or small, requires the ability to measure incoming and outgoing energy. The lack of necessary meters is probably the largest single deterrent to the widespread utilization of energy accounting systems.

Levels of Energy Accounting

As in financial accounting, the level of sophistication or detail of energy accounting systems varies considerably from company to company. A very close correlation can be developed between the levels of sophistication of financial accounting systems and those of energy accounting systems.

Performance Measures

Energy Utilization Index

A very basic measure of a facility's energy performance is called the Energy Utilization Index (EUI). Energy auditors use EUI to enable comparisons between different buildings and energy types. EUI is calculated by converting all energy used in a building to a common unit, and then dividing it by the square footage of the heated/cooled space in the building. The Energy Use Index (EUI) is the most common means of expressing the total energy consumption for each building.

Energy Cost Index

Another useful performance index is the Energy Cost Index (ECI). To compute ECI, all of the energy used in the facility must be identified, the total cost of that energy tabulated, and the total number of square feet of conditioned spacedetermined. The ECI is then found as the ratio of the total annual energy cost for a facility to the total number of square feet of conditioned floor space of the facility.

One-Shot Productivity Measures

This measure enables us to observe the variance of EUI with respect to time. In this measure, EUI is plotted over time, and trends can be noted.

Significant deviations from the same period during the previous year should be noted and explanations sought. This measure is often used to justify energy management activities or at least to show their effect.

Some other Performance Measures:

- Energy per unit of production
- Energy per degree day
- Energy per unit sales
- Energy per unit sales or profit or value addition
- Energy per unit direct labour hour or machine hour

An Example of Energy Accounting System

General Motors Corporation has a strong energy accounting

system which uses an energy responsibility method. According to General Motors, a good energy accounting system is implemented in three phases:

1. Design and installation of accurate metering
2. Development of an energy budget
3. Publication of regular performance reports including variances

Phase 1—Metering: For execution of a successful energy accounting program, energy flow must be measured by cost center. The designing of cost center boundaries requires care; the cost centers must not be too large or too small. However, the primary design criterion is—how much energy is involved? For example, a bank of large electric induction heat-treating furnaces might need separate metering even if the area involved is relatively small, but a large assembly area with only a few energy consuming devices may require only one meter. Flexibility is important since a cost center, that is too small today may not be too small tomorrow as energy cost change tremendously.

The choice of meters is also important. Meters should be accurate, rugged, and cost effective. They should have a good turndown ratio. Turndown ratio is defined as the ability to measure accurately over the entire range of energy flow involved.

Having the meters is not enough. A system must be designed to gather and record the data in a useful form. Meters can be read manually, they can record information on charts for permanent records, and/or they can be interfaced with microcomputers for real-time reporting and control. Many energy accounting systems fail because the data collection system is not adequately designed or utilized.

Phase 2—Energy Budget: There are two ways to develop the energy budget: statistical manipulation of historical data or utilization of engineering models.

The Statistical Model: Using historical data, the statistical model shows how much energy was utilized and how it compared to the standard year(s), but it does not show how efficiently the energy was used.

Multiple linear regression could be used to develop the parameters for the model as:

Energy forecast = a (production level) + b (ft^2) + c (degree days)

Multiple linear regression estimates the parameters in the universal regression model from a set of sample data. Using the base years, the procedure estimates values for parameters a, b, and c in order to minimize the squared error. However, regardless of the analytical method used, a statistical model does not determine the amount of energy that ought to be used. It only forecasts consumption based on previous year's data.

The Engineering Model

The engineering model attempts to remedy the deficiency in the statistical model by developing complete energy balance calculations to determine the amount of energy theoretically required. By using the first law of thermodynamics, energy and mass balances can be completed for any process. The result is the energy required for production. Similarly, HVAC and lighting energy needs could be developed using heat loss equations and other simple calculations. Advantages of the engineering model include improved accuracy and flexibility in reacting to changes in building structures, production schedules, etc.

Phase 3—Performance Reports: The next step is the publication of energy performance reports that compare actual energy consumption with that predicted by the models. The manager of each cost center should be evaluated on his/her performance as shown in these reports. The publication of these reports is the final step in the effort to transfer energy costs from an overhead category to a direct cost or at least to a direct overhead item.

Sometimes more detail on variance is needed. For example, if consumption were shown in dollars, the variation could be shown in dollars and broken into price and consumption variation. Price variation is calculated as the difference between the budget and the actual unit price times the present actual consumption. The remaining variation would be due to a change in consumption and would be equal to the change in consumption times the budget price. Other categories of variation could include fuel switching, pollution control, and new equipment.

IMPROVED INSULATION

Introduction

Unwanted heat loss or gain through the walls or roofs of buildings, and heat loss from the pipes, tanks and other equipment in buildings or plants can significantly increase energy use and energy costs. Thermal insulation plays an important role in reducing these energy costs in many situations. Good engineering design of insulation systems will reduce undesirable heat loss or gain by at least 90% in most applications and will often improve environmental conditions at the same time. Consequently, it is highly beneficial to understand insulation theory and applications, and to recognize when cost-effective insulation EMOs can be implemented.

Insulation Theory

Heat Transfer

Heat transfer occurs through three modes: conduction, convection and radiation. A basic understanding of the modes of heat transfer is required to visualize the impact of insulation on energy and monetary savings.

Since conduction, convection and radiation are in itself a very broad topic, it is impossible to cover them in this single chapter. Therefore we confine ourselves to the concept of overall heat transfer coefficient. Overall heat transfer coefficient (U) takes care of the total heat transfer, be it conduction, convection or radiation. Therefore, the rate of heat transfer (Q) involved in a process is

$$Q = UA\,(\Delta T)$$

where A is the area of heat transfer and T is the temperature difference.

Once the rate of heat transfer is known, D the amount of heat loss that can be avoided through insulation can be estimated. From the knowledge of the amount of insulation required and the amount of heat loss avoided, the annual cost and savings can be worked out and hence the payback period. With the knowledge of payback period, an energy manager can decide whether to go for insulation or not.

Insulation Type

Before an energy manager can select the proper type of insulation for a particular application, he or she must know the properties of various kinds of insulating materials.

Properties of Materials Used for Insulation

Some of the more important properties of materials that would be used to provide insulation properties include the following:

- *Cell Structure:* Cell structures are either open or closed. A closed cell is relatively impervious to moisture, especially in a moderate environment, so insulation with a closed cell structure may not need any additional moisture barrier. Open cells pass moisture freely and therefore probably require vapour barriers. For extremely cold applications where a lot of condensation occurs, a vapour barrier is probably required regardless of cell structure.
- *Temperature Use:* Different insulating materials react to extreme temperatures in different ways. In some cases, high temperatures can destroy the binders and render the insulation useless. All insulation materials have temperature ranges for which they are recommended.
- *Thermal Conductivity (k):* k values vary with the temperature—sometimes significantly. The energy manager must be familiar with the different types of insulation, their k values, and how the temperature affects the k values. In all cases, the k value chosen to reflect the appropriate conductivity should be that for the mean temperature (t_m) experienced by the insulation:

$$t_m = (t_h+t_s)/2$$

- *Fire Hazard:* Fire hazard ratings measure a product's contribution to flame spread and smoke development in a fire. The rating is measured on a flame spread-smoke spread scale where 100/100 is the rating for red oak.
- *Forms:* Insulation is available in a number of different forms. Flexible blankets, batts, rigid board, blocks, and pipe half sections are some of the more popular ones.

Insulation is also available in a number of sizes and thicknesses. Therefore, an energy manager must select one according to his/her requirement.

Common Insulating Materials

Some of the more popular types of materials with a discussion of some of their specific properties are given below:

- *Mineral Fiber-rock Wool:* Mineral fiber insulation is made from molten rock. It is fairly impervious to heat and can be used in relatively high temperatures.
- *Fiberglass:* Probably the most popular type of insulation, fiberglass can be obtained in blankets, batts, boards, and pipe covering. Although organic binders are frequently used which limit temperature ranges somewhat, cell structure is such that the limitations can sometimes be exceeded and still has acceptable results
- *Foams:* Several types of foam insulation are available; some types have problems meeting fire hazard classifications but have very good k values. Others meet the fire hazard requirements but do not offer very good k values. Foams are particularly applicable to cold applications.
- *Calcium Silicate:* A very popular type of insulation for high-temperature use, calcium silicate is spun from lime and silica. It is extremely durable and offers a high thermal resistance.
- *Refractories-ceramic Fiber:* An alumina-silica product, ceramic fibers are available in blankets or felts that can be used alone or added to existing fire brick.
- *Refractories-fire Brick:* Fire bricks are made for high-temperature applications. Made of a refractory clay with organic binders which are burned out during manufacture, they offer good thermal resistance and low storage of heat.
- *Others:* Other types of insulation include cellular glass, perlite, and diatomaceous earth. Earth has advantages and disadvantages with which the energy manager must become familiar.

Economic Thickness

Insulation has an optimum thickness that can be calculated using the principles of engineering economy.

As thickness of insulation is increased, the cost of material and installation goes up. The cost of lost energy, on the other hand, goes down, but at a decreasing rate. Said in other terms, the energy cost savings also goes up, but at a slower rate of increase than the cost of materials and installation. At some point, then, the total cost, which is the sum of the lost energy cost and the material cost, reaches a minimum point. That amount of insulation is called the economic thickness.

The total cost curve is relatively flat in the immediate neighborhood of the economic thickness. This means that the energy manager does not have to use the exact optimum amount of insulation. A small deviation to either way will not affect the resulting annual cost too much.

To determine this economic thickness, the energy manager needs to construct cash flow diagrams for the different alternative thicknesses and calculate the annual equivalent cost for each increment. Since the cash flows include future fuel costs, careful handling of inflation is required.

PROCESS ENERGY MANAGEMENT

Introduction

In many facilities, energy management is simply a matter of managing the energy required for lighting and space conditioning. In many others, however, energy management is much more complex and involves large motors and controls, industrial insulation, complex combustion monitoring, unique steam distribution problems, significant amounts of waste heat, etc. Typical facilities offering large energy management opportunities include industrial facilities, large office and commercial operations, and government institutions such as schools, hospitals, etc. Such facilities generally have specialized industrial, commercial or institutional processes. These processes require thorough analytical evaluations to determine the appropriate energy-saving measures.

The energy manager must be careful in process energy

management. Processes can be quite complex, so a full understanding of the entire process is necessary.

Steps for Process Improvement

Readers who have studied work simplification and improvement may remember the suggested order of changes as (1) eliminate; (2) combine; (3) change equipment, person, place, or sequence; and (4) improve.

The same order of change is appropriate for process energy management, but as mentioned earlier, the analyst must understand the entire system and the cascading impacts that changes might effect. In terms of energy management, examples of the preceding changes include the following:

- *Eliminate* Does that cooling water need to be there? Sometimes process cooling water is not really necessary; eliminating it saves pumping and chilling costs. Is the paint oven really necessary? Some newer paints will air dry quite well, and paint oven costs can be substantial.
- *Combine:* Machining operations can often be combined with jig and fixture modifications or changes in equipment. This saves the energy used by the additional machines; it also reduces material handling and may save process storage energy. Sometimes combining processes also saves the energy necessary to bring the material back to a required workability.
- *Change Equipment, Person, Place, or Sequence:* Equipment changes can offer substantial energy savings as the newer equipment may be more energy efficient. For example, new electric welders are considerably more energy efficient than older ones. Changing persons, place, or sequences can offer energy savings as the person may be more skillful, the place more appropriate, and the sequence better in terms of energy consumption. For example, bringing rework back to the person with skill and to the place with the correct equipment can save energy.
- *Improve:* Most energy management work today involves improvement in how energy is used in the process

because the capital expenditure required is often minimized. Examples include reducing excess air for combustion to a minimum, reducing temperatures to the minimum required, and removing excess lighting. Improving does sometimes require large amounts of capital. For example, insulation improvements can be expensive, but energy savings can be large, and there can be improved product quality.

Motors and Adjustable Speed Drives

Motor energy use represents well over half of all the electric energy consumed by industrial, commercial and institutional facilities. Motors are found on almost every piece of equipment used to perform a process in manufacturing, mining and agriculture. Even pieces of equipment that perform special functions often have motors as their principal part—for example chillers and air compressors.

Because of the widespread application of electric motors in almost every facility, they are excellent candidates for improvements to their efficiencies and improvements in their utilization in machines and processes. Just a small improvement in electric motor efficiency can produce significant savings in the energy cost of operating a piece of equipment. The annual cost of operating a motor can often be five to ten times the original purchase price of the motor.

Many motor applications require variable speeds, should use variable speeds to match the actual loads, and thus the area of motor controls is also very important. Adjustable speed drives- or variable-speed drives—are motor control systems that reduce the energy input to a motor when it is not fully loaded. These ASDs or VSDs can produce substantial savings in the operational costs of motors, and can often improve the operation of the system that previously used a motor without a speed control.

High Efficiency Motors

Electric motors account for about three-quarters of all the electrical energy used by industry, and almost half of all electrical energy use by commercial facilities. Energy efficient motors are now readily available that are two to eight percent more efficient than the standard motors they would replace. Since typical motors last over twenty years, using high efficiency motors offers business and industry substantial energy and dollar savings.

Motor efficiency is a measure of the effectiveness with which electrical energy is converted to mechanical energy. Motor losses occur in five major areas: core losses, stator losses, rotor losses, stray load losses, and windage and friction losses. High efficiency motors are designed and manufactured to reduce these losses. High efficiency motors are designed and manufactured to reduce these losses. In addition to having lower losses, high efficiency motors also have higher power factors during operation. Cost premiums for high efficiency motors range from 10% to 30%, but since a motor may use 75 times its initial cost in electric energy over its lifetime, the savings potential is great. Many motors in commercial facilities, industries and institutions run 6000 to 8000 hours per year, so very cost-effective paybacks can be achieved.

The original purchase cost of a motor can be a small part of the life-cycle cost. Thus, it is important to consider other factors besides the initial cost when buying a new motor for a piece of equipment.

Motor Load Factors

The full load horsepower output rating of a motor is stamped on the motor's nameplate. However, just because we find a motor that is stamped 20-hp des not mean that the motor is running at full load—which is 20-hp. A motor is a load driven machine, and will supply only that amount of power needed by the load. For example, a 20-hp motor may be driving a fan that needs only 15-hp. The load on the motor can be expressed as a percent of full load, and this is called the load factor for the motor. In this case, the load factor would be 15/20 or 75%.

Only few motors run at anywhere near full load. A common assumption made by many energy auditors and analysts is that motor load factors are around 80%. This value is rarely seen in motors other than those specifically sized for known loads in heating, ventilating and air conditioning systems for buildings. In most other applications, motors experience variable loads that average well below 80%. One energy analyst presented data to show that 75% of all motors in his experience have load factors less than 60%.

Individual motors, such as found on a wall ventilating fan, may well have load factors of 80%. However, many other pieces of equipment such as some air compressors, conveyors, pumps, dust collector fans, saws, drills and punches have extremely variable load factors which are generally much less than 50%. Pumps and fans with variable loads are usually ideal candidates for use of adjustable speed drives to reduce the energy input when the motor load is low.

To account for the fact that motors typically operate with load factors less than one, the basic motor equation for computing the electrical load must be modified to include a load factor term.

Actual power consumption, kW = [hp*0.746 kW* LF] / Efficiency

For example, if we have a 100-hp motor that is 95% efficient and is running at 60% load, its electrical power consumption is:

kW = [100*0.746*0.6] / 0.95 = 47.1 kW

If the motor had been operating at full load, its power consumption would have been 78.5 kW.

Rewinding Electric Motors

There is at least one other important factor in motor replacement selection, and that is the potential for rewinding a motor that has failed. There are three options available for a facility that has just experienced a motor failure. One, they can buy a high efficiency replacement. Three, they can send the failed motor out to be repaired, and potentially rewound.

The cost of rewinding a motor is often substantially less than the cost of purchasing a new motor—whether it is a standard-efficiency model or a high-efficiency model. However, it is fairly common for motors to be damaged during the rewinding process, and to suffer losses in efficiency of 1-2%. Often, a 1 percentage point loss in efficiency will result in the cost of the additional electricity being greater than the total cost of rewinding. Thus it is important to consider this factor when replacing a motor. Not all rewinding operations damage motors, but the loss of efficiency is quite common.

Motor Drives and Controls

In addition to improving the efficiency of the motor itself, there are many other opportunities for energy savings in the complete motor system. One opportunity is in the use of solid-state, electronic controls that can provide soft-starts, speed control and power factor correction.

For large motors that have variable loads, the addition of electronic speed controllers—or adjustable speed drives (ASDs)—can be very cost effective. ASDs are electronic devices that vary the speed of a motor to match that of the load being put on the motor. The size of a motor is usually based on maximum load, even though normal design conditions seldom require this full load size. An ASD will reduce the speed of the motor by adjusting the frequency, voltage, or current of the motor input so that the motor performance exactly matches the present load. ASDs are also called Variable Speed Drives (VSDs) or Variable Frequency Drives (VFDs).

Fans and pumps are typical applications where ASDs can improve motor performance. Since the energy used in many fan and pump applications is proportional to the cube of the flow rate, then small reductions in the required flow rates translate to large savings in energy needed. In addition, many motors are purposefully over-sized to have a safety factor in handling the required load. This over-sizing is not beneficial to energy efficiency, and results in many motors running at conditions that unnecessarily waste energy. Properly sizing motors is probably one of the most cost-effective EMOs that a facility could implement.

Other Factors in Motor System Efficiency

- In addition to the efficiency of the motor itself and the use of adjustable speed drives, there are still several other factors that affect the overall motor system efficiency. One of these factors is the mechanism for the transmission of power from the motor to the load. In particular, care should be taken to insure that efficient pulleys, drives, belts and gears are used to couple the motor to the load.
  - *Belts:* Many motors are coupled to their loads with belt drives. There are several types of belts, including

V-belts, cogged V-belts, and synchronous belts. Standard V-belts are the most common type of drive belt, and have transmission losses that occur because of flexing and slippage of the belt. The cogged V-belts and the synchronous belts are more efficient because they do not allow the same amount of flexing and slippage as the standard V-belts. Motor system performance can be improved by 2-4% with the use of these more efficient belts.

- *Lubrication:* Motor lubrication is also a factor in motor efficiency. There are synthetic lubricants available that reduce the friction losses in motor-driven equipment. Savings of 1-2% are common, and much larger savings are possible for some equipment. Often, however, manufacturers recommend that these synthetic lubricants be used only in new pieces of equipment, so that there is no contamination of the synthetic lubricant.
- *Maintenance:* Motor maintenance is also a factor. The operating temperature of a motor should be checked periodically, as well as its mechanical and electrical condition. Each motor in a facility should be inspected periodically to determine the condition of its bearings and its pulley and belt alignment if it uses a belt drive.

Utility Rebates for Motors and Drives

A general discussion of electrical utility company rebates and incentives has already been discussed. However, since most utilities offer rebates and incentives for electric motor system improvements, it is worth mentioning again. There are generally two forms that the rebates and incentives take for motor systems: an incentive based on kW savings, or an incentive based on the horsepower of the motor involved. The level of the rebate or incentive for a peak load reduction due to a motor system improvement depends greatly on the individual utility. If the utility is working hard to limit its peak demand so that it will not have to add new power generation capability, the incentives may be quite large. Incentives of a few hundred dollars per kW of motor load reduced are common.

The incentive may also be related to the horsepower of the motor replaced or the horsepower of the motor that an adjustable speed drive was added onto. For a high efficiency motor replacement, the utility usually has a list of minimum efficiencies that qualify for rebates.

Air Compressors

Many facilities use substantial quantities of compressed air to power machinery, process operations and control systems. This becomes a large energy cost, and the compressed air system should be designed and operated so that it is as energy efficient as possible. Selecting the best types and sizes of air compressor units is important in achieving this goal. A high efficiency motor should be specified for any air compressor, unless it is one that will only be used for short periods of time.

Types of Air Compressors

There are two major classifications of air compressors: positive displacement compressors and dynamic compressors. A reciprocating compressor is an example of a positive displacement compressor. In this type of compressor, successive volumes of air are trapped in a closed space, and the pressure is increased as the piston moves toward the top of the cylinder and reduces the size of the closed space. Reciprocating air compressors have good energy efficiency characteristics at both part-load and full-load. It is more difficult to capture the waste heat from a reciprocating compressor than from a rotary screw or centrifugal air compressor since the pistons in the reciprocating unit are exposed to the open air around the machine.

The rotary screw compressor is another example of a positive displacement air compressor. In this unit, air enters the inlet and is trapped between mating male and female rotors and compressed to the required discharge pressure. Rotary screw compressors have excellent efficiencies at full-load conditions, and average efficiencies at part-load conditions. Heat recovery is easiest from the rotary screw compressors since the entire compressor section is enclosed.

The centrifugal air compressor is an example of a dynamic compressor, where air is compressed by the dynamic action of rotating impellers or vanes imparting velocity and pressure to the air. Almost all large air compressors are centrifugal compressors. The efficiency of these centrifugal compressors is lower than either the reciprocating or rotary screw models, so smaller air compressors are almost never the centrifugal type. Heat recovery is also somewhat difficult from these compressors.

Designing the Compressed Air System

Most facilities have a number of air compressors that can be operated in combinations to satisfy the demand for compressed air at any time. Large units are needed for periods of high demand, and smaller units are needed to supply reduced amounts of compressed air during weekends or periods of slack production. A centralized air compressor facility together with a common-header and a computer control system for managing the load should provide efficient, cost-effective operation for most plants. In some cases there are large distances between parts of a facility that need compressed air. In those cases it might be more efficient to provide a small compressor at each location to minimize the energy lost in transmitting the compressed air through long pipelines.

Air compressors operate most efficiently when they use cool air for the intake. One of the factors that should be considered in designing the compressed air system is the access to cool intake air. Air compressors are often located in parts of a facility which are quite warm, and the air intakes use this warm air. In these cases, an outside air intake vent should be installed to allow the compressors to use cooler air.

Waste Heat Recovery from Air Compressors

Nearly 90% of the energy that goes into an air compressor becomes waste heat. Thus, it is important to recognize the value of air compressors as waste heat sources. Warm air

can be recovered for space heat or process drying, or water can be heated for washing parts, cleaning equipment or for bathroom use. Air compressors can often be located next to the place where their waste heat will be utilized. This can save on costs of ducting and piping that would have been needed to move the waste heat from a compressor located some distance away.

It is very cost-effective to install the ducting to transfer the hot exhaust air from the compressor to the warehouse where it can reduce the need for using gas to provide space heat. Since the heat is only needed for a few months of the year, it must be vented outside during the other months.

Improving the Operation of the Compressed Air System

One way to determine how much energy is being used in the compressed air distribution system is to attach a recording ammeter to one leg of the motor driving the air compressor. This gives both the time and the amount of energy consumption and can point to excess usage or to leaks as possible problems. The assignment of dollar values to air leaks of various sizes is possible, and the amount of air lost to leakage can be a significant fraction of the total air used. In facilities where the air leaks are small, more attention should probably be paid to the ways in which the air is used. In any case, monitoring the electrical consumption of the compressor motor can determine whether this use of energy is worth the attention of the auditor. Replacing standard-efficiency motors with high-efficiency motors for air compressors is usually a very cost-effective EMO.

While considering the compressed air system, think of replacing air-powered equipment by equipment powered by electricity. An air-powered hoist, for example, uses 5-hp in the air compressor for every hp that would be used if the hoist were electrical. When the main function of the air compressor is to control HVAC equipment, water or oil in the control air can wreck the controls on the equipment. Most air compressors have water or oil traps at the bottom, and they can be inspected to see if they are acting as the manufacturer intended. Obtain the operating manual before attempting the inspection; otherwise you may manipulate the safety valve rather than the water trap, with hazardous results. If water or oil is not removed at the compressor, it may travel to the thermostats and impede their operation. Each thermostat operates differently, however, and inspecting a thermostat for oil or water is a task best left to a vendor or to a trained service person.

In addition, clean dry air is so important for the proper operation and longevity of air-powered controls and tools, that most facilities have an air dryer that is placed in the air supply line after the compressor. This may be a mechanical vapor-compression cycle dryer, or it can be a desiccant-type dryer where the desiccant material is periodically reconditioned on an autumn basis.

Electric motors transmit power to compressors through belts, and a misalignment of the belt pulleys can cause severe damage and early failure of both bearings and belts. Other problems that can occur with compressors include inoperable switches, gauges that do not work, loose or frayed wiring, and leaks. Look for these problems, and listen for sounds of escaping air. If compressor problems persist, the cost savings of a working control system more than pays for the help of a trained technician.

Common Energy Management Opportunities

- *Switch to Energy Efficient Lamps:* Switch existing lamps to the energy-efficient ones, such as 34 W energy-efficient fluorescent lamps for conventional 40 W ones, or replace T-12 lamps with T-8 or T-10 lamps.
- *Switch to Energy-efficient Light Sources:* Change to more efficient sources usually requiring fixture changes. Change from incandescent lights to fluorescent or from mercury vapor or fluorescent to high-pressure sodium for in-plant lighting, a very frequent conversion.
- *Use Night Setback-setup:* Turn temperatures up or down at night when needs are reduced. Examples include large ovens that cannot be turned off, large refrigeration units where night operations involve less infiltration (fewer people going in and out), and space conditioning.
- *Turn off Equipment*: Turn off exhaust fans, ovens, motors, or any other equipment when not needed.
- *Move Air Compressor Intake to Cooler Locations*: Move air intakes from hot equipment rooms to cooler rooms (often outside) locations. Efficiency improvements are large and paybacks attractive.
- *Eliminate Leaks in Steam and Compressed Air Systems*: Steam and compressed air leaks are very expensive and should be fixed. Technology exists for repairing leaks

without shutting the equipment down. Night audits (when noise is minimized) often turn up large numbers of these leaks.

- *Control Excess Air:* Careful control of combustion air can lead to significant energy savings.
- *Optimize Plant Power Factor*: Depending on the utility billing schedule and the company's power factor, large savings may be available through power factor improvement.
- *Insulate Bare Tanks, Vessels, Lines, and Process Equipment*: Good savings are often available through insulation of process lines and tanks. Condensate return lines and tanks are often not insulated.
- *Install Storm Windows, Doors, and Weather Stripping:* Although these are often difficult to justify, sizable savings are sometimes available. This is especially true for large glass exposures in cold climates.
- *Use Energy-efficient Electric Motors:* When replacement is necessary or for new applications, energy-efficient motors can usually be justified. Electric utilities often provide rebates to customers who replace standard motors with energy-efficient models.
- *Preheat Combustion Air:* Recuperators can save large amounts of energy and money. Sometimes they are highly cost effective.
- *Reduce the Pressure of Compressed Air and Steam:* If the pressures have been over designed, a reduction will not harm the process. In such cases, large savings are possible.
- *Insulate Walls, Ceilings, Roofs, and Doors:* Industrial plants are frequently poorly insulated. Insulation in dropped ceilings, on roofs or walls, and doors may be cost-justified.
- *Recover Heat from Air Compressor:* Larger air compressors reject large amounts of heat through air or water cooling. Proper design can allow this waste heat to be used for space conditioning in the winter and to be exhausted in warm weather. Sometimes the payback is

very attractive.

- *Insulate Dock Doors:* Plastic strips, dock bumpers, vestibules, or air screens all help block infiltration through large dock doors. If the space is heated and/or air-conditioned, the savings can be very large.
- *Install Economizers on Air Conditioners:* In some areas of the country, economizers can be very attractive. They allow the optimum use of outside air in air conditioning. Sometimes outside air can be used and the air conditioner turned off.
- *Use Radiant Heat:* Sometimes infrared heaters can be used to spot-heat rather than heat entire areas. Infrared heat (like the sun) warms objects and people but not space. The payback can be very attractive.
- *Return Steam Condensate to the Boiler:* Returning hot condensate can yield dramatic savings in energy, water, and water conditioning costs. Return lines should probably be insulated.
- *Change Product Design to Reduce Energy Requirements:* Product redesign can often reduce the energy necessary in heat treating, cleaning, coating, painting, etc.
- *Explore Waste Heat Recovery for Space Exhaust Systems:* Large amounts of exhaust in buildings that are heated and/or air-conditioned offer the potential for waste heat recovery
- *Install Devices to Improve Heat Transfer in Boilers:* Turbulators and other devices designed to reap more energy out of the combustion process are often very cost effective.
- *Reschedule Operations to Reduce Peak Demand:* Sometimes simple changes in equipment scheduling can dramatically reduce demand charges.
- *Cover Open Heated Tanks:* Covering open heated tanks can often lead to big energy savings. Floating balls, cantilevered tops, and rubber flaps have all been used as covers.
- *Spot-ventilate or Use Air Filters:* In wielding areas or other areas where large amounts of ventilation are

required, spot ventilation can often reduce the amount needed. Also, electronic or other types of air filters can sometimes allow reuse of the air. Savings are especially large if the space is heated and/or air-conditioned.

STEAM GENERATION AND DISTRIBUTION

Introduction

One major use of fuel in many facilities is to generate steam which is then used to provide space heat, process heat and mechanical power. Many significant opportunities for energy cost reduction can be found in a good technical examination of the steam generation and distribution systems in buildings and industries. Such an examination first estimates the amount of energy coming into a steam generation system and then determines where the energy goes. These estimates provide a guide to possible waste heat utilization and other ways to improve the efficiency of a boiler, and can be used to evaluate the insulation possibilities for steam distribution lines.

The Heat Balance

An underlying principle of energy analysis is that the most effort should be placed where the largest opportunity exists. For boiler operations, there are two areas with significant energy savings potential—where the boiler energy comes from—the energy sources—and where it goes—the energy sinks. The fundamental tool for analyzing boilers and steam distribution systems is the heat balance which is used to determine the energy sources and energy sinks within the system.

A heat balance equates the energy entering a system to the energy leaving the system. The energy sources are ranked by the amount of heat they exhaust to the environment. Then the source components are examined to see whether each of their functions can be performed with less energy, and the sink components are examined to see if they can feed their energy back in some useful way to one or more of the source components. Because this process shows where energy is utilized or wasted in the boiler and steam distribution system, the benefits to be gained from insulation and from waste heat utilization can be determined.

A heat balance is intended to account for all the heat that goes into a system and to find where all of it leaves the system. Using the heat balance requires understanding the heat content of steam—a concept embodied in the term enthalpy, and understanding the basic principles of heat transfer.

Enthalpy

The sum of the latent heat, the sensible heat, and the mechanical work is called enthalpy. When water is present with the steam, as in most steam distribution systems, the steam is said to be saturated, and the pressure increases as the temperature increases. Furthermore the specific volume decreases as the temperature increases.

In some applications, steam is present without water. Such steam is said to be superheated, and its enthalpy and specific volume at various temperatures and pressures are available in the form of tables.

Heat Gains

To estimate the heat energy entering a steam generation and distribution system, the first step is to determine the amount and form of all heat entering the boiler and the second, to express heat inputs in the same units as outputs. The greatest source of heat input to a boiler (except for some waste heat boilers) is the boiler fuel itself. The heat energy per pound of fuel is generally known because it is a part of the designing criteria for the boiler.

The boiler system also contains heat in the combustion air, the returned condensate, and the boiler makeup water. The enthalpy in each of these sources is used as the measure of the heat energy the source contributes to the system.

Heat Losses

Enthalpy is a useful way of describing the amount of energy contained in steam in steam condensate. Much of the energy lost from boilers, however, is radiated to the environment, and this loss must be calculated to complete the heat balance.

First, consider the problem of heat losses from hot pipes or boiler surfaces. These heat losses are associated with convection (usually treated as if it were the free convection associated with still air) and with radiation. This kind of heat loss must be considered whenever boilers or piping are contained within the system being analyzed, and it must be calculated for all surfaces. Useful formulas for these heat losses are:

Radiative loss = $\sigma A (T_s^4 - T_r^4)$
and
Convective loss = $h A (T_s - T_r)$

where

A = surface area
σ = Stefan-Boltzmann constant
h = Convective heat transfer coefficient
T_s, T_r = surface and room temperatures, respectively (in case of radiative loss calculation, both the temperatures are absolute temperatures in Kelvin)

A second major heat loss occurs in the energy removed in the steam itself. The enthalpy values of the lost steam could be estimated from the tables and thus the heat lost is known.

Any other material leaving the system must be accounted for in the heat balance. For example, flue gas carries with it both latent and sensible heat, and the energy lost this way must be calculated as a significant factor in the heat balance. Any water used in blowdown contains heat that must also be counted as lost heat. Boiler blowdown is required periodically in order to remove some of the dirt, scale and other contaminants in the boiler water that build up over time. Some of the boiler water is drawn off and replaced with chemically purified makeup water. The blowdown process might be continuous, and if so, there would be a continuous loss of heat in this water.

WASTE HEAT RECOVERY

Waste heat is that heat which goes into the atmosphere or to some other heat sink without providing any appreciable benefit to the user. Examples of such heat loss include flue gases, boiler blowdown exhausted to the air, heated air exhausted directly to the environment by vents, and heat lost from pipes that pass through unheated spaces. (Note that when these pipes provide protection against freezing, the heat radiated from the pipes is not waste heat.) Waste heat can be used to generate steam, to provide a source of energy for turbines, or to provide a source of the waste heat is a boiler, an industrial process, or an HVAC system. Benefits from waste heat recovery often include fuel savings and lower capital cost of heating and cooling equipment. Other benefits can include increased production capacity and, under some circumstances, revenue from the sales of recovered heat or energy.

Analyzing the Potential for Waste Heat Recovery

Waste heat sources and their uses can be conveniently categorized by the temperature at which the heat is exhausted.

The use of waste heat to power a turbine or pump should be considered if turbine work or pumping is needed and if enough energy is available to justify the cost involved. If the economics justify the production of electricity, cogeneration, may be a possibility. The use of waste heat to heat a fluid stream should be considered if (1) the waste heat source is close enough to the fluid stream that the fluid temperature will still be high enough to be useful even after taking into account all heat lost in transporting the fluid from source to stream, (2) using waste heat from the source will not create problems at the source, and (3) the transfer of heat from the source to the stream is technically feasible.

The first step in analyzing an industrial process for possible waste heat recovery is the collection of data sufficient to describe the process with a heat balance. The next step is to find all point sources of heat use or exhaust, to determine the annual energy and mean temperature for each, and to show this information on an input-output diagram of the facility. The most promising candidates for heat recovery are then examined in detail. If at all possible, the waste heat from a process should be used to improve the efficiency of that same process at its heat source. This practice avoids transportation losses and helps keep each process as independent from another as possible.

The Economics of Waste Heat Recovery

The benefits from waste heat recovery can be substantial; therefore, the benefits included in the economic analysis must be as complete as possible.

The analysis must also include complete details of the costs involved and the amount by which these costs are reduced by any tax benefits.

Waste Heat Recovery Equipment

The factors that determine which equipment to select for waste heat recovery are the fluid temperature at the source, the intended use for the waste heat, and the distance the heated fluid (if any) must be transported.

- *Recuperators*: A recuperator is a heat transfer device that passes gas to be heated through tubes that are surrounded by a gas that contains excess heat. The heat is transferred from the hot gas to the tubes and through the tube walls to the cool gas inside the tubes.
- *Air Preheaters/Economizers*: In an air preheater or economizer, hot gas flowing through a series of closed channels transfers heat to cooler gas in adjacent channels. This kind of equipment allows the use of hot flue gas to preheat combustion air and reduces the amount of heat that must be supplied by the fuel.
- *Run-around Coils:* A run-around coil heat exchanger consists of two heat exchanger coils connected by piping; a pump is also usually required. The heat is picked up by the heat exchange fluid in one coil. The fluid is then pumped to the other coil where the heat is removed and used. This heat transfer method makes waste heat recovery possible when the source and sink are somewhat separated.
- *Finned-tube Heat Exchangers:* This type of heat exchanger is a tube surrounded by perpendicular fins. The fins help to transfer heat from the tube to the surrounded air by enlarging the heat transfer surface area. If the surrounding fluid has a higher temperature than the tube, the transfer works in the opposite way and transfers heat from the fluid to the material inside the tube. This type of heat exchanger is very common and is often used on boilers to recover some of the heat that would otherwise be lost in the stack gas. It is also used in baseboard heating and automobile radiators.

- *Heat Pipe Heat Exchangers:* Heat pipes are applied for moisture removal in air conditioning systems. A heat pipe is a gas-to-gas heat exchanger, and it has more widespread uses than just in air conditioning systems. They can be used as air preheaters for a boiler or furnace, as heat reclaimers from waste streams, and as heat exchangers in drying and curing ovens. Heat pipes have a variety of applications in industrial waste heat recovery because of their high efficiency and compact size.
- *Waste Heat Boilers*: If gas leaving some industrial process is sufficiently hot to vaporize water or some other working fluid, it may be possible to use a waste heat boiler. Such a boiler uses waste heat to produce vapour or steam which can be used directly in the industrial processes or can be run through a turbine, pump, or generator to generate electricity or shaft power. Water has been the customary fluid for this purpose, but working fluids with lower boiling points are becoming more common.

Boiler Efficiency Improvement

We have discussed combustion in boilers with particular attention to combustion air. In addition to monitoring combustion air closely, good boiler management requires close attention to the boiler control system and to balancing the load economically between boilers. There are also other opportunities for saving money and increasing production with boilers, and they are discussed in this section.

Inspecting the Boiler System

The boiler system often provides clear indications of opportunities to save energy and money. In a visual inspection of a boiler, look at the gauges first. If the gauges do not work, the boiler control system is probably not functioning correctly; this provides an opportunity for a substantial savings in fuel costs. If the boiler has not been professionally inspected and adjusted within the past two years, the same opportunity exists. If the boiler has not been professionally inspected and adjusted within the past two years, the same opportunity exists. If the boiler stack temperature exceeds the boiler water temperature by more than 150 °F, the boiler is not operating as efficiently as it should; in that case, a professional adjustment is usually worthwhile. Look for rust in water gauges. This means that the pipes and tubes need to be cleaned for optimum operating efficiency. Check the boiler exhaust gas. If it is black, too little outside air is being used in combustion; if it is clear, too much outside air is being used.

A boiler can explode, so it is very important that all the safety features be in operating condition. Most building safety codes require that a boiler be inspected periodically; make sure that these inspection requirements have been complied with. Also make sure that outside air can get to the boiler to provide oxygen for combustion. Insufficient combustion air causes incomplete combustion and the generation of carbon monoxide. This is not only an inefficient use of energy, it is potentially dangerous.

Load Management

Boilers differ in efficiencies, and, in a system with several boilers, it makes sense to determine which boilers are the most efficient and to develop a method for allocating the load to them in order of decreasing efficiency. This allocation can be done either manually, by turning boilers down or off during off-peak seasons, or on a real-time basis through computer control. A boiler operates inefficiently with low loads, and it is usually worthwhile to operate one boiler at 90% capacity rather than two boilers at 45% capacity or three at 30%.

Insulation

One common method for reducing heat loss from boilers is the addition of pipe and surface insulation. The choice of insulation type and thickness, together with the economics of insulation has already been discussed.

Components

Boiler efficiency can also be improved by replacing the burners and other components with more efficient models as they are developed. Besides burners, other components that should be examined are those where the heat balance indicates that waste heat may be successfully used, such as in units for preheating fuel oil or other fuels. As with other products, efficiency claims for boilers and their components are often over-stated; any new product should be evaluated carefully before deciding to buy it.

Improving the Steam Distribution System

Steam distribution systems consist of piping from a boiler to points of use, together with the steam traps, condensate return lines, and any pumps needed for condensate return. The main function of the steam distribution system is to get the steam to where it is needed and to return the condensate to the boiler, doing both as efficiently as possible. Energy management can affect this system by improving the insulation, detecting and repairing steam and condensate leaks, maintaining the steam traps and condensate pumps, and providing water treatment. The steam distribution system should be inspected at the same time the boiler is inspected.

Insulation

Energy can be saved by insulating the pipes that carry either steam or condensate. The condensate return tanks should also be checked to see whether they need to be insulated.

Steam Leaks

Steam leaks can be expensive if large amounts of steam are lost; condensate leaks represent lost heat and loss of treated water. In many environments, steam leaks can be detected by their hissing; in very noisy environments, it may be necessary to use an industrial stethoscope or an ultrasonic leak detector. Evidence of possible condensate leaks includes pools of hot water, dripping pipes, and rust spots on pipes. While looking for leaks, put your hand close to the pipes. If a pipe is too hot to touch, it probably should be insulated.

STEAM TRAPS

The main function of steam traps is to drain condensed steam from the steam distribution network so that it can be returned to the boiler. However, anything that reduces heat transfer from the steam to the pipe walls can be a source of inefficiency. In particular, air and dissolved gases act as insulators and should be removed, along with any condensed steam, as soon as possible within the steam distribution system. This removal is also a function of a steam trap.

The maintenance of steam traps is important in energy management because the condensate, dissolved air, and certain gases must be removed from the steam lines if the lines are to transmit steam. If condensate is not removed, the steam lines become lines carrying water but transmitting little heat. If dissolved air is not removed, the steam carries significantly less heat per pound since the pressure of the steam is reduced by the pressure of the air. If dissolved CO_2 is not removed, carbonic acid is formed, and this has a corrosive effect upon pipes. Any of these things can happen if steam traps fail closed. If steam traps fail open and they are open to the air, the effect is the same as if there were a large leak in a steam line. Thus, steam trap maintenance can be a very important source of energy cost savings.

Water Treatment

Scaling also has an adverse effect on heat transfer. The more scale buildup, the less heat is transmitted through pipe walls. For example, a layer of $CaSO_4$ only 0.024 inch thick caused a temperature drop of 362°F in a boiler, leading to an outer tube temperature of 1004°F and to ultimate failure of the boiler tubes. This scaling can be prevented by proper water treatment, making water treatment one of the essential elements in boiler management. The amount of water treatment needed depends on the hardness of the water and the quantity of water used. Because the condensate is pure water, returning it to the boiler saves money on additional water treatment.

COGENERATION

Cogeneration is the process of sequentially producing both electricity and steam from a single fuel source. A cogeneration facility uses some of the thermal energy that a plant producing only electric power would otherwise reject to the environment. Thus, cogeneration can produce a given amount of electric power and thermal energy for 10 to 30% less fuel than a plant which produces the same amount of electricity alone. The specific fuel savings is highly dependent on both the cogeneration technology used and the quantity of thermal energy used. For many facilities, cogeneration offers a way to provide both low-cost electric power and the large amounts of thermal energy needed for thermal energy.

Cogeneration has become more attractive because any cogenerated electricity that contributes to the total peak deliverable capacity of an electric utility enables the utility to avoid building an equal amount of new capacity, and the utility is obligated to buy such electricity from the cogenerator. (There are strict conditions on this purchase: The company must use some of the electricity it produces, the cogenerated electricity must be controlled and interconnected in such a way that it will not damage the utility network, and it must not force a net loss of revenues upon the utility.) Cogeneration also offers additional benefits to the utility, since the electric power is produced with less environmental pollution than it came from a central station utility plant.

Cogeneration offers a number of benefits to the facility, particularly if it is an industry that has a source of waste fuel. Wood chips, black liquor, bagasse, garbage, and waste heat are all sources of fuel that would replace the need for a facility to purchase expensive oil, gas or coal. High efficiency cogeneration helps industries and businesses compete in national and international markets, and helps keep more jobs in these industries and businesses. A facility can reduce its energy cost by lowering its need to buy expensive power from the electric utility company. It may also get some income from selling excess power to the utility.

Chapter 4

Energy Audit

ENERGY AUDIT PROCESS

Introduction

Once a commercial or industrial facility has designated its energy manager and given that person the support and authority necessary to develop an adequate energy management program, the first step the energy manager should take is to conduct an energy audit. Also called an energy survey, energy analysis, or energy evaluation, the energy audit examines the ways, it is currently used in that facility and identifies some alternatives for reducing its costs. The goals of the audit are:

- to clearly identify the types and costs of energy use,
- to understand how that energy is being used and possibly wasted,
- to identify and analyze alternatives such as improved operational techniques and/or new equipment that could substantially reduce energy costs, and
- to perform an economic analysis on those alternatives and determine which ones are cost-effective for the business or industry involved. This chapter addresses the three phases of an energy audit: preparing for the audit visit; performing the facility survey and implementing the audit recommendations.

Phase One- Preparing for an Energy Audit

The energy audit process starts with an examination of the historical and descriptive energy data for the facility. Specific data that should be gathered in this preliminary phase includes the energy bills for the past twelve months, descriptive information about the facility such as a plant layout, and a list of each piece of equipment that significantly affects the energy consumption. Before the audit begins, the auditor must know what special measurement tools will be needed. A briefing on safety procedures is also a wise precaution.

Gathering Preliminary Data on the Facility

Before performing the facility audit, the auditors should gather information on the historical energy use at the facility and on the factors likely to affect the energy use in the facility. Past energy bills, geographic location, weather data, facility layout and construction, operating hours, and equipment lists are all part of the data needed.

Analysis of Bills

The audit must begin with a detailed analysis of the energy bills for the previous twelve months. This is important for several reasons: the bills show the proportionate use of each different energy source when compared to the total energy bill; an examination of where energy is used can point out previously unknown energy wastes; and, the total amount spent on energy puts an obvious upper limit on the amount that can be saved.

The energy bill data must be analyzed by energy source and billed location. Each area of the country and each different industry type has a unique pattern of energy consumption, and presenting the data as said before helps in defining and analyzing these patterns.

A complete analysis of the energy bills for a facility requires a detailed knowledge of the rate structures in effect for the facility. To accurately determine the costs of operating individual pieces of equipment, the energy bills must be broken down into their components, such as demand charge and energy charges for the electric bill. This breakdown is also necessary to be able to calculate the savings from Energy Management Opportunities

(EMOs) such as high-efficiency lights and high-efficiency motors, and off-peak electrical use by rescheduling some operations. This examination of energy rate structures is explained in detailed in Chapter 3.

Geographic Location/Degree Days/Weather Data

The geographic location of the facility should be noted, together with the weather data for that location. The local weather station, the local utility or the state energy office can provide the average degree days for heating and cooling for that location for the past twelve months. This degree-day data will be very useful in analyzing the energy needed for heating or cooling the facility. Heating degree days (HDD) and cooling degree days (CDD) are given separately, and are specific to a particular geographic location. The degree day concept assumes that the average building has a desired indoor temperature of 70°F, and that 5°F of this is supplied by internal heat sources such as lights, appliances, equipment, and people. Thus, the base for computing HDD is 65°F.

Example: If there were a period of three days when the outside temperature averaged 50°F each day, then the number of HDD for this three day period would be

$$\text{HDD} = (65°\text{-}50°) * 3 \text{ days} = 45 \text{ degree days.}$$

HDD for a year are found out by taking the outside temperature each hour of the heating season, subtracting that temperature from 65 °F, and summing up all of these hourly increments to find the total number of degree hours. This total is then divided by 24 to get the number of HDD. Cooling degree days are similar, using 65°F as the base, and finding the number of hours that the outside temperature is above 65 °F, and dividing this by 24 to get the total CDD.

Facility Layout

Next the facility layout or plan should be obtained, and reviewed to determine the facility size, floor plan, and construction features such as wall and roof material and insulation levels, as well as door and window sizes and construction. A set of building plans could supply this information in sufficient detail.

Operating Hours

Operating hours for the facility should also be obtained. Knowing the operating hours in advance allows some determination as to whether any loads could be shifted to off-peak times. Adding a second shift can often reduce energy bills because the energy costs during second and third shifts are usually substantially cheaper (as off-peak power rate is substantially lower than on-peak power rate).

Equipment List

Finally, the auditor should get an equipment list for the facility and review it before conducting the audit. All large pieces of energy-consuming equipment such as heaters, boilers, air conditioners, chillers, water heaters, and specific process-related equipment should be identified. This list, together with data on operational uses of the equipment allows the auditor to gain a good understanding of the major energy-consuming tasks or equipment at the facility.

Tools for the Audit

To obtain the best information for a successful energy cost control program, the auditor must make some measurements during the audit visit. The range of equipments needed depends on the type of energy-consuming equipment used at the facility, and on the range of potential EMOs that might be considered. Tools commonly needed for energy audits are:

Tape measures: It is used to check the dimensions of the walls, ceilings, doors, and windows, and the distances between pieces of equipment for purposes such as determining the length of a pipe for transferring waste heat from one piece of equipment to another.

Lightmeter: It is used to measure illumination levels in facilities. It can be used for direct analysis of lighting systems and comparison with recommended light levels specified by the Illuminating Engineering Society. Many areas in buildings and plants are still significantly over-lighted, and measuring this excess illumination allows the auditor to recommend a reduction in lighting levels through lamp removal programs or by replacing inefficient lamps with high efficiency lamps that may supply slightly less illumination than the old inefficient lamps..

Thermometer: It is used to measure temperature. Several thermometers are generally needed to measure temperatures in offices and other worker areas, and to measure the temperature of operating equipment. Knowing process temperatures allows the auditor to determine process equipment efficiencies, and also to identify waste heat sources for potential heat recovery programs.

Voltmeter: It is useful for determining operating voltages on electrical equipment, and especially useful when the nameplate has worn off of a piece of equipment or is otherwise unreadable or missing.

Wattmeter/Power Factor Meter: A portable hand-held wattmeter and power factor meter is very handy for determining the power consumption and power factor of individual motors and other inductive devices, and the load factors of motors.

Combustion Analyzer: Combustion analyzers are portable devices which estimate the combustion efficiency of furnaces, boilers, or other fossil fuel burning machines. Two types are available: digital analyzers and manual combustion analysis kits. Digital combustion analysis equipment performs the measurements and reads out combustion efficiency in percent. These instruments are fairly complex and expensive.

The manual combustion analysis kits typically require multiple measurements including the temperature, oxygen content, and carbon dioxide content of the exhaust stack. The efficiency of the combustion process can be calculated after determining these parameters. The manual process is lengthy and frequently subject to human error.

Ultrasonic Leak Detector: Ultrasonic compressed air leak detectors are electronic ultrasonic receivers that are tuned very precisely to the frequency of the hissing sound of an air leak. These devices are reasonably priced, and are extremely sensitive to the noise a small air leak makes. The detectors can screen out background noise and pick up the sound of an air leak. All facilities which use compressed air for applications should have one of these devices, and should use it routinely to identify wasteful air leak.

Airflow Measurement Devices: Measuring air flow from heating, air conditioning or ventilating ducts, or from other sources of air flow is one of the energy auditor's tasks. Airflow measurement devices can be used to identify problems with air flows, such as whether the combustion air flow into a gas heater is correct. Typical airflow measuring include are velometer, an anemometer, or an airflow hood.

Blower Door Attachment: Building or structure tightness can be measured with a blower door attachment. This device is frequently used in residences and in office buildings to determine the air leakage rate or the number of air changes per hour in the facility. This often helps determine whether the facility has substantial structural or duct leaks that need to be found and sealed.

Smoke Generator: A simple smoke generator can be used in residences, offices and other buildings to find air infiltration and leakage around doors, windows, ducts and other structural features. Care must be taken in using this device, since the chemical "smoke" produced may be hazardous, and breathing protection masks may be needed.

Safety Equipment: The use of safety equipment is a vital precaution for any energy auditor. Safety glasses, hearing protectors, electrically insulated gloves, thermally insulated gloves, breathing protection masks, steel-shank safety shoes, etc are the most commonly recommended safety equipment.

Phase Two—the Facility Inspection

Once all of the basic data has been collected and analyzed, the audit team should tour the entire facility to examine the operational patterns and equipment usage, and should collect detailed data on the facility itself as well as on all energy using equipment. This facility inspection should systematically examine the nine major systems within a facility, using portable instrumentation and common sense guided by an anticipation of what can go wrong. These systems are: the building envelope; the boiler and steam distribution system; the heating, ventilating, and air conditioning system; the electrical supply system; the lighting system, including all lights, windows, and adjacent surfaces; the hot water distribution system; the compressed air distribution system; the motors; and the manufacturing system. Together, these systems account for all the energy used in any facility. Examining all of them is a necessary step toward understanding and managing energy utilization within the facility.

The facility inspection can often provide valuable information on ways to reduce energy use at no cost or at low cost. Actually, several inspections should be made at different times and on different days to discover if lights or other equipment are left on unnecessary, or to target process waste streams that should be eliminated or minimized. These inspections can also help identify maintenance tasks that could reduce energy use. Broken windows should be fixed, holes and cracks should be cleaned, and HVAC filters should be cleaned or replaced.

The facility inspection is an important part of the overall audit process. Data gathered on this tour, together with an extensive analysis of this data will result in an audit report that includes a complete description of the time-varying energy consumption patterns of the facility, a list of each piece of equipment that affects the energy consumption together with an assessment of its condition, a chronology of normal operating and maintenance practices, and a list of recommended energy management ideas for possible implementation.

Introductory Meeting

The audit leader should start the audit by meeting with the facility manager and the maintenance supervisor. He should briefly explain the purpose of the audit and indicate the kind of information the team needs to obtain during the facility.

Audit Interviews

Getting the correct information on the facility equipment and operation is important if the audit is going to be the most successful in identifying ways to save money on energy bills. The company philosophy towards investments, the impetus behind requesting the audit, and the expectations from the audit can be determined by interviewing the general manager, chief operating officer, or other executives. The facility manager or plant manager can provide operational data on the facility. The finance officer can provide any necessary financial records, such as utility bills for electric, gas, oil, other fuels, water and waste water, expenditures for maintenance and repair, etc.

The auditor must also interview the floor supervisors and equipment operators to understand the building and process problems. Line or area supervisors usually have the best information on the times their equipment is used. The maintenance supervisor is often the primary person to talk to about types of lighting and lamps, sizes of motors, sizes of air conditioners and space heaters, and electrical loads of specialized process equipment. Finally, the maintenance staff must be interviewed to find the equipment and performance problems.

Initial Walk-through Tour

An initial facility/plant tour should be conducted by the facility/plant manager, and should allow the auditor or audit team to see the major operational and equipment features of the facility. The main purpose of the initial tour is to obtain general information, and to obtain a general understanding of the facility's operation. More specific information should be obtained from the maintenance and operational people during a second and more detailed data collection tour.

Gathering Detailed Data

Following the initial facility or plant tour, the auditor or audit team should acquire the detailed data on facility equipment and operation that will lead to identify the significant Energy for this facility. This data is gathered by examining the nine major energy-using systems in the facility.

As each of these systems are examined, the following questions should be asked:

1. What function(s) does this system serve?
2. How does this system serve its function(s)?
3. What is the energy consumption of this system?
4. What are the indications that this system is probably working?
5. If this system is not working, how can it be restored to good working condition?
6. How can the energy cost of this system be reduced?
7. How should this system be maintained?
8. Who has the direct responsibility for maintaining and improving the operation and energy efficiency of this system?

As each system is inspected, this data should be recorded on individualized data sheets that have been prepared in advance.

The Building Envelope

The building envelope includes all building components that are directly exposed to the outside environment. Its main function is to protect employees and materials from outside weather conditions and temperature variations; in addition, it provides privacy for the business and can serve other psychological functions. The components of the building envelope are outside doors, windows, and walls; the roof; and, in some cases, the floor.

As the building envelope is examined, insulation levels in various parts of the facility, the condition of the roof and walls, the location and size of any leaks or holes, and the location and size of any door or windows that open from conditioned to unconditioned space, should be recorded. The Boiler and Steam Distribution System

A boiler burns fuel to produce heat that converts water into steam, and the steam distribution system takes the steam from the boiler to the point of use. Boilers consume much of fuel used in many production facilities. The boiler is thus the first place to look when attempting to reduce natural gas or oil consumption. The steam distribution system is also a very important place to look for energy savings, since every kilogram of steam lost is another kilogram of steam that the boiler must produce.

The Heating, Ventilating, and Air Conditioning System

All heating, air conditioning and ventilation (HVAC) equipment should be inventoried. Prepared data sheets can be used to record type, size, model numbers, age, electrical specifications or fuel use specifications, and estimated hours of operation. The equipment should be inspected to determine the condition of the evaporator and condenser coils, the air filters, and the insulation on the refrigerant lines. Air velocity measurements may also be made and recorded to assess operating efficiencies or to discover conditioned air leaks. This data will allow later analysis to examine alternative equipment and operations that would reduce energy costs for heating, ventilating, and air conditioning.

The Electrical Supply System

This system consists of transformers, wiring, switches, and fuses—all the components needed to enable electricity to move from the utility-owned wires at the facility boundary to its point of use within the company. By our definition, this supply system does not include lights, motors, or electrical controls. Most energy problems associated with the distribution of electricity are also safety problems, and solving the energy problems helps to solve the safety-related problems.

Electricity from a utility enters a facility at a service transformer. The area around the transformer should be dry, the transformer fins should be free from leaves and debris so that they can perform their cooling function and the transformer should not be leaking oil. If a transformer fails to meet any one of these conditions there is a serious problem which should justify a call to the local electrical utility, or if the transformer is company-owned, to the person or department in charge of maintaining the electrical system. A more detailed audit of transformer should also be carried out.

A person performing an energy audit should examine the electrical supply panels and switch boxes. Danger signs and symptoms of wasted energy include signs of arcing such as burned spots on contacts, burned insulation, arcing sounds, and frayed wire. Other concerns are warm spots around fuse boxes and switches and the smell of warm insulation. Any of these symptoms can indicate a fire hazard and should be checked in more detail immediately.

Lights, Windows, and Reflective Surfaces

The functions of this system are to provide sufficient light for necessary work, to enable people to see where they are going, to assist in building and area security at night, to illuminate advertising, and to provide decoration. Making a detailed inventory of all lighting systems is important. Data should be recorded on numbers of each type of light fixture and lamp, the wattages of the lamps, and the hours of operation of each group of lights. A lighting inventory data sheet should be used to record this data.

The Hot Water Distribution System

The hot water system distributes hot water for washing, for use in industrial cleaning, and for use in kitchens. Its main components are hot water heaters, storage tanks, piping, and faucets. All water heaters should be examined, and data recorded on their type, size, age, model number, electrical characteristics or fuel use. What the hot water is used for, how much is used, and what time it is used should all be noted. The temperature of the hot water should be measured and recorded.

Air Compressors and the Air Distribution System

Air compressors and the air distribution system provide motive power for tools and some machinery, and often provide air to operate the heating, ventilating, and air conditioning system. Compression of air to high pressures involves lot of input energy. So, any leakage of compression system is expensive and requires immediate attention.

Motors

Electric motors account for between two-thirds and three-fourths of all the electric energy used by industry and about two-fifths of all electric energy use by commercial facilities. Replacement of existing motors with more efficient models is usually cost effective for applications where the motor is heavily used.

All electric motors over 1 hp should be inventoried. Prepared data sheets can be used to record motor size, use, age, model number, estimated hours of operation, other electrical characteristics, and possibly the full load power factor. Measurement of voltages, currents, power factors, and load factors may be appropriate for larger motors. Notes should be taken on the use of motors, particularly recording those that are infrequently used and might be candidates for peak load control or shifting use to off-peak times. All motors over 1 hp and with times of use of 2000 hours per year or greater, are likely candidates for replacement by high-efficiency motors—at least when they fail and must be replaced. It should be noted that few motors run at full load. Typical motor load factors are around 40-60%.

Manufacturing Processes

Each manufacturing process has opportunities for energy management, and each offers ways for the unwary to create operating problems in the name of energy management. The best way to avoid such operating problems is to include operating personnel in the energy audit process and to avoid rigid insistence on energy conservation as the most important goal.

The generic industrial processes that use the most energy are combustion for process steam and self-generated electricity, electrolytic processes, chemical reactors, combustion for direct heat in furnaces and kilns, and direct motor drive.

Any other equipment that consumes a substantial amount of energy should be inventoried and examined. Commercial facilities may have extensive computer and copying equipment, refrigeration and cooling equipment, cooking devices, printing equipment, water heaters, etc. Industrial facilities will have many highly specialized process and production operations and machines. Data on types, sizes, capacities, fuel use, electrical characteristics, age, and operating hours should be recorded for all of this equipment.

Preliminary Identification of Energy Management Opportunities

As the audit is being conducted, the auditor should take notes on potential EMOs that are evident. As a general rule, the greatest effort should be devoted to analyzing and implementing the EMOs which show the greatest savings, and the latest effort to those with the smallest savings potential. Therefore, the largest energy and cost activities should be examined carefully to see where savings could be achieved.

Identifying EMOs requires a good knowledge of the available energy efficiency technologies that can accomplish the same job with less energy and less cost. For example, over-lighting indicates a potential lamp removal or lamp change EMO, and inefficient lamps indicate a potential lamp technology change. Motors with high use times are potential EMOs for high efficiency replacements. Notes on waste heat sources should indicate what other heating sources they might replace, and how far away they are from the end use point. Identifying any potential EMOs during the walk-through will make it easier later on to analyze the data and to determine the final EMO recommendations.

The Energy Audit Report

The next step in the energy audit process is to prepare a report which details the final results of the energy analyses and provides energy cost saving recommendations. The length and detail of this report will vary depending on the type of facility audited.

The report should begin with an executive summary that provides the owners/managers of the audited facility with a brief synopsis of the total savings available and the highlights of each EMO. The report should then describe the facility that has been audited, and provide information on the operation of the facility that relates to its energy costs. The energy bills should be presented, with tables and plots showing the costs and consumption. Following the energy cost analysis, the recommended EMOs should be presented, along with the calculations for the costs and benefits, and the cost-effectiveness criterion.

Regardless of the audience for the audit report, it should be written in a clear, concise and easy-to understand format and style. An executive summary should be tailored to non-technical personnel, and technical jargon should be minimized. The reader who understands the report is more likely to implement the recommended EMOs. An outline for a complete energy audit report is shown below in table as form

The Energy Action Plan

An important part of the energy audit report is the recommended action plan for the facility. The energy action plan lists the EMOs which should be implemented first, and suggests an overall implementation schedule. Often, one or more of the recommended EMOs provides an immediate or very short payback period, so savings from that EMO—or those EMOs—can be used to generate capital to pay for implementing the other EMOs. In addition, the action plan also suggests that a company designate one person as the energy monitor or energy manager for the facility if it has not already done so. This person can look at the monthly energy bills and see whether any unusual costs are occurring, and can verify that the energy savings from EMOs is really being seen. Finally, this person can continue to look for other ways the company can save on energy costs, and can be seen as evidence that the company is interested in a future program of energy cost control.

Phase Three—Implementing the Audit Recommendations

After the energy consumption data has been collected and analyzed, the energy-related systems have been carefully examined, the ideas for improvement have been collected, and management commitment has been obtained, the next steps are to obtain company support for the program, to choose goals, and to initiate action.

The Energy Action Team

These preliminary audits have uncovered some energy management measures that can save significant amounts of money or can substantially improve production, funding for the changes and employee support are two additional critical ingredients for success. These can best be obtained with the help of a committee, preferably called something like the energy action team. The functions of this committee are:

- To create support within the company for energy management.
- To generate new ideas.
- To evaluate suggestions.
- To set goals.
- To implement the most promising ideas.

Goals

At least three different kinds of goals can be identified. First, performance goals, such as a reduction of 10% in Btu/unit product, can be chosen. Such goals should be modest at first so that they can be accomplished—in general, 10-30% reduction in energy usage for companies with little energy management experience and 8-15% for companies with more. These goals can be accompanied by goals for the reduction of projected energy costs by a similar amount. The more experienced the company is in energy management, the fewer easy saving possibilities exist; thus lower goals are more realistic in that case.

A second type of goal that can be established is an accounting goal. The ultimate objective in an energy accounting system is to be able to allocate the cost of energy to a product in the same way that other direct costs are allocated, and this objective guides the establishment of preliminary energy accounting goals. A preliminary goal would therefore be to determine the amount of electricity and the contribution to the electrical peak from each of the major departments within the company. This will require some additional metering, but such metering pays for itself in energy saving (induced by a better knowledge of the energy consumption patterns) in six months or less.

The third type of goal is that of employee participation. Even if an energy management program has the backing of the management, it will still fail without the support and participation of the employees.

Implementing Recommendations

In addition to providing and evaluating ideas, setting goals, and establishing employee support, the energy action committee has the duty of implementing the most promising ideas that have emerged from the energy evaluation process. Members of the committee have the responsibility to see that people are assigned to each project, that timetables are established, that money is assigned, and that progress monitoring and reporting procedures are set up and followed.

Monitoring discloses what measures contributed toward the company goals, what measures were counterproductive, and whether the goals themselves were too low or too high. Monitoring consists of collecting and interpreting data. The data to collect are defined by the objectives chosen by the energy action committee. At the very least, the electrical and gas bills and those of other relevant energy sources must be examined and their data graphed each month.

The monitoring data should provide direct feedback to those most able to implement the changes. Monitoring should result in more action. Find what is good, and copy it elsewhere. Find what is bad and avoid it elsewhere. If the goals are too high, lower them. If the goals are too low, raise them. Wherever the difference between the planned objectives and the achievements are great, initiate an analysis to determine the reasons and then develop new objectives, initiate new action, and monitor the new results. In this way, the analysis, action, and monitoring process repeat itself.

Chapter 5

Managing Energy Bills

UNDERSTANDING ENERGY BILLS

Introduction

Energy management is all about maximizing the profit of an organization by minimizing energy consumption per unit product. Energy has various costs attached to it. To be able to maximize profit, the cost aspect of the energy has to be understood.

Managers should know what electric rate schedule they are under and how much they are under and how much they are charged for the various components of their electric bill: demand, consumption, power factor, sales tax, etc. They should also know the details of their other energy rate structures.

Electric Rate Structures

Utility Costs

The best way to understand electric utility billing is to examine the costs faced by the utility. The major utility cost categories are the following:

- *Physical Plant:* This is often the single biggest cost category. Because electric power plants have become larger and more technologically sophisticated with more pollution control requirements, the cost of building and operating an electric power generation facility continues to increase. Furthermore, the utility is required to have sufficient capacity to supply the peak needs of its customers while maintaining some equipment in reserve in case of equipment failures. Otherwise brownouts or even blackouts may occur. This added capacity can be provided with expensive new generating facilities. Alternatively, instead of building new facilities, many utilities are urging their customers to reduce their peak demand so that the existing facilities will provide sufficient capacity.

- *Transmission Lines:* Another major cost category is the cost of transmission lines to carry the electricity from where it is produced to the general area where it is needed. Electricity is transmitted at relatively high voltage—often 500 to 1000 kV—to minimize resistance (I^2R) losses. This loss can be large or small depending on the transmission distances involved.
- *Substations:* Once the electricity reaches the general area where it is needed, the voltages must be reduced to the lower levels which can be safely distributed to consumers. This is done with step-down transformers at substations. A few customers may receive voltage at transmission levels, but the vast majority do not.
- *Distribution Systems:* After the voltage is reduced at a substation, the electricity is delivered to the individual customers through a local distribution system typically at a voltage level around 12 kV. Most residential customers are supplied electricity at 120 and 240 volts, single-phase. In addition to these two voltages, commercial customers often take 230 V, three-phase service. Some larger customers must also have 480 V, three-phase service in order to power their large motors, ovens, and process equipment. The desired voltages are provided through the use of appropriate step-down transformers at the customer's specific location. Components of the distribution system which contribute to the utility's costs include utility poles, lines, transformers, and capacitors.
- *Meters:* Meters form the interface between the utility company and customer. Although the meter costs are relatively small, they are considered a separate item by

the utility and are usually included in the part of the bill called the customer charge. The cost of a meter can range from under $ 50 for a residential customer to $ 1500 or more for an industrial customer requiring information on consumption, demand and power factor.

- *Administrative:* Administrative costs include salaries for executives, middle management, technical and office staff, as well as for maintenance staff. Office space and office equipment, taxes, insurance, and maintenance equipment and vehicles are also part of the administrative costs.
- *Energy:* Once the generation, transmission and distribution systems are in place, some form of primary energy must be purchased to fuel the boilers and generate the electricity. In the case of hydroelectric plants, the turbine generators are run by water power and the primary energy costs are small. Fossil fuel electric plants have experienced dramatic fluctuations in fuel costs depending on how national and world events alter the availability of oil, gas, and coal. The cost of fuel for nuclear power plants is reasonable, but the costs of disposing of the radioactive spent fuel rods, while still unknown, are expected to be relatively large.
- *Interest on Debt:* This cost category can be quite large. For example, the interest on debt for a large power plant costing $ 500 million to $ 1 billion is substantial. Utilities commonly sell bonds to generate capital, and these bonds represent debt that the company must pay interest on.
- *Profit:* Finally the utility must generate enough additional revenue above costs to provide a reasonable profit to stockholders. The profit level for private utility companies is determined by the state utility regulatory commission and is called the rate of return. Public-owned utilities such as municipal utilities or rural electric cooperatives usually set their own rates and their profit goes to their customers in the form of reduced municipal taxes or customer rebates.

Once the costs contributing to an electric bill are understood, the next step is to learn how these costs are allocated to the various customers. The billing procedure, also called the rate schedule, should be designed to reflect the true costs of generating the electric power. If the customers understand the problems faced by utilities, they can help the amenities in minimizing these costs. Recent rate schedules and proposed new ones capture the true costs of generation much better than has been done in the past, but more changes are still needed.

Regulatory Agencies

Private electric and gas utilities are chartered and regulated by individual states, and are also subject to some central regulation. The state utility regulatory agencies are most often called Public Utility Commissions or Public Service Commissions. Private utilities are called Investor Owned Utilities (IOUs), and their retail rates for residential, commercial and industrial customers are subject to review and approval by the state utility regulatory agencies.

Utility rates are set in two steps: first, the revenue requirements to cover costs plus profit are determined; second, rates are designed and set to recover these costs or revenue requirements. The state regulatory agencies set a rate of return for utilities. The rate of return is the level of profit a utility is allowed to make on its investment in producing and selling energy. In developing rates, the costs of serving different classes of customers must be determined and allocated to the customer classes. Rates are then structured to recover these costs from the appropriate customer class. Such rate designs are called cost-based rates. Often, these costs are average, or embedded costs, and do not consider the marginal costs associated with providing electricity at different times of the day and different seasons of the year. Rate design is subject to many competing viewpoints, and there are many different objectives possible in rate setting.

When an IOU requests a rate increase, the state regulatory agency holds a public hearing to review the proposed rate increase, and to take testimony from the utility staff, consulting engineers, customers and the public at large. The utility presents its case for why it needs a rate increase, and explains what its additional costs are. If these costs are judged "prudent" by the state regulatory agency and approved the utility, the utility is allowed to recover the costs, plus adding some of that cost to its rate base—which is the accumulated capital cost of facilities purchased or installed to serve the customers and on which the utility can earn its rate of return.

Many large utility customers participate actively in the rate hearings for their utility. Some state regulatory agencies are very interested in comments from utility customers regarding quality of service, reliability, lengths of outages, and other utility service factors. State regulatory agencies vary greatly in their attitude toward utility rate increases. Some states favor the utilities and consider their interests to be first priority, while other states consider the interests of the customers and the public as paramount.

Two other major categories of utilities exist: public or municipal utilities owned and operated by cities and local government entities; and Rural Electric Cooperatives (RECs). State regulatory agencies generally do not exercise the same degree of control over public utilities and RECs, since these utilities have citizens and customers controlling the rates and making the operating decisions, whereas the IOUs have stockholders making those decisions. Municipals and RECs also hold public hearings or public meetings whenever rate increases are contemplated. Customers who have an interest in participating in these meetings are usually encouraged to do so.

Customer Classes and Rate Schedules

An electric utility must serve several classes of customers. These classes vary in complexity of energy use, amount of consumption, and priority of need. The typical customer class categories are residential, commercial and industrial. Some utilities combine commercial and industrial customers into one class while other utilities divide the industrial class into heavy industrial and light industrial customers.

The state regulatory agencies and utilities develop different rate schedules for each customer class. Electric rate structures vary greatly from utility to utility, but they all have a series of common features. The most common components of rate schedules are described below, but not all of these components are included in the rate schedule for every customer class.

- *Administrative/Customer Charge:* This fee covers the utility's fixed cost of serving the customer including such costs as providing a meter, reading the meter, sending a bill, etc. This charge is a flat monthly fee per customer regardless of the number of kWh of electricity consumed.
- *Energy Charge:* This charge covers the actual amount of electricity consumed measured in kWh. The energy charge is based on an average cost, or base rate, for the fuel (natural gas, fuel oil, coal, etc.) Consumed to produce each kWh of electricity. The energy charge also includes a charge for the utility's operating and maintenance expenses.
- Many utilities charge a constant rate for all energy used, and this is called a flat rate structure. A declining block approach may also be used. A declining block schedule charges one price for the first block of energy (kWh) used and less for the next increment(s) of energy as more energy is used. Another approach is the increasing block rate where more is charged per increment as the consumption level increases.
- *Fuel Cost Adjustment:* If the utility has to pay more than its expected cost for primary fuel, the increased cost is "passed on" to the customer through use of a prescribed formula for fuel adjustment cost. In times of rapidly increasing fuel prices, the fuel adjustment cost can be a substantial proportion of the bill. This concept was adopted when fuel costs were escalating faster than utility commissions could grant rate increases. However, utilities can also use the fuel adjustment cost to reduce rates when fuel costs are lower than the cost included in the base rate.
- *Demand Charge:* The demand charge is used to allocate the cost of the capital facilities which provide the electric service. The demand charge may be "hidden" in the energy charge or it may be expressed as $ 6.25 per kW per month for all kW above 10 kW. For large customers, the demand charge is generally based on their kW demand. For small users such as residential and small commercial customers this charge is usually averaged into the energy charge.

- The value of the power or demand a utility uses to compute an electric bill is obtained from a peak power measurement that is averaged over a short period of time. Typical averaging times used by various electric utilities are 15 minutes, 30 minutes and one hour. A demand meter is generally installed by the utility when a customer's monthly demand exceeds 10 kW. Demand is usually averaged over a 15-minute period. This continues all month long as the 15-minute "rolling average" and the highest average demand recorded is retained. The meter reader then reads the demand at the end of the monthly billing period and resets the meter so the whole process can begin again.
- *Demand Ratchet:* An industrial or commercial rate structure may also have a demand ratchet component. This component allows the utility to adequately charge a customer for creating a large kW demand in only a few months of the year. Under the demand ratchet, a customer will not necessarily be charged for the actual demand for a given month. Instead the customer will be charged a percentage of the largest kW value during the last 11 months, or the current month's demand, whichever is higher.
- *Power Factor:* If a large customer has a poor power factor, the utility may impose another charge, assessed as a function of that power factor. Although the term "power factor" does not appear on power bill, it does affect energy costs. This can be thought of as a measure of "wasted" energy. Whenever power is supplied to an inductive load, such as an electric motor or a transformer, some of that power is used to create a magnetic field necessary to operate the equipment. This "reactive" power is, in effect, wasted as it does not produce any useful work. When kW = kVA, power factor is 1, and all power is being used to produce useful work. Power used indirectly increases the overall cost of the electricity system, therefore, customers with low power factor face higher costs.
- *Load Factor:* "Load factor" is another term that does not

appear on your utility bill, but does affect electricity costs. Load factor indicates how efficiently the customer is using peak demand. A high load factor means power usage is relatively constant. Low load factor shows that occasionally a high demand is set. To service that peak, capacity is sitting idle for long periods, thereby imposing higher costs on the system. Electrical rates are designed so that customers with high load factor are charged less overall per kWh.

All of these factors are considered when a utility sets its base rates—the rates the utility must charge to recover its general cost of doing business. The base rates contain an energy charge that is estimated to cover the average cost of fuel in the future. The fuel adjustment charge keeps the utility from losing money when the price of their purchased primary fuel is higher than was estimated in their base rates.

In addition, there are also a number of other features of electric rates incorporated in the rate structure which includes the relationship and form of prices within particular customer classes. The rate structure is set to maintain equity between and within customer classes, ensuring that there is no discrimination against or preferential treatment of any particular customer group. Some of the factors considered in the rate structure are: season of use; time of use; quantity of energy used—and whether increased consumption is encouraged, discouraged, or considered neutral; and social aspects such as the desire for a "lifeline" rate for low-income or elderly customers.

Residential Rate Schedules

A residential user is often a small consumer. A typical residential bill includes an administrative/customer charge, an energy charge which is large enough to cover both the actual energy charge and an implicit demand charge, and a fuel adjustment charge. Residential rates do not usually include an explicit demand charge because the individual demand is relatively inconsequential and expensive to meter.

Standard Residential Rate Schedule

A typical monthly rate schedule for a residential customer

includes customer charge, energy charge and fuel adjustment charge.

Low-use Residential Rate Schedule

A typical low-use residential service rate is an attempt to meet the needs of those on fixed incomes, is used for customers whose monthly consumption never exceeds 500 kWh. In addition, it cannot exceed 400 kWh more than twice a year. This rate is sometimes referred to as a lifeline rate.

Residential Rate Schedules to Control Peak Uses

Although individual resident demand is small collectively residential users place a peak demand burden on the utility system because the majority of them use their electricity at the same times of the day during the same months of the year. Some utilities charge more for energy during peaking months in an attempt to solve this problem. Many utilities have an optional time-of-day or time-of use rate which is suppose to help alleviate the daily peaking problem by charging customers more for electric use during these peak periods. A number of utilities also have a load management program to control customer's appliances.

Take the example of a Florida utility's residential demand profile over a given 24-hour period during the weekdays. The utility experiences one large peak around 9.00 am and another somewhat smaller peak near 9.00 pm. The first peak occurs when people get up in the morning and start using electricity. They all turn up their electric heat, cook breakfast, take a shower, and dry their hair at about the same time on weekday mornings. Then in the evening, they all come home from work, start cooking dinner, turn the heat back up (or use it more because nights are colder) and turn on the TV set at about the same time.

- *Seasonal Use Rate Schedule:* In a residential rate schedule, the season of use may be a factor in the rate structure. The utility may chose to attack its residential peaking problem by charging more for electricity consumed in the summer months when the highest peaks occur.
- *Time-of-day or Time-of-use Pricing:* To handle the daily peaking problem, some utilities charge more for energy

consumed during peak times. This requires the utility to install relatively sophisticated meters. It also requires some customer habit changes. Time-of-use pricing for residential customers is not very popular today; however, most utilities are required by their state regulatory agencies to provide a time-of-use rate for customers who desire one, so most utilities have some form of time-of-use pricing.

- *Peak Shaving:* Some utilities offer a discount to residential customers if the utility can hook up a remote control unit to cycle large electricity using appliances in the home (usually electric heaters, air conditioners and water heaters). This utility load control program is also called load management. This way the utility can cycle large appliance loads on and off periodically to help reduce demand. Since the cycling is performed over short periods of time, most customers experience little or no discomfort. This approach is rapidly gaining in popularity. This provides a rebate to the customers who agree to allow the utility to turn off their electric water heaters or air conditioners for short periods of time during peak hours.

General Service Rate Schedules

A general service rate schedule is used for commercial and small industrial users. This is a simple schedule usually involving only consumption (kWh) charges and customer charges. Sometimes, demand (kW) charges are used; this requires a demand meter.

The energy charge for this customer class is often substantially higher than for residential users for various non-economic reasons. Some of these reasons include the fact that many businesses have widely varying loads depending on the health of the economy, and many businesses close after only a few months of operation—sometimes leaving large unpaid bills. In additional, some regulatory agencies feel that residential customers should have lower rates since they cannot pass on electric costs to someone else.

Small Industrial Rate Schedules

A small industrial rate schedule is usually available for small industrial users and large commercial users. The service to these customers often becomes more complex because of the nature of the equipment used in the industry, and their consumption tends to be higher. Consequently, the billing becomes more sophisticated. Usually, the same cost categories occur as in the simpler schedules, but other categories have been added. Some of these are outlined below.

- *Voltage Level*: One degree of complexity is introduced according to what voltage level the customer needs. If the customer is willing to accept the electricity at transmission voltage levels (usually 50,000 volts or higher) and do the necessary transforming to usable levels on-site, then the utility saves considerable expense and can charge less. If the customer needs the service at a lower voltage, then the utility must install transformers and maintain them. In that case, the cost of service goes up and so does the bill.
- The voltage level charge can be handled in the rate schedule in several ways. One is for the utility to offer a percentage discount on the electric bill if the customer owns its own primary transformer and accepts service at a higher voltage than it needs to run its equipment. Another is to increase the energy charge as the voltage level decreases.
- *Demand Billing:* Some companies have almost constant demand whereas some have steep peaks in demand profile. This means the utility must maintain and gear up equipment which will only be needed for a short period of time. This is quite expensive, and some mechanism must be used by the utility to recover these additional costs.
- To properly charge for this disproportionate use of facilities and to encourage companies to reduce its peak demand, an electric utility will usually charge industrial users for the peak demand incurred during a billing cycle, normally a month. Often a customer can achieve substantial cost reductions simply by reducing peak

demand and still consuming the same amount of electricity. A good example of this would be to move the use of an electric furnace from peaking times to non-peaking times (may be second or third shifts). This means the same energy could be used at less cost since the demand is reduced.

- *Ratchet Clause:* Many utility rate structures have a ratchet clause associated with their demand rate. To understand the purpose of the ratchet clauses, one must realize that if the utility must supply power to meet a peak load in July, it must keep that equipment on hand and maintain it for the next peak load which may not occur for another year. To charge for this cost, and to encourage customers to level their demand over the remaining months, many utilities have a ratchet clause.
- A ratchet clause usually says that the billed demand for any month is a percentage (usually greater than 50%) of the highest maximum demand of the previous 11 months or the actual demand, whichever is greater. For a company with a large seasonal peaking nature, this can be a real problem. A peak can be set in July during a heavy air-conditioning period that the company in effect pays for a full year. The impact of ratchet clauses can be significant, but often a company never realizes this has occurred.
- *Power Factor*: Whenever power is supplied to an inductive load, such as an electric motor or a transformer, some of that power is used to create a magnetic field necessary to operate the equipment. This "reactive" power is, in effect, wasted as it does not produce any useful work. Since the utilities have to maintain the equipments for providing actual (used) power as well as reactive power, it must penalize companies with low power factor. Most utilities do build in a power factor penalty for industrial users. However, the way of billing varies widely. Some of the more common ways include:
  - Billing demand is measure in kVA instead of kW. As the power factor is improved, kVA is reduced, providing a motivation for power factor

improvement.

- Billing demand is modified by a measure of the power factor. Some utilities will increase billed demand one percent for each one percent the power factor is below a designated base. Others will modify demand as follows:
- Billed demand = (Actual demand) * [(Base power factor)/(Actual power factor)]
- In this way, if the actual power factor is lower than the base power factor, the billed demand is increased. If the actual power factor is higher than the base power factor, some utilities will allow the fraction to stay, thereby providing a reward instead of a penalty. Some will run the calculation only if actual power factor is below base power factor.
- The demand or consumption billing schedule is changed according to the power factor. Some utilities will change the schedule for both demand and consumption according to the power factor.
- A charge per kVAR is used. Some companies will charge for each kVAR used above a set minimum. This is direct billing for the power factor.

In addition, since a regular kW meter does not recognize the reactive power, some other measuring instrument must be used to determine the reactive power or the power factor. A kVA meter can be supplied by the utility, or the utility might decide to only periodically check the power factor at a facility. In this case a utility would send a crew to the facility to measure the power factor for a short period of time, and then remove the test meter.

Large Industrial Rate Schedules

Most utilities have very few customers that would quality for or desire to be on a large industrial rate schedule. Sometimes, however, one or two large industries will utilize a significant portion of a utility's total generating capacity. Their size makes the billing more complex; therefore, a well-conceived and well-deceived rate schedule is necessary.

Typically a large industrial schedule will include the same component as a small industrial schedule. The difference occurs in the amount charged for each category. The customer charge, if there is one, tends to be higher. The minimum kW of demand tends to be much higher in cost/kW, but all additional kW may be somewhat lower (per kW) than on small industrial schedules. Similarly, the charge per kWh for consumption can be somewhat less. The reason for this is economy of scale; it is cheaper for a utility to deliver a given amount of energy to many smaller customers.

Cogeneration and Buy-Back Rates

There has been significant renewed interest in on-site-generated power. This can be from cogeneration (on-site generation of thermal heat with concurrent generation of electricity), windmills, solar thermal, solar photovoltaics, or other sources. Generation of this energy for use only on site is often not cost effective due to variability of loads. Resale of excess electricity to local utility, however, often makes a non-utility electric generation project economically feasible. Utilities have developed buy-back rates for this excess electricity. Since the value of this energy may be either less than or greater than the generating cost to the utility, buy-back usually requires a separate meter and a separate rate schedule.

Others

Many other rate schedules are being developed as the needs dictate. For example, some utilities have a rate schedule involving interruptible and curtailable loads. An interruptible load is one that can be turned off at certain times of the day or year. A utility offers a lower rate as an incentive to companies willing to help decrease the system demand during peaking times of the day or year.

A curtailable load is one that the company may be willing to turn off if given sufficient notice. For example, the utility may hear of a weather forecast for extreme heat or extreme cold which would result in a severe peaking condition. It may then call its curtailable customers and ask that all the curtailable loads be turned off. Of course, the utility is willing to compensate the customers for this privilege too.

Natural Gas

Natural gas rate schedules are similar in structure to electric rate schedules, but they are often much simpler. Natural gas companies also experience a peaking problem. Theirs is likely to occur on very cold winter days and / or when supply disruptions exist. Due to the unpredictable nature of these peak problems, gas utilities normally do not charge for peak demand. Instead, customers are placed into interruptible priority classes.

A customer with a high priority will not be curtailed or interrupted unless absolutely necessary. A customer with the lowest priority, however, will be curtailed or interrupted whenever a shortage exists. Normally some gas is supplied to keep customer's pipes from freezing and pilot lights burning. To encourage use of the low-priority schedules, utilities charge significantly less for this gas rate.

Like electric rates, fuel cost adjustments do exist in gas rates. Sales tax also apply to natural gas bills.

Fuel Oil and Coal

Fuel oils are a very popular fuel source in some parts of the country, but they are rarely used in others. Natural gas and fuel oil can generally be used for the same purpose so the availability and price of each generally determines which is used.

Billing schedules for fuel oils vary widely among geographical areas of the country. The prices are set by market conditions (supply vs demand), but within any geographical area they are fairly consistent. Within each fuel oil grade, there is a large number of sulfur grades, so shopping around can sometimes pay off. Basically, the price is simply a flat charge per gallon, so the total cost is the number of gallons used times the price per gallon.

Like fuel oil, coal comes in varying grades and varying sulfur content. It is, in general, less expensive than fuel oil per Btu, but it does require higher capital investments for pollution control, coal receiving and handling equipment, storage, and preparation. Coal is priced on a per ton basis with provisions for or consideration of sulfur content and percent moisture.

Steam and Chilled Water

In some areas of the country, customers can purchase steam and chilled water directly instead of buying the fuel and generating their own. This can occur where there are large-scale cogeneration plants (steam), refuse-fueled plants (steam), or simple economics of scale (steam and / or chilled water). In the case of both steam and chilled water, it is normal to charge for the energy itself (pounds of steam or ton-hours of chilled water) and the demand (pounds of steam per hour or tons of chilled water).

Monthly Energy Bill Analysis

Once the energy rate structures have been examined, management should now understand how the company is being charged for the energy it uses each month. This is an important piece of the overall process of energy management at a facility. The next step in the examination of energy costs should be to review the bills and determine the average, peak and off-peak costs of energy used during at least the past twelve months.

Energy bills should be broken down into components that can be controlled by the facility. These cost components can be listed individually in tables and then plotted. Electricity bills should be categorized by demand costs per kW per month, and energy costs per kWh. The energy analyst must be sure to account for all the taxes, the fuel adjustment costs, the fixed charges, and any other costs so that the true cost of the controllable energy cost components can be determined.

The utility cost data are used initially to analyze potential Energy Management Opportunities (EMOs) and will ultimately influence which EMOs are recommended.

The energy consumption should be plotted as well as tabulated to show the patterns of consumption pictorially. The graphs often display some unusual feature of energy use, and may thus help highlight periods of very high use. These high-use periods can be further examined to determine whether some piece of equipment or some process was being used much more than normal. The energy auditor should make sure that any discrepancies in energy use are accounted for.

Actions to Reduce Electric Utility Costs

Typical actions to reduce kWh consumption involve replacing existing lights with more efficient types; replacing electric heating and cooling equipment with more efficient models; adding insulation to walls and ceilings; replacing motors with high efficiency models and using variable speed drives; recovering heat from air compressors, refrigeration units, or production processes to heat water for direct use or to pre-heat water for steam production; and replacing manufacturing or process equipment by more energy efficient models or processes.

Most of these actions will also result in demand reductions and produce savings through lower kW charges. Other actions that specifically reduce demand involve controlling and scheduling existing loads to reduce the peak kW value recorded on the demand meter.

Utility Incentives and Rebates

Many utility rate structures include incentives and rebates for customers to replace old, energy inefficient equipment with newer, more energy efficient models. Utilities offer such incentives and rebates because it is cheaper for them to save the energy and capacity for new customers than it is to build new power plants or new gas pipelines to supply that additional load. In addition, stringent environmental standards in some areas make it almost impossible for electric utilities to build and operate new facilities—particularly those burning coal. Helping customers install more energy efficient electrical and gas equipment allows utilities to delay the need for new facilities, and to reduce the emissions and fuel purchases for the units they do operate.

Direct incentives may be in the form of low interest loans that can be paid back monthly with energy savings resulting from the more efficient equipment. Incentives may also be in the form of lower rates for the electricity used to run higher efficiency lights and appliances, and more efficient process equipment. Other incentives include free audits from the utilities and free technical assistance in identifying and installing these energy efficiency improvements.

Indirect incentives also exist, and are often in the form of a special rate for service at a time when the utility is short of capacity, such as a time of day rate or an interruptible rate. The time of day rate offers a lower cost of electricity during the off-peak times, and often also during the off-season times. Interruptible rates allow large use customers to purchase electricity at very low rates with the restriction that their service can be interrupted on short notice.

Rebates are probably the most common method that utilizes use to encourage customers to install high efficiency appliances and process equipment. Utilities sometimes offer a rebate tied t the physical device—such as $ 1.00 for each low-wattage fluorescent lamp used or $ 10.00 per hp for an efficient electric motor. Other rebates are offered for reductions in demand—such as $ 250 for each kW of demand that is eliminated.

Incentives or rebates can substantially improve the cost effectiveness of customer projects to replace old devices with new, high efficiency equipment. In some cases, the incentives or rebates may be great enough to completely pay for the difference in cost in putting in a high efficiency piece of equipment instead of the standard efficiency model.

Chapter 6

Economics of Energy Management

ECONOMIC ANALYSIS AND LIFE CYCLE COSTING

Introduction

Once an energy management opportunity (EMO) has been identified, the energy manager must determine the cost-effectiveness of the EMO in order to recommend it to management for implementation, and to justify any capital expenditure for the project. If a group of EMOs have been identified, then they should be ranked on some economic basis, with the most cost-effective ones to be implemented first. There are many measures of cost-effectiveness, and sometimes businesses and industries use their own methods or procedures to make the final decisions. The basic elements of cost-effectiveness analysis are discussed in this chapter and some of the common techniques or measures of cost-effectiveness are presented.

Cash Flow Diagrams and Tables

It is often helpful to present costs visually. This can be accomplished with a tool called a cash flow diagram. Alternatively a cash flow table could be used. A cash flow diagram is a pictorial display of the costs and revenues associated with a project. Costs are represented by arrows pointing down, while revenues are represented by arrows pointing up. The time periods for the costs dictate the horizontal scale for the diagram. In a cash flow table, costs are marked as negative cash flow and revenues are marked as positive cash flows. Although some costs occur at different points in time, most of the time, an end-of-year approach is followed.

Simple Payback Period Cost Analysis

One of the most commonly used cost analysis methodologies is the Simple Payback Period (SPP) analysis. Also called the Payback Period (PBP) analysis, the SPP determines the number of years required to recover an initial investment through project returns. The formula is:

SPP = (Initial cost) / (Annual savings)

The advantage of the SPP is its simplicity, and it is easily understood by workers and management. It does provide a rough measure of the worth of a project. The primary disadvantages are: (1) the methodology does not consider the time value of money; and (2) the methodology does not consider any of the costs or benefits of the investment following the payback period.

Economic Analysis Using the Time Value of Money: Discounted Cash Flow Analysis

Introduction

Most people understand that money changes value over time. The change in worth is due to two primary factors: interest (opportunity cost) and inflation. Interest is the return earned on money when someone else uses it. Inflation is a decrease in the purchasing power of money. The effects of both interest and inflation are important to consider in a full economic analysis of energy projects.

Energy management expenditures are typically justified in terms of avoided energy costs. Expenses come at the beginning of a project, while savings/benefits occur later. The sums of money for costs and revenues that need to be compared are paid or received at different points in time. Because money changes value over time, these sums of money, or cash flows, should not be directly added together unless they occur at the same point in time. In order to correctly add these cash flows at different times, we need to reduce them to a common basis through the use of the interest rate, also called the discount rate. This method of treatment is called discounted cash flow analysis.

Simple Interest

There are two primary types of interest: simple and compound. Simple interest is earned (charged) only on the original principal amount, and paid once, at the end of the time period. The formula is:

$I = P*n*i$, where
I = the interest accumulated over n years
P = the original principal amount
n = the number of interest periods (often measured in years)
i = the interest rate per period

The general formula for the total amount owed or due at the end of a loan (investment) period of n years when using simple interest is:

$$
\begin{aligned}
F_n &= P + I \\
&= P + (P*n*i) \\
&= P\,(1 + n*i)
\end{aligned}
$$

Compound Interest

Interest which is earned (charged) on the accumulated interest as well as the original principal amount is said to be compounded. In other words, the interest which accumulates at the end of the first interest period is added to the original principal amount to form a new principal amount due at the end of the next period. Compound interest is used far more commonly in practice than simple interest.

Discounted Cash Flows: Basics and Single Sum Analysis

Once we understand the effects of interest or discounting, we can proceed with our goal of finding a method which correctly allows the addition of two cash flows occurring at different points in time. The general approach used is to reduce cash flows occurring at different times to a common basis through the use of the interest rate or discount rate. This method of treatment is called discounted cash flow analysis, and it is a fundamental approach that is necessary to use to correctly account for energy costs and savings in different years.

This section presents the formulas and compound interest factors used to convert a sum of money from its value in one time period to its corresponding value in another time period. Here, interest is assumed to be compounded annually, and cash flows are assumed to occur at the end of the year. The following notation will be used:

i = Annual interest rate (or discount rate. Also known as the minimum attractive rate of return or MARR)
n = The number of annual interest periods (in our case, the number of years)
P = A present value (or present worth)
A = A single payment in a series of n equal annual payments
F = A future value (or future worth)

Four important points apply in the use of discounted cash flow analysis:

- The end of one year is the beginning of the next.
- P is at the beginning of a year at a time regarded as being the present.
- F is at the end of the nth year from a time regarded as being the present.
- An A occurs at the end of each year of the period under consideration.

When P and A are involved, the first A of the series occurs one year after P.
When F and A are involved, the last A of the series occurs simultaneously with F.

Single Sum, Future Worth

The first task is to determine how to convert a single sum of money from a present amount to a future amount. In this problem, the present amount, P, and the interest rate are known. The unknown is the future amount, F. The formula for finding F is:

$$F = P\,(1 + i)^n$$

The term $(1+i)^n$ is known as the single sum, future worth factor, or the single payment, future worth factor. Although we are only discussing yearly interest and yearly time periods in this chapter, it is important to note that other interest periods can occur, such as quarterly. Since the compound interest factors are used extensively in Discounted Cash Flow analysis, numerical tables have been developed for various combinations of I and n.

Using the formula for future worth, the formula for finding the present worth of a single sum is found by solving for P. Thus, the single sum, present worth formula, or single payment, present worth formula, is:

$$P = F(1 + i)^{-n}$$

The term $(1 + i)^{-n}$ is called the present worth factor.

Discounted Cash Flows: Uniform Series

The next type of cash flow pattern to understand is a uniform series of costs or savings. A uniform series is a cash flow pattern with cash flows that are of the same magnitude, occurring at the end of several consecutive periods. We will be using years for our periods. Examples of uniform series of costs are car payments, house payments, or any other type of regular payment. Most of our energy management projects, or EMOs, produce a uniform series of savings in future energy costs. Four types of "conversions" will be addressed:

1. Given a present amount, find the equivalent uniform series. This is known as find A, given P, and is denoted by the factor $(A/P_{i,n})$.
2. Given a future amount, find the equivalent uniform series. This is known as find A, given F, and is denoted by the factor $(A/F_{i,n})$.
3. Given a uniform series, find the equivalent present worth. This is known as find P, given A, and is denoted by the factor $(P/A_{i,n})$.
4. Given a uniform series, find the equivalent future worth. This is known as find F, given A, and is denoted by the factor $(F/A_{i,n})$.

The following relations will help us to deal with the above conversions.

$$F = A\,[\{(1+i)^n - 1\}/i]$$
$$A = P\,[\{i(1+i)^n\}/\{(1+i)^n - 1]$$

A Cost Analysis Methodology Using Discounted Cash Flows

It is important to have a methodology to follow when performing a discounted cash flow analysis. The following methodology is recommended for performing economic analyses using cash flows:

- *Define the Alternatives:* State the problem, and list all feasible solutions or alternatives which have been selected for economic analysis.
- *Estimate the Relevant Costs:* Each alternative is defined in terms of its cash flows. Vital information includes the amount, timing, and direction (benefit or cost) of each cash flow.
- *Analyze the Alternatives:* Identify the most cost-effective alternative by analyzing each alternative using the discounted cash flow methodologies.
- *Perform Sensitivity Analyses:* Since the analysis mentioned earlier is generally based on estimated costs, these costs can be varied, depending on the uncertainty of the estimates, to see if the uncertainties have a pronounced effect.

The three pieces of data needed for the above methodology are:

(1) an estimate of the cash flows,
(2) an estimate of the interest rate or discount rate, and
(3) an estimate of the life of the project.

Once the concept of converting money from one time period to another is understood, then a method is needed to compare sums of money which are paid or received at different points in time. To accomplish this, cash flows are "moved around" in time using a discount rate, or MARR, and then compared. If two cash flows have the same present value, future value, or annual worth, they are said to be equivalent (equal in value). Normally, the concept of equivalence is applied to two or more cash flows. The choice of time period is arbitrary. In other words, if two sums of money with the same MARR are found to be equivalent at one point in time, they will be equivalent at any other.

Cost Effective Measures Using Discounted Cash Flows

The goal of this section is to present methods that help energy managers, or other decision makers, determine whether a project is economically feasible or cost effective. Multiple methodologies exist for deciding whether a project is worth pursuing. We have discussed the simple payback period. Because this method does not consider the time value of money, SPP should be used in combination with a method that explicitly considers the time value of money.

We cover five economic decision making methods which consider the time value of money in this section: present worth, future worth, annual worth, benefit/cost ratio or savings to investment ratio, and internal rate of return.

Present Worth, Future Worth, and Annual Worth

A present worth comparison converts all the cash flows to a present worth value (PW); a future worth (FW) comparison converts all the cash flows to a future value at a common future time; and an annual worth (AW) analysis converts all the cash flows to a uniform annual series over the study period.

The different cash flow patterns are converted using the compound interest factors discussed earlier. Costs carry a negative sign, while benefits carry a positive sign.

The decision rules for present worth, future worth, and annual worth are the same: a positive PW, FW or AW indicates the project is economically feasible and cost effective for a given MARR. It is important to note that the three measures are economically equivalent. This means that if the AW value were converted to either FW or PW, the same numerical value for FW or PW would be obtained. The ultimate result is that only one of these three measures needs to be calculated. However, different organizations and different people have their own preferences for which of these methods to use.

Benefit/Cost Ratio, or Savings/Investment Ratio

A benefit/cost ratio (BCR), also known as a savings/ investment ratio (SIR), calculates the present worth of all benefits, then calculates the present worth of all costs, and takes the ratio of the two sums. The BCR or SIR is another alternative economic decision-making criterion. A careful definition of "benefits" and "costs" is important. Benefits are defined to mean all the advantages, less any disadvantages, to the users. Costs are defined to mean all costs, less any savings, that will be incurred by the sponsor. With these definitions, a salvage value would reduce the costs for the sponsor, rather than increase the benefits for the user.

A BCR greater than one is necessary for the project to be cost-effective.

Internal Rate of Return

A final method in this section is to base a project decision on the Internal Rate of Return or IRR of the project. IRR is defined to be that value of the interest rate or discount rate that makes the present worth of the costs of a project equal to the present worth of the benefits of the project. If the computed IRR is greater than the MARR for an organization, the project is cost effective. Many private organizations prefer the IRR method since it produces a rate of return to compare to their MARR that they have already established.

Life Cycle Costing

The life cycle cost (LCC) for a project or a piece of equipment is its total cost of purchase and operation over its entire service life. This total cost includes the costs of acquisition, operation including energy costs, maintenance and disposal. Most of these costs occur at some future time beyond the purchase date, and must be analyzed using the time value of money. Thus, the discounted cash flow analysis form a fundamental part of the LCC analysis.

Many businesses and organizations still use economic analysis methods that do not include all costs, and do not use the time value of money. The SPP method is commonly used by businesses and their organizations, but it is not a life cycle cost analysis method. Some organizations still make purchase decisions based on lowest initial costs and do not consider the operating and maintenance costs at all. Costs that occur after the project or equipment are purchased and installed are ignored. This mission can create a very inaccurate view of the economic viability of a project in many cases. Use of LCC can lead to more rational purchase decisions, and can often lead businesses to higher profits.

The primary criterion for assessing the effectiveness of energy conservation investments is the minimization of life cycle costs. Thus, it is important for all energy managers or energy analysts who deal with projects to understand life cycle costing.

Most life cycle analyses involve choosing between more than one alternative. Therefore, a simple methodology for making valid economic comparisons between alternatives is necessary. This section uses the present worth method for this comparison. Several other methodologies exist, including future worth, annual worth, internal rate of return, and benefit/cost. Future worth and annual worth are economically equivalent to present worth, and can be interchanged if desired. IRR and BCR methods require an "incremental" approach to make valid comparisons between projects. Since present worth is considered the standard against which other methods are judged, present worth is recommended.

The LCC method using present worth, when applied properly, allows the analyst to compare projects with different cash flows occurring at different times. The present worth of the total costs of each alternative is calculated, and the alternative with the lowest LCC is selected. If multiple projects can be selected, then the projects can be ranked by LCC and the project with the next lowest LCC can also be selected.

The present worth analysis in life cycle costing has two important requirements. First, when comparing multiple alternatives, different pieces of equipment may have different lifetimes. In this case, a common "study period" must be chosen so that all alternatives are considered over the same time line. There are four choices for this common time line. They are: shortest life, longest life, least common multiple of the two lives, and an arbitrary choice.

If the shortest life is used, a salvage value must be estimated for the longer lived alternatives. If longest life is used, shorter lived alternatives are assumed to be repeatable. If the least common multiple life is used, projects with lives of 3 years and 5 years would be compared over a 15-year study period. Both projects would have to be repeatable. An arbitrary choice results in possibly having to assume both repeatability, and a salvage value. The critical point is that all projects must be compared over the same time horizon.

The second important requirement of the analysis is that the interest rate used (MARR) must be the same for all alternatives.

Taxes and Depreciation

Depreciation and taxes can have a significant effect on the life cycle analysis of energy projects, and should be considered for all large-scale projects for organizations that pay taxes. Depreciation is not a "cash flow", but it is considered a business expense by the government, and therefore, lowers taxable income. The effect is that taxes are reduced, and taxes are a cash flow. A detailed treatment of tax considerations as they apply to life cycle analysis is beyond the scope of this chapter, and generally requires the assistance of a tax professional.

Inflation

One of the fundamental principles supporting a life cycle cost analysis is the recognition that dollars change value over time. There are two primary reasons for this. First is the "opportunity cost", or the interest loss that is incurred when dollars are not invested. The second reason is inflation. Inflation is the term for the loss in purchasing power of a dollar over time, and should be accounted for in any life cycle analysis.

Terminology

Several additional terms must be defined before the term inflation can be explained clearly. They are:

Constant Dollars: Constant dollars reflect the purchasing power (not face value) of the cash flow. These dollars are generally stated in relation to purchasing power at some base year, for example 1990 dollars.

Current Dollars: These are the out-of-pocket dollars that will actually change hands at any point in time.

Inflation Rate (f): Rate published by the government; based on the Consumer Price Index.

Real Interest Rate (j): The amount of real growth is the earning power of money. This is also known as the inflation-free interest rate.

Market Interest Rate (i): Opportunity to earn as reflected by the rates of interest available in finance and business. This rate contains both the inflation effect and the real earning power effect. This is the interest rate quoted by banks and other financial institutions.

The mathematical relationship between market interest rate, the inflation rate, and the real interest rate is:

$$i = (f + j) + (f^*j)$$

The key to proper analysis under inflation is to match the type of cash flow with the proper interest rate. If cash flows are estimated in current dollars, there are two effects contained in the cash flows: inflation, and real earning power. Therefore, the market interest rate, which includes both effects, is used to discount the cash flows. If cash flows are estimated in constant dollars, they do not contain inflation effects, and the real (inflation-free) interest rate should be used.

Current cash flow and Constant cash flow are interconvertible. The equation to be used is:

$$\text{Constant \$} = (\text{Current \$})/(1 + f)^n$$

where f is the inflation rate, and n is the number of years between the "base year" (usually the present), and the time the money is to be spent.

It should be noted that most energy commodities, such as electricity, inflate at a different rate than the overall inflation rate quoted by the government. This rate is called the escalation rate, k. In this case, f has to be substituted by k.

The PW obtained using constant dollar analysis and current dollar analysis will remain the same. Thus, it does not matter whether a constant dollar, or current (actual) dollar analysis is used.

Energy Financing Options

Once an energy management opportunity is found to be economically attractive, the next step is to obtain financing to implement the project. Many facilities find it difficult to obtain this financing. In fact, lack of financing is a primary reason EMOs are not implemented. There are, however, a number of methods available for paying for the energy efficiency improvements, and the energy manager should be prepared to present these at the same time he/she presents the EMO. The following are the some of these options:

- In-house Capital
- Utility Rebates/Incentives
- Debt Financing/Loans
- Leases
- Performance Contracts (Shared saving, ESCO, Guaranteed savings)

Chapter 7

Concerns of Energy Trading

ENERGY TRADING

Introduction

What is Energy? Energy is the Ability To Do Work.

All of these sources provide us the energy we need to live our busy lives.

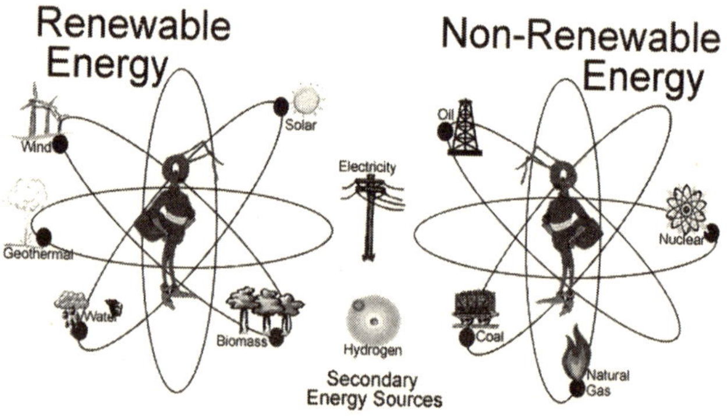

Fig. 7.1

It comes in different forms—heat (thermal), light (radiant), mechanical, electrical, chemical, and nuclear energy. Energy is in everything. We use energy to do everything we do, from making a jump shot to baking our favorite cookies to sending astronauts into space—energy is there, making sure we have the power to do it all. There are two types of energy—stored (potential) energy and working (kinetic) energy. For example, the food you eat contains chemical energy, and your body stores this energy until you release it when you work or play. Learn more about these different forms of energy.

All forms of energy are stored in different ways, in the energy sources that we use every day. **These sources are divided into two groups –**

- **renewable** (an energy source that can be replenished in a short period of time), and
- **nonrenewable** (an energy source that we are using up and cannot recreate in a short period of time).

Renewable and nonrenewable energy sources can be used to produce secondary energy sources including electricity and hydrogen.

Renewable energy sources include solar energy, which comes from the sun and can be turned into electricity and heat. Wind, geothermal energy from inside the earth, biomass from plants, and hydropower and ocean energy from water are also renewable energy sources.

However, we get most of our energy from nonrenewable energy sources, which include the fossil fuels—oil, natural gas, and coal. They're called fossil fuels because they were formed over millions and millions of years by the action of heat from the Earth's core and pressure from rock and soil on the remains (or "fossils") of dead plants and animals. Another nonrenewable energy source is the element uranium, whose atoms we split (through a process called nuclear fission) to create heat and ultimately electricity.

We use all these energy sources to generate the electricity we need for our homes, businesses, schools, and factories. Electricity "energizes" our computers, lights, refrigerators, washing machines, and air conditioners, to name only a few uses.

We use energy to run our cars and trucks. Both the gasoline used in our cars, and the diesel fuel used in our trucks are made from oil. The propane that fuels our outdoor grills and makes hot air balloons soar is made from oil and natural gas.

Energy Commodities such as Oil and gas are of paramount

importance in economies worldwide. Oil, gas, hydro electricity, nuclear power and coal are the five constituents of primary oil. Oil and gas account for about 60 per cent of the total world's primary oil consumption. Crude oil is a mixture of hydrocarbons that exists in a liquid phase in natural underground reservoirs. Nations struggle to explore for oil, and import it at almost any cost. It is also an important contributor to the export realizations of many countries. In countries like Russia, nearly half the hard currency earnings come from crude oil exports. The figure rises to about 80% for Venezuela and 95% for Nigeria and Algeria.

Oil has many applications and it is hard to imagine the modern world without it. Almost all industries including agriculture are dependent on oil in one way or other. Of the industries, oil & lubricants, transportation (including road, rail, sea and air), petrochemicals (some of the end products of petrochemicals include plastics, synthetic fibres, detergents and chemical fertilizers etc.), pesticides and insecticides, paints, perfumes, etc. are largely and directly affected by the oil prices as several products derived from crude oil are basic inputs in the production in these industries. The impact on these industries would result in spiraling effect on other industries and people. Without oil or its close associate natural gas, urban domestic life will become miserable. Oil light homes and streets and serves as a fuel for cooking. In cold countries, oil or gas is needed for heating homes. Metals are being progressively replaced by plastic, a product of oil and artificial fibres have made inroads into the domain of cotton. The indispensable ropes for agriculture and fishing, hitherto made from jute, are now being made from plastics. Polythene (plastic) bags, sheets and covers become indispensable in modern day's packaging and shopping. A wide range of chemicals, medicines and toiletry items is derived from oil.

There are in fact many products obtained from the processing of crude and other hydrocarbon compounds. These include aviation gasoline, motor gasoline, naphtha, kerosene, jet fuel, distillate fuel oil, residual fuel oil, liquefied petroleum gas, lubricants, paraffin wax, petroleum coke, asphalt and other products. The prices of crude are highly volatile. High oil prices lead to inflation that in turn increases input costs; reduces non-oil demand and lower investment in net oil importing countries.

India, which is a net importer of oil, thus is often subject to the vagaries of price volatility in crude. Given this scenario, crude futures will come as a boon to everyone, ranging from the government and corporate to retail users. Crude oil is marketed principally in New York, London and Singapore. Futures are sold promising next-month delivery at agreed amount, price and location, in a minimum of 1000 bbl, and are settled daily. Oil is priced relative to certain standard kinds of crude. In London, it is Brent blend crude from the North Sea; about 2/3 of the world's crude oil is priced in terms of Brent. In New York, West Texas Intermediate light, sweet crude is the standard. OPEC prices its oil in terms of a basket of seven crudes: Saudi Arab light, Emirates Dubai crude, Nigerian Bonny light, Algerian Saharan blend, Indonesian Minas, Venezuelan Tia Juana, and Mexican Isthmus. Individual crudes are sold at a discount or premium, depending on quality and difficulty of transport. Crude oil is a very variable commodity.

World Wide Energy Scenario

In the past four years the world has witnessed oil prices move from low of around $12 per barrel to $70. Some analysts suggest that oil prices may cross $100 per barrel by next year, but even at $100 the oil price will be in keeping with the adjusted real price at the time of first oil shock. Within the energy scene, the 20th Century clearly belongs to oil. In this period, the share of oil has increased from practically nothing to as high as 35-40%. This excludes non-commercial energy sources. During 1950-2000, demand for oil grew from 50 million barrels per day to 75 million barrels per day. In the last five years, the estimated growth was another 10 million barrels per day. The large emerging economies in Asia will further push the demand by another 30 million barrels per day—a total of 115 million barrels per day by 2030.

The global population has increased from 1.6 billion in 1990 to 6.4 billion in 2005. The average per capita supply of commercial energy has matched this increase. However, the global mean hides enormous regional and national inequalities. Per capita energy consumption in India is less than one tenth of that of industrialized nations. Consequently, there is appalling loss of economic activity, productivity and efficiency.

Word Energy Demand

The IEO2006 reference case projects increased world consumption of marketed energy from all sources over the next two and one-half decades. Fossil fuels continue to supply much of the increment in marketed energy use worldwide throughout the projections. The total world energy consumption of oil is expected to decline from 37.8% percent in 2005 to 33 percent in 2030, largely in response to higher world oil prices which would dampen oil demand, whereas natural gas's share is expected to increase from 23.6% in the previous year to 26.3% in 2030.

Table 7.1: World Marketed Energy Use by Fuel Type (1980-2030) (quadrillion Btu)

	Oil	Natural Gas	Coal	Nuclear	Renewables
1980	131	54	70	7.6	18.4
1990	136.1	75.2	89.4	20.4	24.1
2003	162.1	99.1	100.4	26.5	32.7
2004	165.5	102.2	104.4	26.9	34.5
2005	168.8	105.4	108.5	27.2	36.3
2010*	185.6	121.1	128.8	28.9	45.2
2020*	210.8	156.1	160.1	32.9	53.1
2030*	239.1	189.9	195.5	34.7	62.4

Note: *: Projections.
Source: www.eia.doe.gov.

According to international energy outlook's projections worldwide oil consumption would rise from 83.97 million barrels per day in 2005 to 98 million barrels per day in 2015 and then to 118 million barrels per day in 2030.All the projections have been revised downwards because of the expected higher oil prices path. For many years, it has been projected that natural gas would be the fastest growing energy source; however, higher natural gas prices (linked to oil prices) in IEO2006 make coal more cost-competitive, especially in the electric power sector, and as a result natural gas use and coal use increase at similar rates. Natural gas demand is expected to rise by an average of 2.4 percent per year over the 2003 to 2030 period which is greater than oil and almost equal to the rate of growth of coal.

Reasons For Expected Changes In The Demand Pattern

1. Environmental considerations

In the recent past, increased emphasis on the environment has proved to be one of the major drivers of current and future use of natural gas. The ongoing debate over climate change and how it should be addressed is a prime example of the divergence between concerns about energy supply and the environment.

Table 7.2: Fuel-wise Carbon Intensity

Fuel	Carbon Intensity (Mt C/ EJ)	Ratio to Natural Gas
Natural gas	14.4	100%
Crude oil	19.9	138%
Coal	25.4	177%

Source: EIA.

2. Power generation

Natúral gas is used internationally as fuel by thermal power plants. The introduction of CCGT, which burn gas for energy, has revolutionized power generation technology. Natural gas contains no sulphur and releases substantially less CO_2 than coal. Though generating electricity from coal-based power Natural gas consumption for power generation is projected to grow by 4% per year in the industrialized countries, compared with 0.1% decrease for oil and 0.9% increase for coal; this would account for 56.3% of the projected increase in total energy for power generation. Natural gas is projected to capture 24% of the power generation market in the industrialized countries and 21% in the developing countries in 2020, up from 14% and 13% respectively in 1999. In absolute terms, gas demand for power generation in developing countries is projected to triple from 0.2 tcm in 1999 to 0.6 tcm in 2020, while in industrialized countries; it is projected to grow from 0.6 tcm in 1999 to 1.0 tcm.

INDIAN ENERGY SCENARIO

The energy demand is projected to grow at about 6 to 7% for fuelling the projected demand growth in the country. Hydrocarbon sector will have to play a vital role not only for providing energy security but also have to look after the environmental concern due to global warming. The Hydrocarbon vision document has addressed a variety of issues including enhancing the share of natural gas in the energy basket and improving the quality of petroleum products etc. In this regard the natural gas demand is likely to further grow during the years to come. Large scale import of natural gas in the country have been envisaged both through LNG/pipeline route. The projected share of various energy supplies according to the hydrocarbon vision indicate that coal s share will remain around 53% till 2011-12 before falling to 50% in 2025.Oil's share will fall down from 32% to 25% in 2025 nuclear and hydel will continue to make meager contributions in the entire energy basket and gas's share will rise to 20% in 2025 from the current share of 9%.

Table 7.3: Primary Commercial Energy Consumption in India (mmtoe)

Source	*1999-00*	*2000-01*	*2001-02*	*2002-03*	*2003-04*	*2004-05*
Petroleum products (inc RBF)	110.84	115.53	119.84	120.72	125.29	129.75
Natural Gas	24.2	25.07	25.24	26.96	27.81	27.68
Coal	122.99	126.95	134.39	139.92	148.08	153.75
Lignite	7.3	7.57	8.19	8.59	9.23	10.06
Hydel electricity	6.93	6.41	6.32	5.49	6.35	13.14
Nuclear electricity	3.47	4.4	5.08	5	4.61	3.055
Wind energy	0.12	0.14	0.17	0.21	0.23	-
Total	275.85	286.07	299.23	306.89	321.6	337.435

Source: Ministry of Finance/Economic Survey.

As the above table suggests Commercial energy consumption has grown at a CAGR of 4% from 280 MMTOE in 1999-00 to 327 MMTOE in 2003-04 Coal and lignite form 48% whereas Oil and Gas account for 38.3% and 8.5% respectively of total commercial energy mix.Infact Coal and oil have dominated the energy supply basket during the past five decades with 85-90% of share, leaving natural gas with a small share. This is not in line with the world trend where natural gas occupies nearly 24% share in energy basket. It is only during the last two decades, when large off shore fields were developed and cross country pipelines were laid, the share of natural gas in energy basket could rise but it would still be lower than the world average share of natural gas. In the changing scenario, the focus is on developing and expanding core sectors in which oil and gas industry is at the forefront.

Energy Trading

The original form of trade was barter, the direct exchange of goods and services. Modern traders instead generally negotiate through a medium of exchange, such as money. As a result, **buying** can be separated from **selling**, or earning. The invention of money (and later credit, paper money and non-physical money) greatly simplified and promoted trade. Trade between two traders is called bilateral trade, while trade between more than two traders is called multilateral trade is the voluntary exchange of goods, services, or both. A mechanism that allows trade is called a market. Trade exists for many reasons. Due to specialization and division of labor, most people concentrate on a small aspect of production, trading for other products. Trade exists between regions because different regions have a comparative advantage in the production of some tradable commodity, or because different regions' size allows for the benefits of mass production. As such, trade at market prices between locations benefits both locations.

Trading can also refer to the action performed by traders and other market agents in the financial markets.

Three broad category of trader

1. Hedger
2. Speculator
3. Arbitrager

1. **Hedger** faces risk associated with the price of an asset. They use future, forward and options to reduce or eliminate the risk.
2. **Speculator** wish to bet on future movements in the price of an asset. Future, forward and options can give them extra leverage; that is, they can increase both the potential gains and potential losses in a speculative venture.
3. **Arbitrager** is in business to take advantage of a

discrepancy between prices in the two markets. If for an example, they see future price of an asset getting out of line with the cash price, they will take offsetting in the two markets to lock in a profit.

Oil, Gas & Petrochemical trading has come a long way since OPEC formation. Dramatic growth in the late 1990s was followed by an equally dramatic decline following the collapse of major energy merchants in 2001. With close regulatory oversight, deregulation, and the participation of new players like hedge funds, markets are seeing improved liquidity and better price transparency.

Over the last twenty years oil has become the Major Trading commodity in the world. During this period, oil trading has evolved from a primarily physical activity into a sophisticated financial market. Oil is fungible and traded in world commodities markets, there is much uncertainty associated with projections of future patterns of oil trade; however, anticipated changes in the world's oil trading patterns—particularly, the shifting regional dependence of importing regions on producing regions—may have important geopolitical ramifications. In the process it has attracted the interest of a wide range of participants who now include banks and fund managers as well as the traditional oil majors, independents and physical oil traders.

Gas is moving closer to being a global industry. The geographical dislocation of reserves to market is being partly mitigated by new cost-effective ways of linking stranded fields and customers. Progress on integrating supply and demand is likely to accelerate and, as economies of scale increase and new alliances are formed, regional markets will continue to develop and coalesce. At the same time, liberalization of markets is heralding new choice for customers, more dynamic, liquid gas trading conditions for gas companies, a changing balance of risk and reward for all players. Indian economy is developing at 9% per annum. In Indian market the demand of gas is increasing because the increasing demand in cement, infrastructure, power sector, plastic industry and other industries. The depleting reserves of gas are likely to increase the price requiring the betterment of trading activities so trading of gas is becoming a major trading activity.

Forms of Market

The Markets where Trading is done basically classified into two types.

- Physical Markets—Over-the-Counter (Spot & Cash markets)
- Paper Markets—Commodity Exchange (Futures markets)

1. OTC-Over the Counter

Over The Counter means where trading is privately negotiated derivative contracts. The OTC is mostly used in the early days for the trading where two parties do the privately contract and do the trading between them. The OTC have following Characteristics:

- **Forward contract**: The forward means the contract is settled on the forward date with particular specification, on the particular date.
- **Privately negotiated**: The contract is between the two parties with the specification mentioned by them, its price and the time of delivery.
- **Custom made contract:** It means each contract is different from one other its specification changes with the contract size, each contract is different from other as they are specified by two parties who are involved in the contract.
- **No role of clearing corporation:** There is no corporation who settles there contract. It is the basically the trust between the parties and the contract clears on the trust. There is no corporation who involves in the clearing of the contract.
- **No margin payment:** The Contract is between the two parties and contact Price is specified by the seller to the buyer the buyer pays the upfront amount and obliged to take the delivery on that date. As there is no middle man and there is trust between them so there is no margin came into exists in this payment.
- **No M-T-M settlement:** The OTC the buyer is obliged to take the delivery and what gain or loss is on the date of exercise. There is no daily gain or loss which is provide

to it.

- **No Regulation:** There is no regulation and no rules for the trading it is just a contract which is done between two persons for rules and regulation made by them.
- **Settlement in delivery:** In this contract settle in the form of delivery.

(a) Drawbacks:

1. **Counter party Risk:** This arises if parties do not discharge their obligations fully when due or at any time thereafter. This has two components, namely replacement cost risk prior to settlement and principal risk during settlement.
   (a) The replacement cost risk arises from the failure of one of the parties to transaction. While the non-defaulting party tries to replace the original transaction at current prices, he loses the profit that has accrued on the transaction between the date of original transaction and date of replacement transaction. The seller/buyer of the security loses this unrealized profit if the current price is below/above the transaction price. Both parties encounter this risk as prices are uncertain. It has been reduced by reducing time gap between transaction and settlement and by legally binding netting systems.
   (b) The *principal risk* arises if a party discharges his obligations but the counter party defaults. The seller/buyer of the security suffers this risk when he delivers/makes payment, but does not receive payment/delivery. This risk can be eliminated by delivery vs. payment mechanism which ensures delivery only against payment. This has been reduced by having a central counter party which becomes the buyer to every seller and the seller to every buyer.
2. **Liquidity risk** which arises if one of the parties to transaction does not settle on the settlement date, but later. The seller/buyer who does not receive payment/delivery when due, may have to borrow funds/securities to complete his payment/delivery obligations.

3. **Third party risk** which arises if the parties to trade are permitted or required to use the services of a third party which fails to perform. For example, the failure of a clearing bank which helps in payment can disrupt settlement. This risk is reduced by allowing parties to have accounts with multiple banks. Similarly, the users of custodial services face risk if the concerned custodian becomes insolvent, acts negligently, etc.

(b) Exchange

Exchange Trading is trading which done on the exchange. A commodities exchange is an exchange where various commodities and derivatives products are traded. There are many commodity markets across the world that trade energy products and contracts based on them. These contracts can include spot prices, forwards, futures and options on futures.Commodities exchanges, usually trade futures contracts on commodities. Such as trading contracts to receive something, say gasoline, in a certain month. A refiner can sell a future contract on his gasoline, which will not be produced for several months, and guarantee the price he will be paid when he delivers; a large gasoline consuming company buys the contract now and guarantees the price will not go up when it is delivered. This protects the refiner (seller) from price drops and the consuming company (buyer) from price rises.

What are Trading derivatives?

Trading Derivatives are financial instruments (contracts) that do not represent ownership rights in any physical asset but, rather, derive their value from the value of some other underlying commodity or other asset. When used prudently, derivatives are efficient and effective tools for isolating financial risk and "hedging" to reduce exposure to risk. Derivative is a product whose value is derived from the value of one or more basic variables, called bases or underlying asset in a contractual manner. The underlying asset can be equity, forex, or commodity (crude oil, bullion, agri-products). Derivative contracts transfer risk, especially price risk, to those who are able and willing to bear it. Derivatives allow investors to transfer risk to others who could profit from taking the risk.

E.g. An oil producer may wish to sell his output (yet to be produced) at a future date to eliminate the risk of change in price by that date.The price of this derivative is driven by the spot price of oil which is the "underlying asset". person transferring risk achieves price certainty but loses the opportunity for making additional profits when prices move opposite his fears. Likewise, the person taking on the risk will lose if the counterparty's fears are realized. Except for transactions costs, the winner's gains are equal to the loser's losses. Like insurance, derivatives protect against some adverse events. Because of their flexibility in dealing with price risk, derivatives have become an increasingly popular way to isolate cash earnings from price fluctuations.

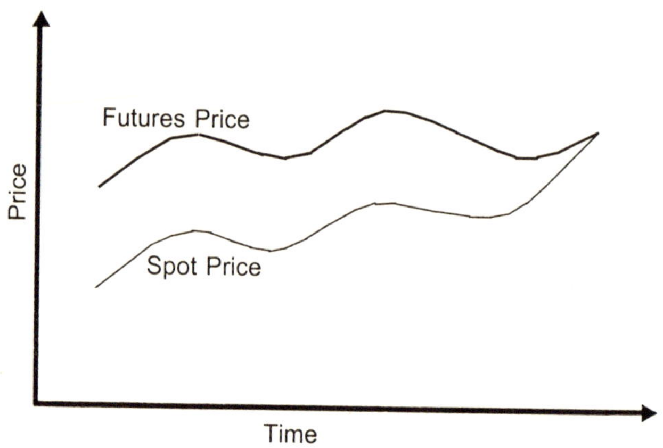

Fig. 7.2

The most commonly used derivative contracts are forward contracts, futures contracts, options, and swaps.

Evolution of Derivatives Markets

In 1974, Congress observed that derivatives trading was about to expand from its traditional base in farm commodities into financial futures—contracts based on bonds, interest rates, currencies, and so on. To ensure that derivatives traders received the same protections whether they were trading pork bellies or T-bonds, P.L. 93-463 created the CFTC to oversee all derivatives trading, regardless of the nature of the underlying commodity. The CFTC was given exclusive jurisdiction: all contracts that were "in the character of" futures contracts had to be traded on a CFTC-regulated futures exchange. There were two major exceptions to this exchange-trading requirement. Forward contracts, where actual delivery of the commodity would take place at the expiration of the contract, were considered cash sales and not subject to the CEA. Second, the so-called Treasury Amendment (part of the same law that created the CFTC) specified that contracts based on foreign currencies or U.S. Treasury securities could be traded off-exchange. Existing markets in these instruments had long used futures-like contracts and appeared to function well without direct government regulation; Treasury saw no public interest in bringing them under the new CFTC.

During the 1980s, a large and active market in OTC derivatives evolved, utilizing swap contracts that served exactly the same economic functions as futures. The first swaps were based on currencies and interest rates; later, OTC contracts based on commodity (including energy) prices were introduced. These OTC **markets** were well established before the CFTC made any move to assert its jurisdiction, despite the fact that swaps were clearly "in the character of" futures contracts. The potential CFTC jurisdiction, however, created legal uncertainty for the swaps industry: if a court had ruled that a swap was in fact an illegal, off-exchange futures contract, trillions of dollars in outstanding swaps could have been invalidated. This might have caused chaos in financial **markets**, as swaps users would suddenly be exposed to the risks they had used derivatives to avoid.

The CFTC issued a swaps exemption in 1989, stating that although it believed the CEA gave it authority to regulate swaps, it would not do so as long as they differed from futures contracts in certain enumerated respects. In 1992, Congress gave the CFTC additional authority to exempt OTC contracts (P.L. 102-546). In response, the CFTC modified the 1989 swaps exemption in 1993, and also issued a specific exemption for OTC derivatives based on energy products.

Under the 1993 exemption, OTC energy derivatives would not be **regulated** if all Trading was between principals whose business involved the physical energy commodities underlying the derivatives, if all contracts were negotiated as to their material terms (unlike futures contracts, where terms are standardized), and if all contracts were held to maturity (rather than traded rapidly, as futures are). This exemption was a matter of regulation, not statute. In May 1998, the CFTC issued a "concept release" that indicated that it was considering the possibility of extending features of exchange regulation to the OTC market. The release solicited comments on whether regulation of OTC derivatives should be modified in light of developments in the marketplace. Among the questions were whether the existing prohibitions on fraud and manipulation were sufficient to protect the public, and whether the CFTC should consider additional terms and conditions relating to registration, capital, internal controls, sales practices, record keeping, or reporting. The concept release drew strong opposition from the swaps industry and from other regulators, especially the Federal Reserve. In December 1998, Congress included in the Omnibus Appropriations Act (P.L. 105-277) a provision directing the CFTC not to propose or issue any new regulations affecting swap contracts before March 31, 1999. In November 1999, the President's Working Group on Financial **Markets** issued a report entitled "Over-the-Counter Derivatives Markets and the Commodity Exchange Act." The report recommended that, to remove uncertainty about the legal and regulatory status of the OTC market, bilateral transactions between sophisticated parties that do not involve physical commodities with finite supplies should be excluded from the Commodity Exchange Act; that is, the CFTC should have no jurisdiction. While the Working Group's report made a distinction between financial commodities and those with finite supplies, and suggested that continuing CEA jurisdiction was appropriate for the latter, the report did *not* recommend that the CFTC should rescind its exemption of OTC energy derivatives. In other words, the Working Group saw no immediate problem with the **unregulated** status of OTC **markets** in energy derivatives.In 2000, the 106thCongress considered two bills (H.R. 4541 and S. 2697) that generally followed the Working Group's recommendations. Energy derivatives were exempted—as a matter of statute—from many of the provisions of the CEA, but were not given a blanket exclusion. The treatment of energy derivatives changed in its wording through the various iterations of the legislation, but the substance remained basically the same, from the bills as introduced to the final passage of the Commodity Futures Modernization Act of 2000 (P.L. 106-554, H.R. 5660). That legislation established three classes of commodities. First, financial variables (inter estrates, stock indexes, currencies, etc.) are defined as "excluded commodities," and OTC contracts based on these are not subject to the CEA (provided that trading is restricted to "eligible contract participants," that is, not marketed to small investors). Second, derivative contracts based on agricultural commodities cannot be traded except on the futures exchanges; these remain under CFTC jurisdiction. Finally, there is an "all other" category—"exempt commodities"—which includes energy products. Contracts in exempt commodities can be traded in the OTC market without CFTC regulation provided that no small investors participate. However, certain antifraud and anti manipulation provisions of the CEA continue to apply. If an OTC exchange is created—defined in the legislation as one where multiple buyers and sellers may post bids and trade with each other—the CFTC has some over sight jurisdiction and may require disclosure of certain market information.

In summary, the OTC energy derivatives market developed outside CFTC jurisdiction in the late 1980s and early 1990s, despite the CEA's apparent prohibition of such a market. As with financial OTC derivatives, however, the CFTC never challenged the legality of this off-exchange market. As concerns about legal uncertainty mounted, the CFTC in 1993 issued an exemption stating that certain OTC energy transactions did not fall under the CEA. In 2000, Congress essentially codified this exemption, by including energy in the category of "exempt commodities."This removed them from even the possibility of CFTC regulation, except for a limited antifraud and manipulation jurisdiction and some oversight if the present dealer market for OTC contracts should evolve into an exchange-like market. Thus, the 2000 legislation did not deregulate the OTC energy derivatives market; that market had been **unregulated** since its beginnings Energy derivatives—financial contracts whose value is linked to changes in the price of some energy product—are traded in two kinds of **markets** in the United States today: the futures exchanges and the off-exchange, or over-the-counter market. The New York Mercantile Exchange (Nymex) offers futures contracts based on prices of crude oil, natural gas, heating oil, and gasoline. (Other futures exchanges offer energy-related contracts, but Nymex is by far the busiest.) Futures exchanges are **regulated** by the An electronic trading system like Enron Online did not meet this definition, because a single dealer—Enron—was involved in all transactions. Enron Online essentially displayed the prices at which Enron was willing to trade.

Commodity Futures Trading Commission (CFTC) under the Commodity Exchange Act (CEA). The CEA imposes a range of mandates on the exchanges (and on futures industry personnel) regarding record keeping (including an audit trail for all trades), registration requirements, market surveillance, financial standards, sales practices, handling of customer funds, and so on.

The second trading venue for energy derivatives is the off-exchange, or over-the-counter (OTC) market. Unlike the futures market, there is no centralized marketplace for OTC derivatives. Instead, a number of firms act as dealers, offering to enter into contracts with others who wish to manage their risk exposure to energy prices. Derivatives contracts based on energy products are generally exempt from regulation under the CEA, so long as the contracts are offered only to "eligible contract participants," defined as financial institutions, professional traders, institutional investors, governmental units, and businesses or individuals with more than $10 million in assets. The law assumes that sophisticated parties such as these do not need the kind of investor protection that government regulation provides for public customers of the futures exchanges. The CFTC has limited jurisdiction over the OTC market if certain CEA provisions against fraud and price manipulation are violated. In addition, if OTC contracts are traded on an electronic exchange-like facility, where multiple buyers and sellers can post bids and offers and trade with each other, the CFTC can require disclosure of certain transaction price and volume data.

At present, however, the OTC market remains primarily a dealer market, and the dealers do not report to the CFTC. The evolution of the two energy derivatives **markets**—one **regulated**, the other largely **unregulated**.

Derivatives and Hedging Instruments (Risk Management Tools)

- Forwards
- Futures
- Swaps
- options
- Caps and Floors
- Collars
- Spread Trades
- Crack Spreads contract
- Crack Spread Options
- Calendar Spreads options
- Volumetric production payment contract.

Major Derivative Markets

In the energy industry, derivatives can be bought and sold in two main ways: on-exchange and over-the-counter (OTC). On-exchange refers to the futures markets which are found on regulated financial exchanges such the New York Mercantile Exchange (NYMEX) and\London's International Petroleum Exchange (IPE). The OTC market is specific to the non-standard swaps and OTC options. These are usually traded directly between two companies (principals, players) in the energy markets.

Although the futures markets are important to the energy industry, it relies much more heavily on OTC derivatives. This is because OTC derivatives are customized transactions, whereas their on-exchange counterpart, the 'futures' contract, is a standard contract. In theory, each deal on the OTC market is unique, so it is important to be alert to contract terms, pricing mechanisms and price reference when using OTC derivatives.

Some companies find that the measurement and control of risks can be more difficult with an OTC contract because of the lack of price and liquidity transparency in the OTC market (unlike regulated futures exchanges, which publish public real-time price data) and this can create the possibility of an unexpected loss. There are also sometimes additional legal, credit and operational risks with OTC derivatives compared to on exchange futures contracts. However, the OTC market remains a popular option for price risk management purposes. Many companies find that there are benefits in the flexibility of an OTC derivative because it can be valued against the same price reference as the energy which is being produced or consumed.

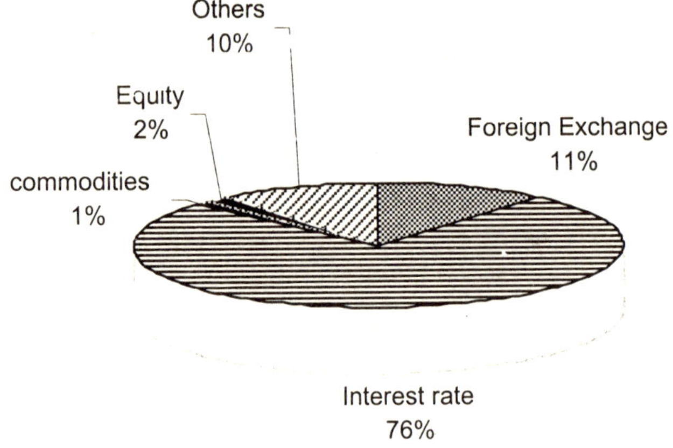

Fig. 7.3: OTC Derivative Contracts (Total Amount Outstanding) Dec. 2005

As the pie chart in Figure shows, energy OTC derivatives markets are far less liquid than most other financial derivatives markets accounting for less than one per cent of the value outstanding on derivatives markets worldwide. This means that those who take part in energy markets whether as market makers, traders or end-users (usually companies with underlying price risk in the energy being hedged either as a producer or consumer), need to have clear policies for derivatives usage, including strong management controls and organizational reporting structures effective before derivatives are employed. They should also provide shareholders with information that will put to rest any unjustified fears associated with their company's use of derivatives. Indeed, as a result of the concerns of regulators and public shareholders around the world, more and more information is now required by international accounting standards.

Futures versus OTC

At one time it was easy to distinguish the futures market from the OTC market and also to establish the pros and cons of using one or the other. As Figure shows, when risk managers or traders used futures contracts they knew that the contract would be traded on an exchange, that they would have an account with their futures broker and that they were operating in a highly regulated market. They could also see the price of the contract on a screen and they could be sure that the security of the contract and its performance would be guaranteed by the clearing house of the exchange. This in turn was guaranteed by 'margins' (good faith payments by everyone with a futures position on that particular exchange), plus, the funding the exchange raised itself and the funds contributed by its clearing broker members.

Margins on a futures exchange can be split into two types: 'initial margins' and 'variation margins'. Initial margins are the good faith deposit that is placed with the clearing house or that a broker finances (at a cost) when a trade is opened, A variation margin is the daily revaluation of a portfolio with the clearing house. If the valuation is negative, you or your broker (if you have a credit line) will have to place a margin to cover that negative variation margin, if the next day the portfolio has a positive variation margin (i.e. it is showing an unrealized profit), because the position has not been traded or closed out yet, some of that margin will be returned.

However when OTC contracts are used there is always the credit risk of the other company in the transaction, as well as a liquidity risk and a lack of price transparency because there is no screen to display a real-time price.

The Convergence of OTC and Futures

The clear distinction between the OTC energy market and the futures markets is now disappearing as the two markets converge. Clearing houses around the world have started to accept OTC trades into their guarantee umbrella. This means that after executing bilateral OTC trades with one another, both counterparts can agree to 'give-in' their OTC deal to a clearing house. This process basically makes the clearing house the counterpart to the OTC deal, so that the two OTC counterparts can benefit from the higher credit quality of the clearing house as well as getting other benefits such as more netting opportunities on settlement and offsetting of positions.

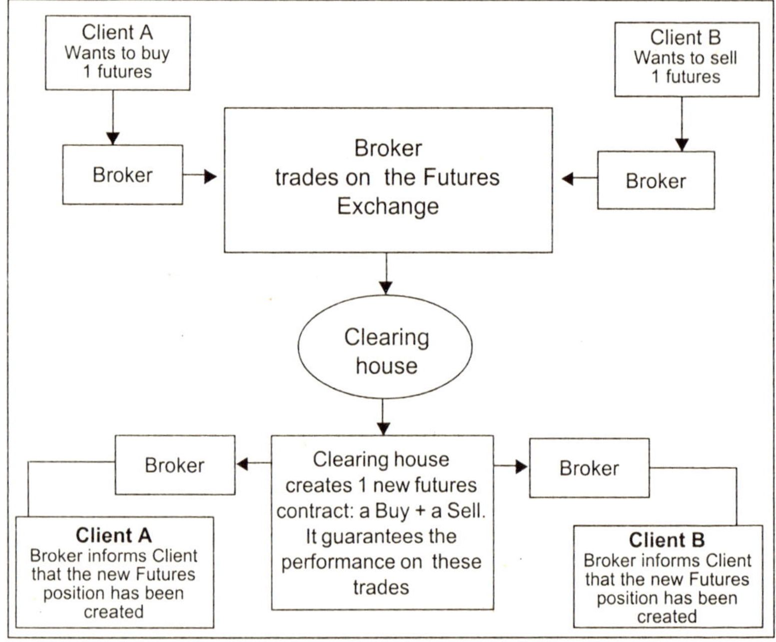

Fig. 7.4: Basic Future Trade Transaction Flow

The usual market approach for two OTC counterparts to trade an OTC derivative contract with one another directly and to take on one another's credit risk.

In the new convergence environment we now sometimes have a situation like this:

In the new convergence environment we now sometimes have a situation like this:

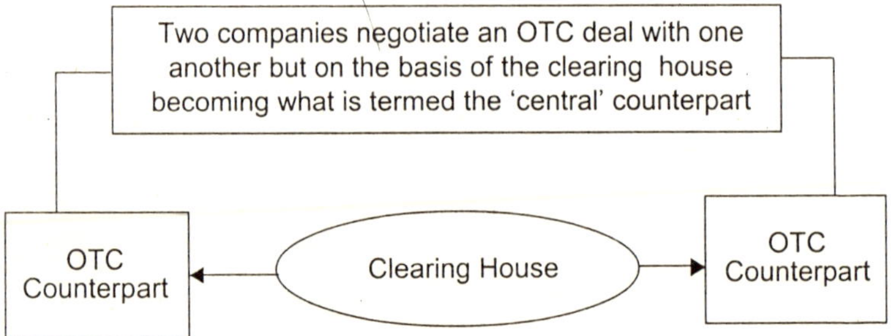

Although market share penetration has been slow in the oil sector, we have seen the newer power and gas markets embracing electronic trading platforms in a big way. This has brought about greater price transparency as users can view and trade prices onscreen like futures markets. As a result, power and gas markets have been the quickest to embrace OTC clearing.

Energy Futures, Past and Present

Energy futures are not nearly as young as you think. In the second half of the 19th century, a Petroleum Exchange flourished in New York. Again in the early 1930s—when market discipline was briefly disrupted by the explosive growth of oil production in Oklahoma and Texas, causing oil prices to fall dramatically—an oil futures market (in West Texas Intermediate) was established in California. It soon collapsed as a formidable alliance of big oil and big government restored discipline to the marketplace. Nearly 40 years of relative price stability ensured, leaving little incentive for the emergence of an oil futures market.

Only with the traumatic price increases accompanying the Arab oil embargo of late 1973 was another attempt made, this time in New York at the cotton Exchange. The contract called for Rotterdam delivery (to avoid the constraints of US price regulations). That attempt was stillborn, however, doomed by continuing US government price controls and a skeptical oil industry.

In the decade that followed, the commercial realities and—equally important—the perceptions of those realities by the international oil industry had gradually changed to the point where oil features could fulfill the industry's need for risk management and provide an outlet for the speculative impulses of investors whose interest in oil had been captured by the commodity's new prominence in daily head -lines and nightly newscasts.

The emergence of oil features markets and their remarkable growth were a natural, indeed inevitable, consequences of three concurrent but only partly interrelated trends in Petroleum, financial and commodity markets. By far the most important determinant was the structural change in oil markets themselves. The nationalization of production by the organization of

Petroleum Exporting Countries (OPEC) and non-OPEC governments alike, and he subsequent pressure to eliminate large third party crude resales, resulted in a disintegration of the oil market that had been highly integrated since the days of J.D. Rockefellet. In the ten years following the 1973 Arab oil embargo, the crude oil available to the major companies fell by nearly 50%, from about 30 million barrels per day (bbl/day) to just more than15 million bbl/day. Equity oil available to the majors fell even more sharply by some 75%.The net result was a drop in the major's share of internationally traded oil from 62% to 37%.

In addition to the newly created national oil companies a host of oil trading firms and independent refineries entered the picture. The links that had traditionally tied upstream and downstream (vertical integration) were weakened to the breaking point. T he reduction of horizontal integration (as large third –party crude sales were curtailed, and joint venture production was nationalized)further eroded the ability of the larger oil companies to exercise control over markets. Simply there were too many actors with divergent commercial and political interests to guarantee market stability. The consequences were not long in coming. After a decade of virtually universal confidence that oil prices would rise, prices began to weaken and fluctuate over an ever-wider range, climaxing in the dramatic events of 1986, when prices fell from nearly $30/bblto less than $10/bbl in a period of only nine months. Although many feel stability(Table1) returned in 1987, it is interesting to note that prices oscillated between $15 and $22/bbl between September and December of that year alone. The fact is that stability has yet to rear its hoary head in current-day oil markets.

Along with the structural change that was reshaping oil markets during the decade, a second important trend was emerging from the financial; markets. High interest rates (along with high oil prices) at the beginning of the 1980s were making inventory maintenance very expensive. This caused oil company managements to rethink traditional approaches to inventory and risk management. Also hedging of financial risk was increasingly becoming a fact of life in foreign currency and interest rate markets. These trends ensured that oil companies were increasingly respective to the hedging potential of the fledging oil future markets.

Finally the third important factor that set the stage for energy futures' ultimate success was the general growth and diversification of futures contracts in a wide variety of new markets, the growing sophistication with which they were being used and modification offering an ever-wider range of hedging tools. For almost 100 years futures markets (then commonly called commodity markets) were largely confined to the traditional agricultural products (especially grains).

In the past two decades, however there has been a explosion in the variety of products served by these markets. The first waves of expansion brought in new agricultural contracts (especially meats) and precious metals. The second phase starting in the 1970s saw the introduction of financial instruments including currency interest rate and stock index contracts. A third phase brought in oil and a number of other industrial products. The fourth stage saw the introduction and rapid acceptance of options on futures contracts. The fifth stage saw an explosion of trading in over-the-counter (OTC) derivatives often in direct competition with exchange traded instruments.

The introduction and success of oil futures was a product of first three trends. The growing volatility and loss of confidence in the future stability of oil prices demanded the emergence of new market structures and institutions. One obvious sign of the change was the rapid growth of spot markets and the trading companies that thrived on price volatility.

Prior to 1979 less than 5% of internationally traded crude moved at spot prices outside of official term supply contracts arrangement. By the end of 1985, virtually all crude moved at some sort of market –related pricing and experts estimated that oil companies were acquiring anywhere from 30 to 50% of their supplies on a spot, non contract basis. Although the proportion of oil sold on a purely spot basis has subsequently shrunk the price risks remain because term contracts today almost universally call for market related prices.

The trading companies' independents refineries and increasingly the companies developed trading techniques to cope with the growing price volatility of these markets. Their first response was to create informal."Forward markets". At first they were only 30 days, then 60 days, and more recently 90days out.

A second response was an explosive growth in the demand for rapid (often real time) pricing and other market information. Against this backdrop futures became inevitable: a time proven and efficient technique for coping with broad market instability.

Energy futures trading in the 1980s focused on growth of the liquid petroleum markets for crude oil, natural gas liquids (NGL), and the major refined products (gasoline, heating oil, and fuel oil). In the 1990s the boundaries of the energy complex have expanded to include natural gas (in 1990) and electricity (in 1996).

While the breadth of energy markets has expanded, their fundamental purposes remain the same. Futures markets basically spot markets for standardized forward contracts, serve three functions:

Price Discovery—Giving an instantaneous reading o0f marginal price movements.

Risk management—Allowing companies to hedge their price risks for limited periods of time. However the hedging opportunity rarely extends more than six months forward as a result of a lack of market liquidity in the more distant months.

Speculative opportunity—Attracting additional risk capital to the market from outside the industry. Low margin requirements—lower than in equity markets enhance the attraction of futures as a vehicle for speculation.

These are the necessary conditions for a successful contract—but they are often not sufficient. In reality new futures contracts often fail. The reason is that the criteria for a successful futures contracts are simply too stringent, with too few physical markets that actually meet those criteria.

Criteria for Successful Futures Markets

In assessing the suitability of any commodity/market for futures trading the following conditions need to be analyzed:

Price volatility: This is perhaps the single most important criterion. It provides the basic economic justification for futures trading which is to provide protection to the hedger against adverse price fluctuation. If a commodity is characterized by a relatively stable—or at least predictable—price there would be little associated risk and there would be no need for a futures market. Price volatility is also necessary to attract risk capital from speculators and essential to ensure sufficient liquidity to maintain the market.

Quantitative indicators: Variations of plus or minus 20% per annum are assumed to be the minimum necessary to sustain futures trading. In general, the greater the degree of volatility the more likely a futures market will survive.

Uncertain supply and demand are generally the cause of price volatility and therefore are generally present when price volatility is found.

Quantitative indicators: In energy markets which markets, which typically display a rather high inelasticity of price demand variations of plus or minus 10% during a two year period should be sufficient to sustain futures trading.

Sufficient deliverable supplies are the Catch-22 of futures trading. If there are not sufficient deliverable supplies of the commodity meeting the quality specifications of the contract, futures trading will fail. However, there must be some uncertainty about the sufficiently of supplies if the previous conditions are to be met. In the U.S., this dilemma is heightened by the regulatory requirements of the Commodity Futures Trading Commission (CFTC), whose fear of market squeezes at times forces exchanges to overstate deliverable supplies in order to gain government approval.

Quantitative indicators: Storage capacity equal to at least 30 days average demand is highly desirable.

Product homogeneity is another prerequisite. Futures contracts are traded on the premise that product taken on a delivery will meet certain quality specifications. The commodity must therefore have certain key characteristics that are quantifiable, allowing the clear differentiation of the product from other grades. Standardized tests and generally accepted procedures are essential. In oil, for example, the various American Petroleum Institute (API), Deutsche Institut fur Normung (DIM), and ASTM standards generally provide the necessary references. In addition, the existence of generally trusted independent inspection agencies or inspectors to administer these tests is an important aspect. A range of different products (*e.g.*, several types of crude oil) may be suitable for delivery, if the price differences between the various grades are relatively stable, and if the technical characteristics of the various deliverable grades are sufficiently close to one another.

This is often a difficult aspect of contract design, since the price variation between various grades of products fluctuates from time to time. For example, it may be desirable to allow several grades to be deliverable, perhaps with price adjustments for quality, in order to ensure sufficient deliverable supplies. However, if buyers are uncertain of what grades they will receive, and if they place different values on the quality differences among the grades, they may be deterred from trading.

Quantitative indicators: The quality of the product must be capable of being described by objective, quantifiable standards.

Product perishability can be a deterrent to trading. In general a product should have a shelf life sufficiently long enough to permit storage and delivery as called for under the contract. ill addition, the maintenance of inventories of the commodity will both facilitate deliveries and provide a ready pool of potential hedgers. While perishability is not usually a major concern in oil and natural gas markets, the stability of some oil product blends is an issue. Long storage of gasoline, for example, can result in separation of blended product.

Quantitative indicators: Products should have a minimum shelf or stock life of 6-12 months.

Market concentration is a difficult factor to quantify. A successful futures market is a highly competitive market, marked by a large number of buyers and sellers. No one market participant, or plausible combination of market participants, should possess sufficient market power to exert unilateral control either on the supply or the demand for the commodity, either in the short or medium term. ill oil, however, the existence of OPEC has not prevented the emergence of highly successful futures markets. The answer lies in the inability of OPEC to act decisively, and in the availability of alternative sources of supply and stocks that seriously limit OPEC's ability to achieve its stated objectives. However, the concentration of producers and/or consumers can be a serious obstacle in specific regional oil markets. Thus, a U.S. west coast gasoline market would be risky, given the relative concentration of production in the hands of a small number of refiners. Similarly, an east coast residual fuel market might be too much dominated by the demand from a small number of very large utilities to sustain liquid futures trading.

Quantitative indicators: ill general, the market share of the top five firms should be less than 50%, and the top 10 firms should have less than 80%.

Readily available price information is critical to market success. It should be noted that the opening of a futures market might stimulate a rapid growth of price information services.

However, at the outset, market participants must have a sufficiently broad base of price information to permit evaluation of spot prices and their relationship to futures prices. Convergence between these two prices as the delivery period approaches is essential. A market in which all products are traded on the basis of long-term contracts where prices remain undisclosed would be a very difficult market in which to establish futures trading.

Quantitative indicators: Daily cash market prices should be available from at least two independent sources.

Unique trading opportunity is another key factor. If an existing market for a commodity has reasonable liquidity and is serving its customers well, it is extremely difficult to launch a copycat contract. Inertia, habit, and personal relationships will tend to keep the traders loyal to the preexisting market. In addition, even if there is no active market at present, recent failures of similar contracts can be a substantial (but not fatal) deterrent.

Quantitative indicators: The ideal candidate would be a commodity that is not currently traded on any futures exchange in the world and has not been the subject of a failed attempt in the previous five years. However, special circumstances may override these concerns.

Market timing (and blind luck) are often critical to the success or failure of a contract. However, they are often impossible to forecast. Ideally, contracts should be introduced to coincide with periods of high volatility and high levels of cash market activity. For example, a heating oil or natural gas contract would be best introduced in the fall months when physical trading is at its yearly high. Conversely, a gasoline contract would be best introduced in the spring, prior to an anticipated surge of summer driving.

Quantitative indicators: Contracts should be introduced to coincide with high levels of cash market activity, to the extent these are predictable. Alternatively, one might just as well consult an astrologer.

FUTURES PRESENT

Since 1974, there have been some 50 attempts to launch energy futures markets. The success rate has averaged about 20%-typical of the experience in other commodity markets. In spite of thorough research by the exchanges, often excruciating governmental reviews (particularly in the U.S.), and extensive marketing campaigns, roughly 80% of all future markets opened fail to reach the critical mass needed for takeoff (commonly defined as reaching an average open interest of 5,000 contracts).

Today-after the smoke has settled from various attempts by exchanges in New York, Chicago, London and Singapore there are seven well-established futures contracts (crude, heating oil, unleaded gasoline, natural gas, and electricity in New York; plus crude and gasoil in London). In addition, options contracts have been successful as extensions of those future markets.

When first introduced in late 1978, heating oil futures attracted smaller, independent marketers and refiners who turned to the Merc as an alternative source of supply. Physical deliveries were initially quite high, as these smaller firms sought alternatives in a marketplace dominated by the larger companies. These initial participants were quickly joined by the spot oil traders and by a growing number of pure speculators on and off the trading floor, drawn from other financial and commodity markets. This phase lasted until well into 1983. Then, with the introduction of crude oil futures and the increasing instability of prices, the larger refiners and integrated companies reluctantly entered the market.

By 1984, more than 80% of the 50 largest companies were using futures. Larger end-users, such as airlines and other major energy consumers, also appeared. ill addition, a far wider range of speculators entered the scene, as trading volume and open interest rose high enough to meet the minimum liquidity requirement of the commodity funds.

Finally, another phase, dating from 1986, brought in almost all the remaining holdouts among the larger U.S. companies, more foreign participation, and a new group of traders-the Wall Street Refiners. These were companies such as Morgan Stanley and Bear Steams, which were attracted by the rising volatility of oil prices and the speculative opportunities presented by that price instability, particularly relative to other markets.

As one Bear Steams trader put it, "Plywood was dead, so we looked around for some better action and found it in oil." The low internal cost of capital for margin maintenance and a built-in trading infrastructure made these new entrants formidable competitors for the older oil trading and supply companies.

However, even today, participation by independent producers and smaller end-users remains limited. The former's participation is limited by the lack of liquidity in the more distant months; the latter by ignorance of how the markets operate, the high management cost of setting up a futures trading department, and for a number of domestic as well as international companies, a very real basis-risk problem.

Futures trading has thus survived adolescence and entered a period of youthful maturity. Growth in the coming years will have to come from an expansion of futures trading opportunities in the form of new contracts rather than from bringing in new participants. In other words, to continue to grow, the exchanges will have to offer a bigger and more diverse menu, not just put more seats around the table. The recent success of options would seem to confirm this point of view.

TRADING FUTURES: A PRIMER

Many readers of this book will be thoroughly familiar with the basic mechanisms and concepts of futures trading. This section is not for them. However, for those who are new to any type of futures trading, it is important to understand a few fundamentals about futures markets. Futures markets offer both *hedgers* or *commercials (i.e.,* those who use a particular commodity in their business) and speculators the opportunity to buy or sell standardized contracts for a given commodity. In many cases, the same exchanges also offer options contracts on those same commodities. Options contracts as presently traded are options on the futures contract for the same commodity, which is often called the *underlying* futures.

Contract Identification

Both futures and options contracts are identified not only by the particular type of commodity being traded *(e.g.,* heating oil, unleaded gasoline, Brent crude oil), but also by the delivery month called for in the contract. In practice, traders often abbreviate the names of months, so that one should not be surprised to hear references to "Feb Brent" or "Jan gas."

Options contracts are further identified by their strike prices and whether they are options to buy (call) or sell (put). Thus an options trader will talk about "Jan gas 55 puts," meaning options to sell January unleaded gasoline futures contracts at **554 gal.** A buyer of a commodity contract is said to be long while he holds that contract. A seller is said to be short. The Contracts traded are highly standardized with respect to volume, quality, and delivery terms. The terms of selected contracts are printed for reference in the appendices to this book. Exchanges do, however, change the terms of these contracts from time to time, to keep pace with changes in the physical market. The samples included should therefore not be assumed to be up-to-date. Please check with the appropriate exchange to obtain a copy of the latest contract terms.

Placing Orders

Except in the case of exchange members operating on their own account, all transactions must be conducted through a member of the exchange, who must also be registered to accept customer orders by the Commodity Futures Trading Commission (CFTC) in the U.S. or its counterparts in other countries. Orders can be placed any time a broker is willing to answer the telephone, but exchange trading hours tend to fall between 9:00 A.M. and 5:00 P.M., with the New York exchanges closing earlier and the London exchanges closing later. A buyer normally places an order by telephone to the broker, who may be located anywhere in the world. The broker in turn executes this order by telephone through exchange members on the floor of the appropriate exchange. Buyers can place various conditions on their orders, including price limits or time limits, and they may also simultaneously request a broker to close out the position if losses exceed a certain amount. While brokers will generally accept such conditions on orders, they usually offer no guarantees they can execute the order as given. Only a *market order,* in which the buyer (or seller) agrees to accept the prevailing market price, is virtually guaranteed for execution. Brokers will most often execute orders through the employees of their own firm on the floor. ill order to camouflage larger orders, execution will sometimes be shared with independent floor brokers, who execute orders on behalf of others. On the exchange floor, all trading must be by *open outcry,* giving all present-at least in theory-an equal opportunity to take the other side of the trade. Assuming a willing seller is found to meet the buyer's order, the trade is posted with the exchange. In practice, exchanges publish price quotations over the various electronic information services to provide an up-to-date record of pricing trends even before the official record of the transaction is entered. The actual trade is usually entered into the exchange's computer within a few minutes of the transaction. The buyer and seller, however, are not matched permanently. At the end of the day, each broker is assigned an appropriate long or short position with the exchange's clearinghouse. Thus, while there must be an equal number of buyers and sellers each day, their respective positions are maintained totally independently. Thus each buyer and seller is free to close his or her position at any time. To do so, the buyer will simply sell his or her contract back into the market, effectively clearing the position from the exchange's books.

Spreads

In addition to straightforward orders to buy or sell a single commodity for a single month, many traders take *spread* positions, which are positions in several different contracts to profit from the relative price movements between those contracts. For example, spreads can be placed between contracts for different delivery months for a single commodity-they can cover different commodities for delivery in the same month-they can cover different commodities and different months. One popular type of spread position in the energy contracts is the *crack spread,* in which a position in crude oil is balanced against positions in both gasoline and heating oil, to approximate the refining process (in which crude oil is transformed by catalytic cracking into refined products). NYMEX has offered option contracts of such spreads since 1994. A newer type of spread trading is the "spark spread" that pairs positions in natural gas with those in electricity to approximate the gross margin of power generation using natural gas.

Margins and Clearinghouses

Exchanges collect margins (or deposits, as they are called in England) from each broker on behalf of his or her customer (and in most cases, the broker in turn collects similar funds from his or her customer). These margins, which are usually in the range of 5 to 10% of the contract's total face value, are normally designed to be equal to the average daily fluctuation in value of the contract being traded. Exchanges will therefore tend to lower margins in times of low price volatility and raise them in times of high price volatility. Every night, based on the final closing or settlement price, the exchange calculates the effect of that price on each position, and either requests additional margin or pays excess margin to each broker.

If prices go up from one day to the next, a buyer's margin is credited with a gain and a seller's margin is debited. The rules of "margin maintenance" between customers and brokers vary considerably from country to country.

The exchange and its clearinghouse are therefore always in a very strong position to guarantee all outstanding positions. Moreover, the clearinghouse holds its member-brokers-not the ultimate customer-responsible for performing under the contracts. In the unlikely event that a broker is unable to perform as called for under the contract, all the members of the clearinghouse are called upon to guarantee performance. Futures markets therefore offer several levels of financiai performance guarantees.

Prices on an exchange are freely determined by the interplay of buyers and sellers. However, exchanges do place certain limits on both the minimum and maximum amounts of fluctuation that can occur in a given time period. The minimum price is referred to as a *tick*, and in the oil contracts is typically equal to 1.00(Z/ bbl, 25.00(Z/metric ton (MT), or 0.01 (Z/gal in New York. In all cases, there are no limits on the *spot contract*, which is the contract that is next scheduled to go to delivery. All other contracts face limits. In New York, these are typically $1/bbl, $15/MT, or 2.00(Z/ gal. In a given day, no trades may take place outside these ranges. However, if a limit is reached on one day, the limits are expanded by 50% for the next day's trading, and so on, up to a maximum of $2/bbl or 4.00!1/gal. In London, the limits don't apply for a full day, but rather trigger cooling off periods before trading is resumed.

Delivery

These markets should always be thought of primarily as financial markets, being used in parallel to physical movement of oil and natural gas. Nevertheless, delivery does take place and serves to ensure that the prices on futures markets remain closely linked to the real world.

The standardization of contracts and their delivery terms are often unnecessarily rigid for the commercial participants, who prefer greater flexibility in their day-to-day operations. As a consequence, delivery typically occurs in only about 2% or less of all futures contracts. In simplest form, all those holding positions in a given contract at the closing bell on the last day of trading for a given contract are automatically required to take or make delivery of the specified commodity. The timing and methods of delivery are clearly spelled out in each contract and in the exchange's rules. The exchanges' staffs match buyers and sellers, and the matched companies are then obligated to meet their respective obligations.

Exchanges have found it useful, however, to permit several variations of this simple process. Prior to the exchange matching process (typically the day after the end of trading), any two market participants may agree to an exchange for physicals (EFP) and transfer title to oil (or natural gas) by mutual agreement in lieu of closing out their position on the exchange. EFPs can also be used to establish future positions by mutual agreement. In fact, in the U.S. crude markets, this mechanism is widely used as a routine means of buying and selling crude, since it has the attraction of the exchange's financial performance guarantees.

Once trading in a given contract has ended and participants are matched, the two matched companies may elect to use an alternative delivery procedure (ADP), which also allows the two to make alternative arrangements. In the case of both EFPs and ADPs, the exchanges are relieved of *any* responsibility for guaranteeing performance.

Regulation

Exchanges are self-regulating, not-for-profit corporations owned by their members. The degree of governmental oversight and regulation has traditionally been most extensive in the U.S. and least intrusive in the United Kingdom. However, the widespread publicity over the U.S. government's investigation of trading practices in 1989 seems certain to increase government regulations everywhere.

The exchanges maintain active compliance and market surveillance programs to enforce trading rules and to detect any evidence of market manipulation. Traders caught violating rules are typically fined and, in relatively infrequent instances, barred from trading. If evidence of market manipulation is uncovered, exchanges possess a wide range of powers to remedy the situation. These powers include the right to order a given participant to reduce or even eliminate his or her position, to substitute alternative delivery points or additional supplies (*i.e.*, by broadening quality specifications), or even to impose a cash settlement in place of physical delivery (assuming the contract calls for such delivery). These powers are not often used, but their very existence serves as a powerful disincentive to would-be market manipulators.

Perhaps the most controversial aspect of futures trading (particularly in the U.S.) is the permitting of dual trading; *i.e.*, allowing the same individuals to trade for their own account while simultaneously executing orders for customers as a floor broker. Many critics have argued that this practice provides opportunities for floor brokers to jump ahead of large customer orders, profiting from the market movements that those large orders are likely to provoke. While such actions are a clear violation of exchange rules, detection is not always easy. Exchanges counter with the argument that dual trading promotes liquidity and that exchange enforcement activities are sufficient to prevent serious abuses.

As the widespread arrests and prosecutions in both Chicago and New York showed, there will always be temptations. Clearly, exchanges can improve their rules and surveillance. At a minimum, exchanges that want to allow dual trading have an obligation to create dear audit trails so that violations are easier to detect. It seems likely, however, that dual trading will be prohibited in futures trading as it is in securities trading. The exchanges and their floor communities can be expected to resist this development until the bitter end.

That makes it all sound quite simple. All you have to do is figure out whether to go long or short. The following chapters are designed to help you make that decision. If it all seems too simple, just turn to the options chapter and figure out how to do straddles, strangles, fences, and butterfly spreads.

Major Energy Exchanges Across the World

Comprehensive List

Exchange	Abbreviation	Location	Product Types
Brazilian Mercantile& Futures Exchange	BMF	Brazil	Biofuels, Metals
Bursa Malaysia		MDEX	Malaysia Biofuels
Central Japan Commodity Exchange			Nagoya Energy
Chicago Board of Trade	CBOT	Chicago	Biofuels, Metals
Chicago Climate Exchange	CCX	Chicago	Emissions
Chicago Mercantile Exchange		CME	Chicago Biofuels
Dubai Mercantile Exchange	DME	Dubai	Energy
Dubai Gold & Commodities Exchange	DGCX	Dubai	Precious Metals
European Climate Exchange	ECX	Europe	Emissions
HedgeStreet Exchange		California	Energy
London Metal Exchange	LME	London	Industrial Metals
Multi Commodity Exchange	MCX	Mumbai	Energy
National Commodity and Derivatives Exchange	NCDEX	Mumbai	Energy
New York Board of Trade	NYBOT	New York	Biofuels
New York Mercantile Exchange	NYMEX	New York	Energy, Metals
Shanghai Futures Exchange	SFE	Shanghai	Energy
Tokyo Commodity Exchange	TOCOM	Tokyo	Energy, Metals
U.S. Futures Exchange	USFE	Chicago	Energy

Chapter 8

Energy Security

ENERGY SECURITY—THE CONCEPT

Defining Energy Security

The International Energy Agency (IEA) defines energy security primarily in terms of stable supplies of oil and natural gas. However, this definition does not address the multidimensional nature of energy security for the developing world. ESMAP has redefined energy security to address the micro and macro level needs of developing countries as follows: *A country's ability to optimize its energy resource portfolio and supply of energy services for the desired level of services that will sustain economic growth and poverty reduction.* Energy security can also be defined in the following terms:

1. Enabling a certain percentage or number of countries to sustain the provisioning or availability of energy services for poverty reduction and economic growth.
2. Enabling a certain percentage or number of households, businesses and communities to meet their energy needs for consumptive, productive or socially productive uses

Energy security is an umbrella term that covers many concerns linking energy, economic growth and political power (Energy Vision Update-CERA, 2006). The energy security perspective varies depending upon one's position in the value chain. Consumers and energy-intensive industries desire reasonably-priced energy on demand and worry about disruptions. Major oil producing countries consider security of revenue and of demand integral parts of any energy security discussion. Oil and gas companies consider access to new reserves, ability to develop new infrastructure, and stable investment regimes to be critical to ensuring energy security. Developing countries are concerned about the ability to pay for resources to drive their economies and fear balance of payment shocks. Power companies are concerned with the integrity of the entire network. Policymakers focus on the risks of supply disruption and the security of infrastructure due to terrorism, war or natural disaster. They also consider the volumes of security margins—the amount of excess capacity, strategic reserves, and infrastructure redundancy.

Throughout the value-chain, prices and supply diversity are critical components of energy security. In earlier periods, oil was used as a "weapon," and there is concern that natural gas could also be used to gain political leverage at some time in the future. The traditional elements of energy security include: supply sources, demand centres, geopolitics and market structures (and responsiveness of related institutions). In the energy crises of the 1970s, the primary focus for the Western industrial countries was on oil supply sources and geopolitics. These two elements were the underlying causes of energy security concerns, and the demand centres, market structures and new institutions created the solutions to the two energy crises that occurred. In fact, the creation of the International Energy Agency (IEA) was a direct response to the 1973-74 oil disruption by the then-dominant energy-consuming economies.

The definition of energy security has changed over time. In the period post 1970's oil shocks, the definition of energy security related to the avoidance of oil supply risk resulting from potential disruptions of crude oil supply from the Middle-East. In this century, other factors that affect fuel supply stability and increase energy price have been added to the previous energy security definition. These factors include political conflicts, unexpected natural disasters, concern on terrorism, and energy-related environmental challenges.

The study conducted by IEA defines energy security as the ability of an economy to guarantee the availability of energy resource supply in a sustainable and timely manner with the energy price being at a level that will not adversely affect the economic performance of the economy. Thus, there are several factors that can influence the 'security' of energy supply, such as: (1) the availability of fuel reserves, both domestically and by external suppliers; (2) the ability of an economy to acquire supply to meet projected energy demand; (3) the level of an economy's energy resource diversification and energy supplier diversification; (4) accessibility to fuel resources, in terms of the availability of related energy infrastructure and energy transportation infrastructure; and (5) geopolitical concerns surrounding resource acquisition. In terms of energy demand elasticity, an economy that is able to decouple economic growth with energy use—through energy efficiency and conservation–will have an advantage in terms of its energy security.

Following the above definition, there are 3 fundamental elements of energy security that need to be taken into account to evolve future energy security policy as also to ensure long-term sustainability.

(1) PHYSICAL energy security, the availability and accessibility of supply sources;
(2) ECONOMIC energy security, the affordability of resource acquisition and energy infrastructure development; and
(3) ENVIRONMENTAL SUSTAINABILITY, the sustainable development and use of energy resources that "meets the needs of the present without compromising the ability of future generations to meet their own needs."

The Evolution of Energy Security

Background

The concept of energy security evolved from the oil crisis of the 1970's when the OPEC oil embargo and the Iranian revolution threatened to cause price increases and quantity shortages for the United States. Since then energy security has been viewed in terms of reliable and affordable access to oil by western countries that were dependent on oil imports for their energy needs. As natural gas became more important in the energy mix, it was included in this thinking. However, energy security has still remained predominantly a western concept due to the dominance of OECD countries as consumers of the world oil and natural gas production as can be seen in Table 1 below.

Table 8.1: Share of OECD countries in Oil & Gas

(*in %*)

	United States	Europe & Eurasia	Asia-Pacific	Africa
2003 daily oil consumption (share of total world consumption)	25.1	25.9	28.8	3.3
Change in 2003 over 2002 consumption	1.9	1.6	4	2.2
2003 daily natural gas consumption (share of total world consumption)	24.3	41.8	13.3	2.6
Change in 2003 over 2002 consumption	–4.9	3.6	5.7	8.3

Source: British Petroleum Statistical Review, 2003.

Analytical Framework for understanding Energy Security:

The definition of energy security implies that an analytical framework must examine the demand and supply side of the issue. The demand-side analysis includes the following factors:

1. **Understanding the demand structure:** The demand for energy services is generated from four distinct user groups: households, communities, industrial and agricultural users. There is heterogeneity among each of these user groups in terms of their demand for energy services. The present consumption patterns of these groups, along with their projected demand must be studied to ensure adequate investments in capacity building to meet their needs. Demographic trends and their impact on the demand for energy services must be also be studied and documented.
2. **Ability and willingness of users to pay for services:** Utility companies in developing countries face financial constraints which prevent much needed investments in infrastructure upgrades and maintenance. This is in part, due to the amount of "theft" from the transmission infrastructure caused by illegal connections and customers that do not pay. Ensuring financial flows from

customers is critical to sustaining the delivery energy services over the long-term. It is therefore important to gauge the ability and willingness of users during the design and implementation of energy projects.

3. **Securing demand for energy services and incomes:** Viable energy services require users that are able to pay for those services. This implies that securing demand for services is linked to securing incomes at the user level to ensure affordability of services.

The Supply-side analysis, on the other had, includes the following factors:

1. **Macroeconomic indicators:** The ability of oil importing countries to provide a sustained level of energy services is dependant on their level of energy imports and their ability to pay for it. The recent oil price increases have impacted the economies of oil importing developing countries such as Madagascar, Rwanda and Uganda. For example, in Madagascar, the total value of oil imports reached approximately US$213 million in 2001 from US$124 million in 1999. The effect of doubling of petroleum product prices on the already poor population (approximately 70 percent) has been severe. The price of gasoline, which increased 70 percent between April 1999 and October 2000, affects the transportation of all goods. Kerosene used by the poor increased 65 percent and the cost of mass urban transportation increased by 100 percent in the same period. Certain developing countries such as India subsidize certain fuels such as LPG and kerosene to encourage consumption by the poorer sections of the population. An increase in international fuel prices increases the subsidy bill of the governments and affects the overall fiscal stability of the economy. Other macroeconomic factors which affect energy security by impacting the ability of countries to import fuels are the level of foreign exchange reserves and the exchange stability of its currency. An understanding of the various macroeconomic factors affecting energy security is thus important for effective policy making.

2. **Geopolitical strategies:** Thirty percent of the 2003 production of oil came from the Middle East. Approximately 63% of the world's proven oil resources and 40% of the world's proven natural gas resources are concentrated in the Persian Gulf in the Middle-East.

   The geographic concentration of hydrocarbon resources has led to countries entering into bilateral or regional agreements to ensure stable supplies. For example, a study conducted by the Baker Institute at Rice University in 1999 stated that as China's oil import levels rise to levels above 2 million b/d, it will be increasingly difficult for China to meet its crude oil import requirements without concluding large, long-term contracts for the supply of oil. China has indicated intentions to deepen its oil trading relationships with Iraq or Iran, leading to fears that Beijing will form oil for arms, military client relationships with these nations. China's emergence as a major source of demand for hydrocarbons from the Persian Gulf is a source of concern for Japan which fears a "war for resources." It is thus, important to understand the geopolitical supply agreements that exist from each country's perspective to assess its level of energy security.
3. **Institutional capacity:** Developing countries can be categorized as net importers or net exporters of energy. Net exporting countries such as Chad, Algeria, Nigeria and Angola must have corporate and institutional structures in place to sustain gains from their energy exports, especially with the recent oil price increases. This is critical for their economies since they are heavily dependent on oil revenues. A robust institutional structure to invest the oil revenues to promote greater economic growth is therefore very important. Similarly, countries that might be net importers, but have refining and processing capabilities for exporting finished products, must have adequate institutional capacity to sustain revenues from these activities. It is important to understand these institutional capacities to formulate effective policies for enhancing energy security.
4. **Financial resources:** The total investment amount

required for energy infrastructure over the next 25 years is projected to be $16 trillion. To provide the desired level of energy services for their populations, developing countries must be able to mobilize resources in the domestic and international capital markets. Attracting investment requires governments in developing countries to play an active role in promoting good governance and anticorruption measures.

5. **Environmental Impacts:** The rapid increase in energy use in countries like China and India is causing environmental problems such as smog and acid rain, which interfere with other economic sectors such as agriculture. Hence, expanding access to energy must be balanced with environmental considerations.
6. **Natural resource endowment & technological feasibility:** Understanding the energy endowments of each country such as hydrocarbon reserves, hydropower capacity, solar & wind energy capacities are important in assessing the ability of a country to domestically meets its energy requirements. It is equally important to analyze the investment outlays and required technologies to develop these resources which should be based on a framework consisting of: (a) the premise that the level of energy services available to the people of any country is a function of the policies undertaken by the governments at the country level and (b) that the goal of every country's energy policy is to have a resource portfolio that is optimized against constraints that are country or region specific to enable a desired level of services.

Such a framework conceived by CERA can be translated into specific tasks which are outlined below:

Natural Resource Endowment and Technological Feasibility

Natural resource endowment and technological feasibility studies, inter alia, imply mapping the energy resource endowment of each country along with the economics of developing those resources. Factors affecting consumption of energy services for each user group (industrial, agricultural, community and households) may include:

Current consumption levels
Current expenditures on energy services
Impacts of service disruption
Securing demand for energy services
Demand variations due to seasonal changes, transitioning economies, etc
Understanding the demand structure
Ability and willingness of users to pay for services
Demand side analysis
Balance of payments
Budgetary impacts of subsidies
Foreign exchange reserves
Macroeconomic factors
Securing incomes among user groups to pay for services
Ability of a country to attract domestic and international investment
Financial factors
Impact of expanding energy services
Environmental sustainability
Natural resource &technological endowment
Geopolitical supply agreements
Institutional capacity
Supply side analysis

Ability of a country to optimize its energy resource portfolio and supply of energy services for the desired level of services that sustain economic growth and poverty reduction: the detailed framework conceived to optimize the energy resource portfolio and supply of energy services at desired level to sustain economic growth is outlined below:

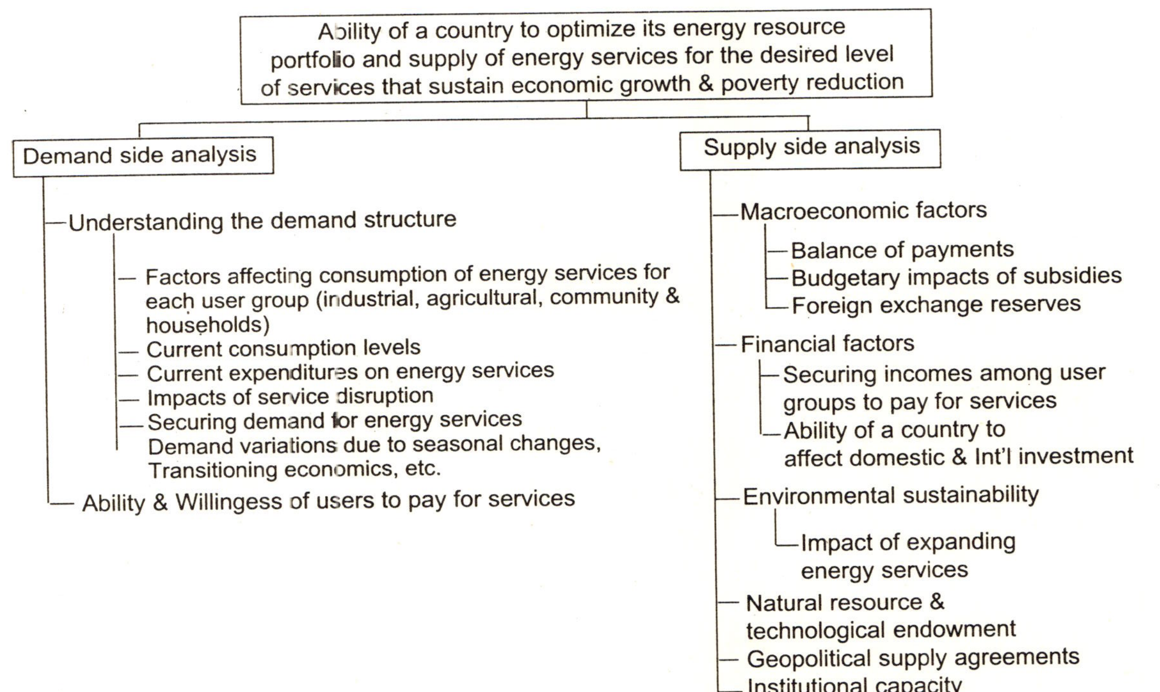
Ability of a country to optimize its energy resource portfolio and supply of energy services for the desired level of services that sustain economic growth & poverty reduction
Demand side analysis
Understanding the demand structure
Factors affecting consumption of energy services for each user group (industrial, agricultural, community & households)
Current consumption levels
Current expenditures on energy services
Impacts of service disruption
Securing demand for energy services
Demand variations due to seasonal changes, Transitioning economics, etc.
Ability & Willingess of users to pay for services
Supply side analysis
Macroeconomic factors
Balance of payments
Budgetary impacts of subsidies
Foreign exchange reserves
Financial factors
Securing incomes among user groups to pay for services
Ability of a country to affect domestic & Int'l investment
Environmental sustainability
Impact of expanding energy services
Natural resource & technological endowment
Geopolitical supply agreements
Institutional capacity

The framework above can be translated into specific tasks which are outlined below:

Energy security-subcategories	Tasks
Macroeconomic factors	Measuring the import dependence of each country to understand its exposure to fuel price volatility.
Demand and demographics	Understanding the demand function of each user group according to consumption patterns and the ability to pay for energy services.
Geopolitics and institutional capacity	Documenting existing geopolitical supply agreements
	Analyzing changes in demand when economies are undergoing restructuring
	Corporate structure required to sustain energy imports or gains from energy exports
Financial resources	Documenting the ability of a country to attract domestic and international investment to expand energy infrastructure and service delivery.
Environmental feasibility	Understanding the impacts of expanding access on the environment and the role of technology (e.g. improved devices such as cooking stoves, renewable energy generation) in mitigating these impacts.
Natural resource endowment and technological feasibility	Mapping the energy resource endowment of each country and the economics of developing those resources.

Geopolitical Dimension of Energy Security

Energy security issues have traditionally focused on crude oil supply disruptions in the Middle-East. The instability of the Middle-East during the 1970s led to rising prices for more than a decade. After oil prices collapsed in the mid-1980s, followed by the end of the Cold War and the resolution of the 1990-91 crisis, the world passed into a decade of lower oil prices and overconfidence about energy security—and, indeed, security overall. But turmoil in the Middle East—accentuated by demographic pressures, generational change and the rise of extremism; by the threat to political order and infrastructure posed by terrorist organizations; by regional conflict; and by rising demand, market pressure and price spikes—all these have brought the issue centre stage again. Yet, over the past 30 years, all four elements of traditional energy security discussions have evolved. Oil and natural gas production occurs today in locations not anticipated 30 years ago.

The expansion of the European Union, the break-up of the Soviet Union and the economic explosion in the Asia Pacific region have meant major shifts in demand and supply and in geopolitics. Terrorist acts by small groups that are more concerned about disrupting economies than on controlling oil were not a consideration in the past. Now, every government must factor in the possibility of terrorist acts that could disrupt some part of the supply chain or systems that support the energy supply chain, including telecommunications. In the 1990s, natural gas became the "fuel of choice" for new power generating plants. Both globalization and the Internet revolution have also created interconnections in the supply chain that squeeze out inefficiencies and yet create new vulnerabilities for disruption. In this section of the report, we explore the major shifts in the world of energy between 1974 and 2005, beginning with oil—the original focus of energy security (Pronishka, 2007).

Energy security—the continuous availability of energy in varied forms, in sufficient quantities, and at reasonable prices—has many aspects. It means limited vulnerability to transient or longer disruptions of imported supplies. It also means the availability of local and imported resources to meet, over time and at reasonable prices, the growing demand for energy. Environmental challenges, liberalization and deregulation, and the growing dominance of market forces all have profound implications for energy security. These forces have introduced new elements into energy security, affecting the traditionally vital role of government. In the past, and especially since the early 1970s, energy security has been narrowly viewed as reduced dependence on oil consumption and imports, particularly in OECD and other major oil-importing countries. But changes in oil and other energy markets have altered that view. Suppliers have increased, as have proven reserves and stocks, and prices have become flexible and transparent, dictated by market forces rather than by cartel arrangements.

Global tensions as well as regional conflicts are lessening, and trade is flourishing and becoming freer. Suppliers have not imposed any oil sanctions since the early 1980s, nor have there been any real shortages anywhere in the world. Instead, the United Nations and other actors have applied sanctions to some oil suppliers, but without affecting world oil trade or creating shortages. All this points to the present availability of abundant oil supplies at all times, an availability that has been greatly enhanced thanks in large part to technological advances. Moreover, in today's market environment energy security is a shared issue for importing and exporting countries. Energy security can be ensured through local adequacy—abundant and varied forms of indigenous energy resources. But for countries that face local shortages, as most do, energy security can be enhanced through:

> The ability, of the state or of market players, to draw on foreign energy resources and products that can be freely imported through ports or other transport channels and through cross-boundary energy grids (pipelines and electricity networks). This is increasingly aided by energy treaties and charters and by investment and trade agreements.

Adequate national (or regional) strategic reserves to address any transient interruption, shortages, or unpredictably high demand.

Technological and financial resources and know-how to develop indigenous renewable energy sources and domestic power generating facilities to meet part of local energy requirements.

Adequate attention to environmental challenges.

Diversification of import sources and types of fuels.

Energy Security-Conservation Nexus

Energy security can also be greatly enhanced by energy conservation and efficiency measures, because reducing energy intensity will reduce the dependence of the economy on energy consumption and imports. But while all this is very encouraging, new threats to energy security have appeared in recent years. Regional shortages are becoming more acute, and the possibility of insecurity of supplies—due to disruption of trade and reduction in strategic reserves, as a result of conflicts or sabotage—still exists, although it is decreasing. All this points toward a need to strengthen global as well as regional and national energy security.

Adequate global energy supplies, for the world as a whole as well as for individual countries, are essential for sustainable development, proper functioning of the economy, and human well-being. Thus the continuous availability of energy—in the quantities and forms required by the economy and society—must be ensured and secured. Energy security—the continuous availability of energy in varied forms, in sufficient quantities, and at reasonable prices—has several aspects. It means limited vulnerability to transient or longer disruptions of imported supplies. It also means the availability of local and imported resources to meet growing demand over time and at reasonable prices.

Beginning in the early 1970s energy security was narrowly viewed as reduced dependence on oil consumption and imports, particularly in OECD and other major oil-importing countries. Since that time considerable changes in oil and other energy markets have altered the picture. Suppliers have increased, as have proven reserves and stocks, and prices have become flexible and transparent, dictated by market forces rather than by cartel arrangements. Global tensions and regional conflicts are lessening, and trade is flourishing and becoming freer. Suppliers have not imposed any oil sanctions since the early 1980s, nor have there been any real shortages anywhere in the world. Instead, the United Nations and other actors have applied sanctions to some oil suppliers, but without affecting world oil trade or creating shortages.

Regional Imbalance-a Potential Threat to Energy Security

New threats to energy security have emerged in recent years. Regional shortages are becoming more acute, and the possibility of insecurity of supplies—due to disruption of trade and reduction in strategic reserves, as a result of conflicts or sabotage—persists, although it is decreasing. These situations point to a need to strengthen global as well as regional and national energy security (some means for doing this are discussed later in the chapter). There is also a need for a strong plea, under the auspices of the World Trade Organization (WTO), to refrain from restrictions on trade in energy products on grounds of competition or differences in environmental or labour standards. Environmental challenges to sustainable development are gaining momentum and have profound implications for energy security, as do the current trends of liberalization, deregulation, and the growing dominance of market forces. These forces have introduced new elements into energy security, affecting the traditionally vital role of government, as described below. They also have consequences for medium-size companies and individual consumers, who may be tempted by cheap competitive prices and lack of information to sacrifice, sometimes temporarily, supply security.

Energy has always been important to humanity. But its importance is increasing each year. Interruptions of energy supply—even if brief—can cause serious financial, economic, and social losses. Some energy products and carriers have become absolutely essential for modern life and business. Interruption of electricity supply can cause major financial losses and create havoc in cities and urban centres. The absolute security of the energy supply, particularly electricity, is therefore critical. With the widespread use of computers and other voltage- and frequency-sensitive electronic equipment, the quality of supply has also become vital. In the electricity supply industry, a significant share of investment goes into reserve generating plants, standby equipment, and other redundant facilities needed to protect the continuity and quality of supply.

Energy Security Linked to Distribution and Supplies

Energy insecurity and shortages affect countries in two ways: they handicap productive activities, and they undermine consumer welfare. Energy insecurity discourages investors by threatening production and increasing costs. Shortages in electricity supplies (as in many developing countries) require more investment for on-site electricity production or standby supplies. For small investors, the cost of operation is increased, since electricity from private small-scale generation is more expensive than public national supplies. Electricity interruptions at home cause consumers great inconvenience, frustration, and loss of productivity, sometimes threatening their well-being. For any economy, an unreliable energy supply results in both short- and long-term costs. The costs are measured in terms of loss of welfare and production, and the adjustments that consumers (such as firms) facing unreliable fuel and electric power supplies undertake to mitigate their losses. Interruptions in supply may trigger loss of production, costs related to product spoilage, and damage to equipment. The extent of these direct economic costs depends on a host of factors, such as advance notification, duration of the interruption, and timing of the interruption, which relates to the time of day or season and to the prevailing market conditions and demand for the firm's output. These direct costs can be very high. In addition, the economy is affected indirectly because of the secondary costs that arise from the interdependence between one firm's output and another firm's input.

New dimensions and Challenges to Energy Security

Energy security needs to be investigated at several levels: globally, to ensure adequacy of resources; regionally, to ensure that networking and trade can take place; at the country level, to ensure national security of supply; and at the consumer level, to ensure that consumer demand can be satisfied (Khatib,2007). At the country level, energy security is based on the availability of all energy consumption requirements at all times from indigenous sources or imports and from stocks. Normally in most countries, this is a state responsibility. However, markets in some OECD countries are increasingly shouldering part of this responsibility. To ensure energy security, projections, plans, and supply arrangements should look beyond short-term requirements to medium- and long-term demand as well. With the increasing deregulation and competition among private and independent suppliers, supply security at the consumer level can become more vulnerable and correspondingly more important in some cases. Consumer demand for energy services can be met by different suppliers competing to deliver different forms of energy at different prices, while the consumer remains unaware of the degree of supply security.

As explained above, environmental challenges deregulation,

and market forces have introduced new players to the energy security scene. This chapter considers energy security at the national (and regional) level as well as consumer security in terms of energy services. In most countries these two levels of security are one and the same. But in some OECD countries, with markets and competition emerging at the consumer level, the two may diverge. The section also covers the geopolitical aspects of energy security as well as the limitations of the resource base and other factors that may affect long-term energy security. Of all energy sources, crude oil and its products are the most versatile, capable of meeting every requirement for energy use and services, particularly in transport. The other fossil fuels, coal and natural gas, are well suited for electricity production and such stationary uses as generation of heat and steam. Coal, increasingly used for electricity production, requires relatively expensive clean technologies, and treatment for liquefaction and gasification to make it more versatile. Natural gas also requires expensive infrastructure, and special treatment to make it useful for transport. Hydropower, newer renewable resources such as wind and photovoltaic, and nuclear energy have limited use beyond electricity production.

Given the versatility of crude oil and its products and the limitations of other energy sources, energy security depends more than anything else on the availability of crude oil in the required amounts (by ship or pipeline) to any importing country in the world. Thus, although energy security has to be interpreted more broadly than in the past, the uninterrupted supply of crude oil in the required amounts and at reasonable prices will continue to be the most important determinant of energy security. Uninterrupted supply—of oil and other forms of Energy—includes uninterrupted transit through third countries.

Security of Electric Power Supply

Chronic energy shortages and poor security of the electric power supply trigger long-term adjustments. If firms expect shortages and unreliable service to persist, they will respond in one or more ways. The most common long-term adjustment by commercial consumers and small industrial firms is to install back-up diesel generator sets. It has been estimated that in many developing countries such standby generation on customer premises accounts for 20 percent or more of the total installed generating capacity (USAID, 1988). The shortages and inadequate maintenance of the grid also add to poor security. In some developing countries half the public electricity supply is inoperable at any given time. Many manufacturing firms have had to purchase their own generators to meet their demand for electricity. In Nigeria about 92 percent of firms surveyed in the mid-1990s had their own generators. This purchase added to their fixed costs, raised production costs, and tended to discourage new investments. For small firms, the investment in generating capacity represented almost a quarter of their total investment, and for large firms, a tenth (ADB, 1999). Moreover, in many developing countries the electric power system losses (technical and non-technical) are very high, exceeding a quarter of generation in some and as much as half in a few. Shortages of electric power and supply interruptions are not uncommon, particularly in many developing countries. They occur for two main reasons:

System inadequacy—shortfalls of delivered electricity under even the best conditions in the electric power system. Such shortfalls, most common in developing countries, usually occur because of an inadequate number of generating facilities capable of meeting peak demand and limitations in the transmission and distribution system, particularly to rural areas.

Supply insecurity—unreliability of supply due to non-availability of generating plants or breakdowns in the transmission and distribution system. This can occur in varying degrees in any power system in the world. To ensure system adequacy—the ability of a power system to meet demand and deliver adequate electricity to consumers— requires investment. Most investments in electric power security are meant to reduce the likelihood of shortages and maintain and improve reliability. Most shortages occur as a result of growth in demand, which necessitates expanding generation capacity and strengthening networks. But even with large investments, interruptions are inevitable. And the costs of improving continuity of supply can become very high once a certain level of reliability has been reached.

The function of the electric power system is to provide electricity as economically as possible and with an acceptable degree of security and quality. The economics of electric power security (reliability) involve striking a reasonable balance between cost and quality of service. This balance varies from country to country and from one category of consumers to another.

To improve supply security, countries invest in redundant facilities. These investments, in reserve generating capacity and other network facilities, normally amount to at least a third of the investments by the electricity supply industry. Low-income developing countries cannot afford such huge investments, leading to supply insecurity. Thus in many developing countries, electricity supplies are enhanced by standby plants on consumer premises. Many industries and commercial outlets have to spend heavily on in-house generation or standby plants to attain a reasonable standard of continuity. This greatly increases the cost of attaining supply security and places an added burden on the limited economic resources of these countries.

Supply interruptions occur not only because of shortages in generating plants or limitations in the grid. They are also attributed to inadequate maintenance due to lack of skilled staff or shortage of spare parts. Attaining a reasonable standard of performance in developing countries' public systems is essential not only to improve electricity supply security but also to limit the wasted resources in standby plants and reserve generating capacity. This can be achieved through proper planning of the system and by investing in training and maintenance rather than only in system expansion. The cost of insecurity of the electricity system in developing countries varies by country depending on the extent of electrification and quality of the supply. However, in industrialized countries the costs of supply insecurity for non-deferrable economic activities are huge. In the United States it was estimated that these costs might exceed $5 billion a year (Newton-Evans Research Company, 1998). Most of these costs are borne by industrial and commercial consumers.

Pathways to Enhanced Energy Security

Energy security can be ensured by local adequacy—abundant and varied forms of indigenous energy resources. In the case of local shortages, which occur in most countries, energy security can be enhanced through: _ The ability, of the state or of market players, to draw on foreign energy resources and products that can be freely imported through ports or other transport channels and through cross boundary energy grids (pipelines and electricity networks).

- Adequate national (or regional) strategic reserves to address any transient interruption, shortages, or unpredictable surge in demand.
- Technological and financial resources and know-how to develop indigenous renewable sources and power generating facilities to meet part of local energy requirements.
- Adequate attention to environmental challenges.

Energy security can also be enhanced through energy conservation and efficiency measures. Reducing energy intensity will reduce the dependence of the economy on energy consumption and imports. To achieve energy security requires first of all ensuring global energy adequacy—the existence of enough energy resources, or other prospects, to meet long-term world energy needs.

Energy Adequacy

Although energy resources are examined in detail elsewhere in this report, a quick review is provided here because energy security depends, to a great extent, on the availability of an adequate resource base. The resource base is the sum of reserves and resources. Reserves are occurrences (of all types and forms of hydrocarbon deposits, natural uranium, and thorium) that are known and economically recoverable with present technologies.

Resources are less certain, are not economically recoverable with present technologies, or are both. In the future, with advances in technology and geophysics, many of today's resources are likely to become reserves (McKelvey, 1972). In 1998, world consumption of primary energy totaled almost 355 exajoules, or 8,460 million tonnes of oil equivalent (Mtoe)—7,630 Mtoe of fossil fuels, 620 Mtoe of nuclear energy, and 210 Mtoe of hydropower. To this should be added around 47 exajoules (1,120 Mtoe) of biomass and other renewables, for a total of 402 exajoules (9,580 Mtoe). The huge resource base of fossil fuels, coal, water, sunshine and nuclear fuels will be adequate to meet such global requirements for decades to come.

Let us examine in brief the potentiality of these resources to meet the growing challenges of Energy Security.

Crude Oil

Proven oil reserves have increased steadily over the past 20 years, mainly because oil companies have expanded their estimates of the reserves in already discovered fields. This optimism stems from better knowledge of the fields, increased productivity, and advances in technology. New technologies have led to more accurate estimates of reserves through better seismic (three- and four-dimensional) exploration, have improved drilling techniques (such as horizontal and offshore drilling), and have increased recovery factors—the share of oil that can be recovered—from 30 percent to 40–50 percent (Campbell and Laherrere, 1998). Huge amounts of untapped unconventional oil also exist, augmenting conventional oil reserves. Some 1.2 trillion barrels of heavy oil are found in the Orinoco oil belt in Venezuela. And the tar sands of Canada and oil shale deposits of the Russian Federation may contain 300 billion barrels of oil.

The U.S. Geological Survey assessed ultimate oil and gas reserves at the beginning of 1993 (IEA 1998; WEC, 1998). The results, which tally with the World Energy Council (WEC) and International Energy Agency (IEA) figures, point to ultimate conventional oil reserves of 2,300 billion barrels, with cumulative production until 1993 amounting to 700 billion barrels and unidentified reserves to 470 billion. No shortage of conventional liquid fuels is foreseen before 2020. Any deficiencies after that can be met by the ample reserves of unconventional oil.

Natural Gas

The U.S. Geological Survey also assessed ultimate natural gas reserves in 1993 (Masters, 1994). It estimated ultimate reserves at 11,448 trillion cubic feet (11,214 exajoules, or 267 gigatonnes of oil equivalent [Gtoe]), with cumulative production until 1993 amounting to 1,750 trillion cubic feet (1,722 exajoules, or 41 Gtoe).

Cumulative world gas production through the end of 1995 was only 17.1 percent of the U.S. Geological Survey's estimate of conventional gas reserves. Natural gas consumption is projected to grow 2.6 percent a year, mostly as a result of growth in electricity generation in non-OECD countries. Despite this growth, cumulative production is expected to be no more than 41 percent of the U.S. Geological Survey's estimate of conventional gas reserves by 2020. This points towards a resource base that is large enough to serve global requirements for natural gas well into the second half of the 21st century.

Coal

Coal is the world's most abundant fossil fuel, with reserves estimated at almost 1,000 billion tonnes, equivalent to 27,300 exajoules, or 650,000 Mtoe (WEC, 1998). At the present rate of production, these reserves should last for more than 220 years. Thus the resource base of coal is much larger than that of oil and gas. In addition, coal reserves are more evenly distributed across the world. And coal is cheap. Efforts are being made to reduce production costs and to apply clean coal technologies to reduce the environmental impact. Coal demand is forecast to grow at a rate slightly higher than global energy growth. Most of this growth will be for power generation in non-OECD countries, mostly in Asia. Although trade in coal is still low, it is likely to increase slowly over time. Long-term trends in direct coal utilization are difficult to predict because of the potential impact of climate change policies. Coal gasification and liquefaction will augment global oil and gas resources in the future.

Nuclear Energy

Although nuclear energy is sometimes grouped with fossil fuels, it relies on a different resource base. In 1998 nuclear energy production amounted to 2,350 terawatt-hours of electricity, replacing 620 Mtoe of other fuels. Uranium requirements amounted to 63,700 tonnes in 1997, against reasonably assured resources (reserves) of 3.4 million tonnes. Ultimately recoverable reserves amount to almost 17 million tonnes. Considering the relative stagnation in the growth of nuclear power, the enormous occurrences of low-grade uranium and the prospects for recycling nuclear fuels, such reserves will suffice for many decades.

Renewable

Renewable energy sources—especially hydroelectric power, biomass, and wind power, and geothermal energy—account for a growing share of world energy consumption. Today hydropower and biomass together contribute around 15 percent. Hydroelectric power contributes around 2,500 terawatt-hours of electricity a year, slightly more than nuclear power does. It replaces almost 675 Mtoe of fuels a year, although its direct contribution to primary energy consumption is only a third of this. But it has still more potential. Technically exploitable hydro resources could potentially produce more than 14,000 terawatt-hours of electricity a year, equivalent to the world's total electricity requirements in 1998 (WEC, 1998). For environmental and economic reasons, however, most of these resources will not be exploited. Still, hydropower will continue to develop. Hydropower is the most important among renewable energy sources. It is a clean, cheap source of energy, requiring only minimal running costs and with a conversion efficiency of almost 100 percent. Thus its annual growth could exceed the growth of global energy demand, slightly improving hydropower's modest contribution towards meeting world requirements.

Renewable energy sources other than hydro are substantial. These take the form mainly of biomass. Traditional biomass includes fuelwood—the main source of biomass energy—dung, and crop and forest residues. Lack of statistics makes it difficult to accurately estimate the contribution of renewable to the world's primary energy consumption. But it is estimated that the world consumed around 1.20 Gtoe in 1998. About two-thirds of this was from fuelwood, and the remainder from crop residues and dung. Much of this contribution is sustainable from a supply standpoint. But the resulting energy services could be substantially increased by improving conversion efficiencies, which are typically very low.

The contribution of biomass to world energy consumption is expected to increase slightly. It is mainly used as an energy source in developing countries. While energy demand in these countries is steadily increasing, some of the demand is being met by switching from traditional to commercial energy sources. Biomass energy technology is rapidly advancing. Besides direct combustion, techniques for gasification, fermentation, and anaerobic digestion are all increasing the potential of biomass as a sustainable energy source. The viability of wind energy is increasing as well. Some 2,100 megawatts of new capacity was commissioned in 1998, pushing global wind generating capacity to 9,600 megawatts.

Wind power accounted for an estimated 21 terawatt-hours of electricity production in 1999. While that still amounts to only 0.15 percent of global electricity production, the competitiveness of wind power is improving and its growth potential is substantial. Use of geothermal energy for electricity generation is also increasing, with a present generating capacity of more than 8,300 megawatts.

To summarize, no serious global shortage of energy resources is likely during at least the first half of the 21st century. Reserves of traditional commercial fuels—oil, gas, and coal—will suffice for decades to come. When conventional oil resources are depleted, the huge unconventional oil and gas reserves will be tapped as new extraction and clean generating technologies mature. Coal reserves are also huge: the resource base is more than twice that of conventional and unconventional oil and gas. Clean technologies for coal will allow greater exploitation of this huge resource base, mainly in electricity production, but also through conversion into oil and gas, minimizing environmentally harmful emissions. The uranium resource base is also immense, and it is unlikely, at least in the short-term, to be tapped in increasing amounts. The ultimately recoverable uranium reserves will easily meet any nuclear power requirements during this century. The renewable resource base is also promising. Only part of the global hydro potential has been tapped. Hydropower plants will continue to be built as demand for electricity grows and the economics of long-distance, extra-high-voltage transmission improve. Biomass has substantial potential and will continue to be used not only as a traditional fuel but also in increasingly sophisticated ways, through thermo-chemical and biochemical applications. New renewable sources, particularly wind power, will gradually increase the contribution of renewables to global energy supplies as the economies and technologies of these environmentally attractive sources continue to improve.

In short, the world's energy supplies offer good prospects for energy security in the 21st century. The fossil fuel reserves amount to 1,300 Gtoe and the fossil fuel resource base to around 5,000 Gtoe amounts sufficient to cover global requirements throughout this century, even with a high-growth scenario.

Supply-side Security

Energy resources are not evenly distributed across the world. Oil in particular, and natural gas to a lesser extent, is concentrated in a few regions. The concentration of oil reserves in the Persian Gulf region has always caused concerns about continuity of supply. Most countries, particularly OECD countries, experienced oil shortages and high prices in the 1970s and early 1980s, with physical disruption in supply leading to economic disruption. Energy importers are anxious not to repeat such experiences.

The oil supply situation has improved significantly since then. OECD countries' share of the energy market is decreasing, while that of developing countries is increasing. This adds to the security of oil supplies because many developing countries are oil producers or have supply arrangements with producers. OECD countries, which accounted for 70 percent of the energy market in the 1970s, will see their market share fall to less than half by 2010.

Technological advance has allowed the discovery and development of new energy reserves and reduced the cost of supplies. It has also helped increase efficiency in energy use, loosening the historically tight link between economic development and energy consumption. Another major favourable development is the reduction in the sources of conflict that can affect global energy security. The cold war is over, and stability in the Middle East, although still precarious, is improving, with the Arab-Israeli conflict moving towards resolution. However, some other global developments present both opportunities and new challenges to the energy sector. The policy emphasis on environmentally sustainable development, particularly in OECD countries, has important long-term implications for energy security. And the market liberalization taking place in most industrialized countries has reduced the state's role in energy security—and increased that of consumers.

Energy security is also important for energy producers and

exporters. History shows that oil supply disruptions have negative effects on oil-exporting economies. As consumers in importing economies shift away from oil, the lower demand causes severe economic damage to the exporters. In addition, many oil-exporting countries have recently obtained stakes in downstream operations in importing countries. This involvement in OECD economies will contribute towards energy security, as supply disruptions could mean a loss of business opportunities for both oil exporters and importers.

Causes of supply disruption are not limited to disturbances in production facilities. Disruptions can also occur in the long supply chains, such as serious tanker accidents in the most heavily travelled zones—the Strait of Malacca, for example. Vulnerability to disruption may grow as energy supplies are increasingly delivered through grids (gas pipelines and extra-high-voltage transmission networks).

Some of these cross national boundaries and are at least theoretically vulnerable to damage through sabotage and other political disturbances. Terrorist actions could damage liquefied natural gas (LNG) conversion and receiving stations and tankers. But such possibilities are remote. Most energy supplies are delivered under long-term contracts that commit governments to ensuring safe transit and security. Despite the favourable developments in the energy market, energy security continues to concern planners and strategists in most importing countries. Long-term energy security can be enhanced in several ways; namely through:

Diversifying sources of supply and forms of energy used

Encouraging international cooperation and agreements among energy-importing countries and between consumer and supplier countries, whether between governments or between companies.

Investing in and transferring technology to developing countries. Enabling developing countries to develop more energy supplies will enhance the availability of global supplies. Helping these countries increase the efficiency of energy use and improve environmental management will have a similar effect.

Enhancing and increasing national and regional strategic reserves of crude oil and its products

Of all the forms of energy, crude oil and its products are still the most important for energy security, because of oil's versatility and because it is the optimal form of energy for the transport sector. Natural gas, because of its affordability and cleanliness, is gaining in importance. Nuclear energy, despite its past promise, faces many difficulties. The security of all these energy forms, as well as coal, is discussed below. Energy intensity is also discussed, because improvements in this area could yield a wider range of benefits for energy security than could provide new sources of energy.

Security concerns of Crude Oil Supply

Over the past 20 years many changes in the oil market have improved the overall security of the energy market. The world economy has become less dependent on oil, as most regions have diversified their energy sources. Oil constituted almost 46 percent of world commercial energy sources in 1973, compared with 40 percent now. There has also been diversification of supply. In the early 1970s the Organization of Petroleum Exporting Countries (OPEC) accounted for more than half the world's oil; today it provides only 42 percent. The world now has 80 oil-producing countries (although very few have the surge capacity needed in emergencies). The oil markets have become more like traditional commodity markets (with futures markets), transparent and able to respond quickly to changing circumstances. Big strides have been made in energy efficiency, gradually reducing the dependence of economic growth on increased oil consumption.

Advances in technology have led to discoveries of more oil, reduced the cost of discoveries, and significantly improved the recovery rate, increasing the oil resource base to an estimated 2,300 trillion barrels. World trade has flourished in recent years. In 1998 it was three times that in 1980, and now accounts for 44 percent of global GDP, compared with 39 percent in 1980. Both energy exporters and importers benefit from trade. Most exporters are low-income countries that badly need oil income for development. Even with the increase in oil-producing countries, the fact remains that almost two-thirds of the world's oil resources are in the

Middle-East, mostly in the Gulf region (the Islamic Republic of Iran, Iraq, Kuwait, Qatar, Saudi Arabia, and the United Arab Emirates). Although these six countries now account for only 27 percent of global crude oil supplies, they are expected to double their share to 52 percent in 2010. The Middle East, particularly the Gulf region, has not been historically known for political stability and security. But as mentioned, the situation is improving.

OECD countries, which account for almost 80 percent of the world's economic activity and 63 percent of global oil consumption, are particularly dependent on oil imports. All OECD countries are expected to increase their dependence on oil imports over the next few years. Their oil imports, 56 percent of their energy requirements in 1996, are expected to rise to 76 percent in 2020.

Asia-Pacific countries' crude oil imports are expected to increase to 72 percent of their requirements in 2005 (up from 56 percent in 1993). The Middle East is expected to account for 92 percent of the region's imports, with the Gulf countries the main source of supply. The Gulf region is expected to supply 18 million barrels a day to Asia-Pacific countries in 2010, far more than its expected total supplies to Europe and the United States of 12 million barrels a day. That is why oil security, particularly for the major oil-importing countries, and the stability of the Gulf region have such importance to overall energy security and the world economy. This importance will only increase in the future.

Differences between regional requirements and regional supplies will be accentuated in the future. Nowhere will this be more serious than in Asia, particularly among the large oil-consuming countries—China, India, Japan, and the Republic of Korea. Competition for supplies may intensify during emergencies, creating a potential for severe strains among Asian powers. Shortages may tempt some of these countries to project political and even military power to ensure adequate oil supplies. Already some of them—as well as the United States—have increased their naval presence in the Asian and Indian oceans (Jaffe, 1998). And U.S efforts for cooperation and conflict resolution are linked to its military planning and presence in the Gulf region and key oil export sea routes (Kemp and Harkavy, 1997).

Threats to security in oil-exporting countries can be both internal and external. Continued supply from Saudi Arabia is the most important element of energy security. Saudi supplies, now more than 9 million barrels a day, will have to increase to 13–15 million barrels a day in 2010 to meet growing world demand and offset resource depletion in non-OPEC suppliers. By that time the United States will be importing more than 60 percent of its oil. Saudi Arabia has both the potential and the reserves to meet projected demand, but the expansion will call for investment resources from that country as well as the world financial community. For a healthy oil sector, the availability of such financing should be no problem.

Over the past few decades the Gulf countries have proved to be stable; continued internal and external stability is crucial to energy security. Disruption of the Gulf oil flow would lead to a deep world-wide recession. This has been presented as one of the gravest threats imaginable to U.S. interests, short of physical attack (David, 1999). The cost of energy security goes beyond investing in redundant facilities and building pipelines, grids, and strategic reserves. Tremendous military expenditures—both visible and invisible—are required to head off any threats to the flow of oil, particularly from the Gulf countries. These costs cannot be easily computed or ascertained. The enormous expenditures on the 1990–91 Gulf-War, totaling several hundred billion dollars, were meant to ensure energy security for major oil importers and the world oil markets in general. The six Gulf Cooperation Council (GCC) states, which control nearly 45 percent of the world's recoverable oil resources, contributed more than $60 billion to the U.S.-led allied offensive to eject Iraqi forces from Kuwait in 1991 (AFP, 1998). The GCC countries' contribution in 1991 exceeded their oil export income in 1998 or 1999. The United States maintains a costly military and naval presence in strategic locations to ensure the uninterrupted flow of GCC oil exports to world markets.

Oil-stocks: Combating Supply Disruptions

Oil-stocks are usually held by oil companies for operational purposes, and by countries and state utilities to provide a cushion against unexpected surges in demand and possible disruptions in imports. Oil companies usually hold stocks that account for 55–65 days of consumption. International Energy Agency (IEA) members are required to hold emergency oil stocks equivalent to at least 90 days of net imports. The European Union requires its members—also IEA members—to hold stocks equivalent to at least 90 days of consumption. It is not easy to estimate oil stocks held by developing countries. Because of the cost, their stocks are relatively smaller than those of OECD countries, but can amount to 25–55 days of consumption, which is also typical for oil companies in these countries. Correspondingly, world oil stocks in 1997 were about 5,500 million barrels, equal to 70–80 days of average global consumption. With the continued growth of non-OECD oil consumption, oil stocks will function less effectively. Their size relative to the global oil market will decline, since most developing countries do not maintain emergency oil stocks (many cannot afford them). If this trend continues, vulnerability to sudden and substantial oil supply disruptions will increase.

Liberalization of Markets: Easing the Flow of Oil

Another aspect of security is the liberalization of energy markets in importing countries. Liberalization and deregulation, coupled with the development of oil futures and forwards markets, mean easier and more secure flow2of oil from exporting to importing countries. Most oil producers are now inviting foreign companies to participate in oil development, which will significantly enhance the security of the oil market. And the strengthening of the World Trade Organization (WTO) will add further to the security of the energy market. Although security in terms of flows of oil and gas to importing countries is improving, the security of supply to consumers faces new challenges. Liberalization, the withdrawal of government responsibility for supply, and competition among private suppliers are creating challenges in securing reliable supply to individual consumers.

Security aspects of Natural Gas supply

Natural gas is slowly gaining importance in the energy market. Between 1987 and 1997 gas consumption increased from 1,756 giga cubic metres to 2,197, for an annual growth rate of 2.27 percent, compared with 1.47 percent for total primary commercial energy consumption. Over the period until 2020 natural gas demand is expected to grow still faster—at an annual rate of 2.6 percent, compared with 1.9 percent for oil. And natural gas supply, since it is starting from a much lower base than oil supply, is not expected to peak until well beyond 2020 (IEA, 1998).

Internationally traded natural gas accounted for 19 percent of gas consumption in 1997, compared with 44 percent for oil. So, just as for oil, though to a lesser extent, there is a mismatch between the location of gas supply and its consumption. Security of supply is therefore critical. But the physical characteristics of natural gas make ensuring security of supply for gas more complicated than for oil. Crude oil is an eminently fungible commodity, portable by ship, pipeline, road tanker, or even barrel. In contrast, gas requires expensive pipelines or LNG infrastructure. These delivery systems are relatively inflexible: pipelines cannot be moved or built overnight, and LNG, although somewhat portable, still requires an expensive receiving terminal.

Crude oil and, more important, refined oil products can be transported to any location that can receive a ship or road tanker. Moreover, gas is difficult to store in significant quantities. The energy content per unit of volume is much lower for gas than for oil. Gas is simply more difficult to handle than liquid. Its storage often depends on the suitability of geological structures, while oil tank farms can be built relatively easily and cheaply. All these factors mean that the solutions used to ensure security of oil supply (storage, diversification of supplies) do not apply as easily to gas. The gas supply system must be configured to give the required flexibility. Security of supply also involves reducing strategic risk, namely, the risk of a major disruption to supplies caused by, for example, political factors or major technical failure, such as the failure of a high-pressure pipeline. This is an extension of operational security, but of a different order of magnitude. Strategic risk is growing in parallel with the growing share of gas in meeting countries' primary energy requirements. It can be reduced through:

Interconnectivity—the degree of physical interconnection with other gas systems is an important factor in ensuring strategic security of supply. Interconnectivity is more than simply a guard against potential failure; it also encourages diversity of supply.

All sources of supply are unlikely to fail at the same time. Countries have often explicitly diversified supply by contracting with several countries. France, for example, buys gas from Algeria, the Netherlands, Norway, and Russia. In recent years there have been a number of spot LNG sales into Europe from LNG suppliers using spare capacity. Security of supply also entails guarding against long-term risk—ensuring that consuming countries can secure future and additional supplies as their existing supplies are depleted. This represents a challenge, as the bulk of the world's gas reserves are in areas that are far from current markets and also often have a high level of country risk. Some gas-importing countries, such as France, use long-term strategic storage to guard against significant disruption of supply. Such storage can be in depleted oil or gas fields, aquifers, salt caverns, or other geological structures.

Security of Coal Supply: Global Scene

Coal presents fewer challenges—other than environmental ones—to energy security than do oil and gas. It is abundant and more evenly distributed around the world than oil or gas. It is cheap, and costs are continuously being reduced by competition. Too many suppliers and the possibility of switching from one to another ensure supply security. The global ratio of coal reserves to production is 225 years; for OECD countries, it is even higher. Coal is still a local fuel, however. International trade in coal is limited, amounting to only 13 percent of production, a smaller share than for gas. The huge reserves of coal and their even distribution contribute to global energy security. Coal will continue to play a major part in ensuring the energy security of large energy consumers, particularly China (the largest coal consumer), the United States, and South Asia.

Over the next few decades the growth in demand for coal is expected to continue to be healthy, exceeding the growth in overall energy demand. Most of that growth will be for electricity generation, with coal consumption in the electricity sector expected to grow in all regions. But this is also the area where the main security challenge arises, because of the environmental effects of coal use—locally, regionally, and also possibly globally. Coal utilization is very inefficient, particularly in power generation, where its efficiency is less than 25 percent (Ecoal, 1998). The efficiency of oil and gas in electricity generation is at least 50 percent higher.

For coal to play its deserved role in global energy security, its many detrimental environmental impacts must be addressed. This will require not only clean coal technologies for new plants, but also rehabilitation and refurbishment of existing inefficient plants. And this must happen not only in industrialized countries, but also in developing countries, which are expected to account for most coal use and all this calls for technology transfer and huge investments.

Nuclear Energy and Energy Security

Nuclear energy could continue to add to the energy security of countries short of hydropower and indigenous fossil fuel resources, for several reasons. Uranium resources are widely distributed and abundant world-wide. Nuclear fuel is cheap: at the price of present long-term uranium supply contracts, the cost of natural uranium per kilowatt-hour is equivalent to an oil price of $0.35 per barrel, so several years' supply could be kept in reserve against possible future supply disruption at a low cost. And the cost of uranium contributes only about 2 percent to the cost of nuclear electricity generation, compared with 40–70 percent for fossil fuels in electricity generation, making the cost of nuclear electricity relatively insensitive to possible future increases in the uranium price. These considerations played a key part in the decisions of such economies as France, the Republic of Korea, Japan, and Taiwan (China) to launch major nuclear power programmes. In all likelihood, such considerations will also be important determinants in similar decisions by countries with a shortage of indigenous resources and a heavy reliance on imports. Moreover, the fact those nuclear power releases virtually no environmentally damaging emissions of carbon-dioxide, sulphur-di-oxide, and nitrogen oxide could make it an attractive option for many countries seeking technologies leading to reduced greenhouse gas emissions or abatement of local and regional pollution.

In the 1960s and 1970s, particularly after the first oil shock nuclear power promised to be a viable solution for industrializec countries looking for energy security and cheap power. Largely as a result of investment decisions made in that period, nuclear power has grown to the point where it dominates electricity generation in several industrialized countries, providing about a sixth of global electricity in 1998. But the outlook for nuclear power is not bright. Most of the promise of nuclear energy has evaporated as a result of loss of investor and public confidence in the technology. There is likely to be growth in nuclear power in some Asian countries in the period to 2020 and modest expansion at the global level until 2010. But most projections show nuclear power accounting for a smaller share of global electricity generation in 2020 than today, and many show its absolute contribution staying the same or even shrinking. The loss of investor and public confidence in nuclear technology is due to concerns about costs, nuclear safety, radioactive waste disposal, and proliferation or diversion. Until these concerns are adequately dealt with, nuclear energy is unlikely to play an expanding role in enhancing global energy security. The energy security benefits provided by nuclear power might even be diminished if there is another reactor accident involving substantial releases of radioactivity or a proliferation or diversion incident that could be plausibly linked in the public mind to nuclear power. Recognition that another major accident might not only diminish prospects for nuclear expansion but also trigger demands to shut down existing nuclear plants has catalyzed private sector-led efforts, under the auspices of the World Association of Nuclear Operators, to instill a culture of safety in the world's nuclear industry. This situation has also prompted an international effort, led by the International Atomic Energy Agency, to bolster national nuclear regulatory regimes. This effort is embodied in the Convention on Nuclear Safety, adopted by the organization's members. The Nuclear Non-Proliferation Treaty and associated international safeguards and nuclear supplier agreements have been implemented to minimize the nuclear weapons link to nuclear power (Murray, 1995). To date, all but a few states (apart from the five nuclear weapons states recognized in the 1968 Non-Proliferation Treaty, these are India, Israel, and Pakistan) have committed themselves to putting all nuclear material, including the material used for uranium enrichment and reprocessing, indefinitely under safeguard of the

International Atomic Energy Agency. Recent events and concerns about the limitations of existing policies have led various experts to call for further efforts to weaken the nuclear weapons link to nuclear power. But because the risk of proliferation and diversion is not at the forefront of public concerns about nuclear power (and may not be until there is an incident), because national policies in this area differ widely, and because there is much disagreement in the technical community about the best approaches for minimizing this risk, there has been less action in this area than there has been in improving reactor safety. Increasing the authority and resources of the International Atomic Energy Agency for monitoring enrichment plants and spent fuel is the principal way immediately available to reduce the proliferation risks associated with existing uranium enrichment and fuel reprocessing capabilities.

In summary, for the next couple of decades the prospects for enhancing energy security through expansion of nuclear power are not bright at the global level, although they are somewhat better in some Asian countries. In the longer term whether nuclear power can contribute to energy security depends not only on technical and economic considerations to be sorted out by the market, but also on the extent to which the public can be convinced that nuclear power is safe and that wastes can be disposed of safely. It also depends on whether the industry can avoid major accidents and proliferation and diversion incidents, and whether national and international policymakers and the technical community can reach consensus on what needs to be done to make nuclear energy technology widely acceptable.

Energy Intensity Aspects

One way to improve energy security in any country is by reducing its energy intensity—the amount of energy required to produce one unit of GDP. The rate of change in energy intensity reflects the overall improvement in energy efficiency as well as structural changes in the economy. Declining rates of energy intensity indicate that economic growth is less tightly linked to increases in energy use. Energy intensity has improved considerably in industrialized countries. In the United States over the past two centuries it has declined 1 percent a year on average.

One unit of GDP now requires only a fifth of the primary energy required 200 years ago (IIASA and WEC, 1998). In the past 15 years energy intensity in the United States has improved 20 percent.

Energy intensity differs depending on the level of economic development. OECD countries generally have an energy intensity that is a fraction of that in developing countries. In 1996 the commercial energy intensity of middle-income developing countries was three times that of high-income countries. This finding remains whether GDP is measured in market dollars or in purchasing power parity (PPP) terms. In most developing countries energy intensity is stagnant or even increasing because these countries are in the early take-off stages of industrialization, when energy-intensive industries and infrastructure are being established. Moreover, low-income developing countries usually show increasing commercial energy intensity because commercial energy sources are replacing non-commercial fuels. The prospects for lowering energy intensity are reduced in many developing countries by the proliferation of energy price subsidies and by the use of inefficient and outdated plants and equipment.

Generally, however, energy intensity in developing countries is similar to that in industrialized countries when they were at an earlier stage of development. Economic growth in developing countries has been relatively high in recent years, averaging 2.8 percent a year in the 1990s, compared with 2.1 percent for industrialized countries and 2.3 percent for the world. This trend is likely to continue. If this growth is matched by measures to conserve energy—such as phasing out subsidies and improving environmental awareness—energy security in developing countries is likely to continue to improve as well. Predicting the future of energy intensity is difficult, particularly for developing countries. In low-income countries energy intensity may increase in the next few years as these countries substitute commercial energy for traditional fuels. But for the world as a whole, energy intensity is likely to improve. Average improvements will range from 0.8 percent to 1.0 percent a year, depending on such factors as environmental awareness and energy prices (IIASA and WEC, 1998). If the world economy continues to grow at the expected average rate of 2.7 percent, energy demand growth will average

1.7–1.9 percent a year. That means that in 2020 global energy demand will be 45–51 percent higher than in 1998. This is a substantial increase. But without the expected efficiency improvements in global energy utilization, the demand could grow as much as 80 percent. The potential for efficiency improvements is high in many energy applications. Some of the most important progress in energy efficiency is that taking place in the conversion of energy to electricity. Modern combined cycle gas turbines burning natural gas have efficiencies approaching 60 percent, and efficiencies of 70 percent are within reach in the foreseeable future. Such efficiencies are more than double the average of 31 percent for the world stock of existing generating plants. As old plants are phased out and new, CCGT-type plants—or the traditional thermal generating plant firing coal at more than 40 percent efficiency—take over, considerable improvements in energy utilization will gradually occur. In addition, the increased use of electricity as an energy carrier world-wide will further improve energy efficiency. In some applications electricity is more efficient than other forms of energy, and its use is now growing 2.8–3.2 percent a year, a rate more than 50 percent higher than that for primary energy overall (Khatib,1997). All this will significantly lower energy intensity and thus improve prospects for global energy security.

The Environment and Energy Security Relationship

The idea of sustainable development is gaining acceptance on the official level as well as among the public. Sustainable development demands environmental preservation. Energy production and utilization, particularly in the case of fossil fuels, can be major sources of environmental degradation. These detrimental environmental impacts have a direct bearing on the future of energy—in terms of fuels and the extent of their use—and on energy security. The United Nations Framework Convention on Climate Change, adopted at the Rio Earth Summit in 1992, and the Kyoto Protocol, signed by more than 160 countries in 1997, call for major reductions of greenhouse gas emissions, which are caused mainly by energy use. Fulfilling the commitments as agreed and at the schedules approved would greatly affect the use of energy resources and could compromise global economic progress. There is a large gap between the commitments and the means for implementation. Targets agreed upon by negotiators were not necessarily implemented by legislators or other policymakers. Implementation of such targets is hindered not only by cost but also by the need to maintain energy security. All indications are that fossil fuels will continue to dominate global energy resources for at least the first decades of the 21st century. Moreover, the demand for energy services will continue to increase. Most of the growth will be in developing countries, which can ill afford the high cost of containment measures. It is therefore essential to find means to contain energy-related emissions without compromising energy security. The environmental effects of energy use occur at the local, regional, and global levels. Local effects consist primarily of heavy hydrocarbons and particulate matter (including sulphur flakes) that are deposited within hours and can travel up to 100 kilometres from the source. Regional effects include emissions and effluents, the most important of which are sulphur and nitrogen oxides, which are converted into acids; these acids, which last for a few days in the atmosphere, may travel up to a few thousand kilometres before being deposited, often after crossing boundaries. Global environmental impacts are exemplified by emissions of carbon dioxide and other gases (mainly methane) that have long residence times in the atmosphere. Local and regional impacts can be addressed by technologies. However, some of these technologies are expensive for developing countries, where growth in the use of low-quality coal will be particularly high. There are no easy answers in dealing with greenhouse gas emissions. Mitigation and sequestration measures are still to be developed. The most practical solution is to reduce the growth in fossil fuel use by increasing efficiency in energy utilization. Enhancing efficiency in energy use not only helps greatly to mitigate emissions; it also improves energy security. But for greater benefits for energy security, energy use should also be made more compatible with the aims of sustainable development through better containment of emissions. Such simple measures as washing coal will rid it of 20–50 percent of its sulphur. Advanced burners and scrubbers remove pollutants and effluent gases from smoke stacks and chimneys. Fuel substitution is another effective measure. A modern CCGT power station, firing gas, will emit only 40 percent as much carbon dioxide as a traditional coal-fired thermal power station. The slow but persistent growth in the use of electricity as an energy carrier will also contribute towards energy security. Besides offering greater efficiency than other forms of energy in many applications, electricity concentrates emissions in a single remote location—the site of the power station—making them easier and cheaper to deal with.

Emerging Global Markets and Energy Security

Approaches to ensuring energy supply security in the 21st century should differ from past approaches that concentrated on oil substitution. Besides sustainable growth challenges, new approaches need to tackle the new energy security issues raised by market liberalization. The enhanced role of markets is tied closely to the process of globalization. Globalization, which is still gaining momentum, has encouraged competition and strengthened markets and regional and international trade, particularly for crude oil and oil products, natural gas, and energy services. Globalization is bringing new opportunities for energy security, such as better access to markets and services and the transfer of technologies that are helping to reduce the cost of energy exploration and expand proven reserves. International trade in energy resources and services is vital for energy security. The creation of the World Trade Organization in 1995, built on the GATT, is the latest multilateral step towards creating an environment conducive to the exchange of goods and services. It will assist in trade liberalization and allow countries greater recourse to trade dispute settlement mechanisms. Foreign trade has grown more quickly than the world economy in recent years, a trend that is likely to continue. For developing countries, trade is growing faster than national income, reaching 50 percent of GDP, and a good share of that trade is in energy. The flow of information has become much easier and more transparent, increasing the resources and services available for trade and reducing prices. All this aids greatly in enhancing energy security. The introduction of a single market in Europe will lead to more competition in energy services and supply of cheaper electricity.

Improvements in transport networks and technology are reducing the cost of energy trade. The liberalization of European gas and electricity markets will initiate major structural changes in European energy enterprises, increasing competition, improving economic performance, and contributing towards fuel diversification and greater energy security (EC, 1999).

In studying the influence of markets, there is a need to distinguish between OECD countries, where free markets prevail, and developing countries, where market liberalization is still at a very early stage. Security of supply is a public policy objective. But in free markets decisions are made by market players rather than by governments. Markets allow even small and medium-size consumers—as well as suppliers—a say in energy decisions. That requires redefining the political dimension of energy security.

Markets clearly produce benefits for consumers: trade, innovation, cost reduction, technological advances, and better allocation of resources. Moreover, unbundling the supply chain enhances transparency and allows tariffs to reflect real costs. Markets have also taught us a few lessons: they have proven that they can adjust more easily than governments to changing circumstances in the energy market and that it is costly to intervene against the market for an extended period.

Market liberalization is leaving much of the decision-making to consumers. Are the consumers capable of making the right choices? Or would they choose cheaper options (such as interruptible supply) even if that compromises their energy supply security? This possibility suggests a need for a government role. Moreover, liberalization will not necessarily cover the entire supply chain. Certain monopolies will remain in transmission and distribution. Governments therefore have a duty to protect consumers at the very end of the supply chain (retail consumers). In addition, the energy market may ignore the interests of other consumer classes, such as remote and isolated consumers. All this necessitates that government continue to be involved in the energy market to a certain extent in almost every country.

The argument applies particularly to the supply side. Energy development entails long-term, capital-intensive investments. Private investors may demand a higher rate of return in a liberalized market than in a government-controlled energy industry. In addition, markets usually look for short-term profits and may therefore forgo diversification of supplies, which is associated with high up-front investment and risk but long-term benefits. How will markets respond to the long-term requirements of sustainable development, which demands heavy investments in research and development? How can they meet societies' long-term interest in secure supplies at reasonable prices when their interest is mainly in the short-term? How can markets respond to an emergency disruption of supply in exporting countries? The division between the production and supply functions does not allow full integration of the security function. Will the energy markets be able to internalize all the costs of security, including political risk?

Having said all that, there are several reasons to believe that regulatory reforms in the energy market that are aimed at enhancing competition would promote energy security. First, as discussed, reforms can lead to increased investment and trade in energy resources, which will, in turn, facilitate expansion of energy production, increase inter-fuel competition, and encourage the construction of trans-boundary energy delivery infrastructure, such as oil and gas pipelines. Second, also as discussed, the participation in downstream operations by firms from oil-exporting economies, and the participation in upstream operations by firms from oil-importing economies (all of which is facilitated by market liberalization), will be mutually beneficial and thus increase both exporters' and importers' interest in energy security. In Asia deregulation and other energy sector liberalization will also promote accelerated growth in energy supplies and a greater sense of energy security. Third, regulatory reforms will enhance efficiency and effectiveness, even in the area of energy supply emergency response. The IEA's oil supply emergency systems place growing emphasis on drawdown of oil stocks compared with such measures as demand restraint. The release of oil stocks into the market is more market-oriented than government intervention to restrain demand. Thus energy sector regulatory reforms could be compatible with or even enhance energy supply security. Governments, while withdrawing from energy investments themselves, need to create a positive climate for trade and investment. With increasing market liberalization, there is a growing need for governments to monitor private sector actors and deal with market failures. Certain investors might be looking for concentration through mergers and joint ventures, for example, which might conflict with government policy of promoting liberalization and fostering competition. In considering the role of markets, the following questions are increasingly asked: Can the important issue of energy security be left entirely to markets? What is the role of the state in ensuring energy security in a liberalized market environment?

European Views on Energy Security

Most European countries are heavily reliant upon imported energy. Today, EU countries as a whole import 50% of their energy needs, a figure expected to rise to 70% by 2030. Russia is a key supplier of oil and natural gas. Germany imports 32% of its energy from Russia. Poland imports two-thirds of its natural gas needs from Russia, and 97% of its oil. As a whole, EU countries import 25% of their energy needs from Russia (EC, 1999).

In one estimate, by 2030 EU countries will import 40% of their gas needs from Russia, and 45% of their oil from the Middle East.4 In addition, oil in particular is found largely in unstable areas of the world such as the Middle East, a factor in U.S. and European concerns over energy security.

European governments view energy security primarily in an economic and political context. The EU floated a proposal meant to build interdependence between EU members and Russia to secure reliable energy supplies from Russia. The EU has discussed with Russia a structured arrangement in which Russia would sell energy not only to its principal customers in central and Eastern Europe, but to more distant customers in Western Europe. In return, the EU is asking Moscow to allow European companies to develop Russian energy reserves. But Russia has rejected key elements of this proposal. Moscow for the most part has not allowed foreign ownership of its pipelines, and has squeezed out some foreign companies that have been developing its energy reserves. At the same time, it has secured access to some European markets, for example, through agreements to sell gas to Hungary and France. Russia has taken steps to build its leverage in European energy markets. In May 2007, Russia, Turkmenistan, and Kazakhstan agreed to build a new gas pipeline around the Caspian Sea. The new pipeline would send Central Asian natural gas to the Russian energy grid; Russia has repriced such gas, from another pipeline, twofold before selling it to European customers. The United States and some European governments have sought instead a trans-Caspian Sea pipeline that would bypass the Russian grid, and provide natural gas more cheaply to Europe, thereby diminishing as well greater potential Russian leverage tied to the supply of energy.7 Russia has also discussed the linking its natural gas supply grid to that of Algeria, which also supplies gas to Europe. EU energy CRS-3 commissioner Andris Piebalgs has charged that the two governments may be planning to develop an energy cartel that would further weaken competitive pricing. To prevent impediments to competition and to improve energy security, the EU Commission is urging new infrastructure, including terminals for receiving liquefied natural gas; the construction of new pipelines from the Caspian region and North Africa; and single European energy grids for both continental electricity and natural gas markets that would challenge the grip of national energy firms on their national markets.9 The Commission has also recommended that companies that produce raw energy not be allowed to own distribution networks, a step intended to encourage competition. Some EU governments, such as France, have large public entities that own both the sources of energy and the distribution network, and oppose this proposal. Should the EU eventually adopt the Commission's proposal, Russian efforts to buy parts of the European energy grid might be set back. Few observers believe that Moscow's pricing agreement for its gas exports to Ukraine indicates that the market process is working successfully. Some EU officials say that the agreement lacks transparency, and may mask involvement by criminal enterprises.

They contend that Russia needs European (and other) firms' good will and continued investment in its decaying energy infrastructure to maintain existing production and develop its oil and gas reserves to sell energy products abroad. Some European and U.S. officials believe that Germany may become too reliant on Russian energy supplies and move away from its EU partners and the United States. East European states in particular, once in

Moscow's sphere, believe that they could find themselves unable to ensure reliable and affordable energy supplies from Gazprom, the powerful state-controlled Russian energy company. They point to the former Schroeder government's deal with Gazprom to involve German companies in the development of a Russian-German gas pipeline under the Baltic Sea as a special arrangement that appears to promise a supply to Germany that other states might not enjoy. Some governments believe that Russia has little interest in market forces in the energy sector. In this view, Russia seeks high energy prices to maximize profits. These governments note that the Russian government has a prevailing control over Gazprom, hardly a model of capitalist entrepreneurship, and that Gazprom was behaving like a monopoly in ratcheting up the price of natural gas to Ukraine. Knowing that Ukraine had no reliable alternatives for gas supply, Gazprom raised prices threefold and threatened a sixfold rise. Gazprom also controls the transit of non-Russian energy supplies to Ukraine, and threatened rapid rises in transit fees as well. Russia has temporarily followed similar policies towards Georgia, Lithuania, and Belarus. Political motives seem apparent in such CRS-4.

NATO and Energy Security

Some U.S. officials believe that NATO could play a role in building international political solidarity in the event of a deliberate disruption of energy flows. In this view, NATO might coordinate policies among member states and with non-member partner governments to share resources and to bring an end to an energy disruption. NATO might also provide security for infrastructure in energy-producing states facing unrest. Iran has threatened to use its energy reserves to attain political objectives. In response to possible sanctions due to its refusal to comply with requirements by the International Atomic Energy Agency on its nuclear program, Iran has threatened to cut off or limit its energy supplies to buyers. Beyond deliberate policies affecting energy security, there are many countries in Central Asia and the Middle East that are unstable, have a need for new energy infrastructure investment, and have insecure transportation systems due to political unrest. Some of these countries are in NATO's Partnership for Peace program, or desire a closer association with NATO (Gallis Paul, 2006).

NATO member states increasingly believe that the alliance must be a global player with global partners. This trend is evident in Afghanistan, for example, where Australia, New Zealand, and Japan are expending resources to bring stability through NATO's International Security Assistance Force, even though the three countries are not NATO members. NATO's role in energy security could be complementary to the EU's effort to strengthen market forces and interdependence in the international energy sector. U.S. officials agree with their EU counterparts that market forces can lead to greater energy security. Diversification of supply, for example, through building more pipelines that are secure, is one course of action. Joint investment efforts to build such pipelines in and with energy producers such as Kazakhstan and Azerbaijan could be an important step in this direction. Both countries are members of NATO's Partnership for Peace program, and are seeking closer relations with the United States and its allies. Development of more Liquefied Natural Gas (LNG) transport and reception facilities from distant suppliers, such as Nigeria, into Europe could be another course of action. Coupled with the development of new oil and gas pipelines could be an offer from NATO (and/or EU) members to provide security for energy infrastructure in periods of unrest or conflict in supplier and transit countries.

NATO is attempting to become a global security organization, still concentrating on protection of the interests of the United States and its Canadian and European partners, but engaging non-member states as global partners. NATO's role in energy security remains uncertain, however, as some individual members may prefer a greater role for the EU. A political role in energy security for NATO seems most likely in the near future. Under NATO's Istanbul Cooperation Initiative of 2004, the allies have begun discussions with Bahrain, Qatar, Kuwait, and the United Arab Emirates to build practical cooperation in the security field, including the fight against terrorism. Some Middle Eastern CRS-6 governments are concerned about terrorist attacks on their oil facilities, but it is not publicly known whether NATO has discussed this issue with the four governments. Partnership for Peace countries, such as Kazakhstan and Azerbaijan, that are important energy producers often seek ways to associate themselves more closely with NATO, in part to diminish Russian influence on their soil, in part to develop reliable partners in an unstable region. It is possible that NATO will seek ways to provide security for the energy infrastructure of such countries. At the same time, the EU may encourage its member states to invest more heavily in that infrastructure. There is division in the EU over management of the Union's growing dependence on Russian oil and gas. Several states, led by Poland, wish to engage NATO more fully in ensuring energy security in this relationship. While in the early stages of discussion, Poland is exploring a role for NATO and the United States, perhaps only diplomatically, in which U.S. leverage on Moscow could be an element for encouraging responsible Russian behavior and deflecting any Russian attempt to divide the Europeans. A NATO role in energy security could prove to be premature. Most EU governments clearly prefer that market forces secure access to energy. A well-structured commercial partnership with Russia might be one mark of such a policy. Another would be the effort of the EU3 (Germany, France, and Britain) and the United States to curtail Iran's nuclear program. The EU3 desire completion of that effort in the UN before there is any discussion of a military organization like NATO assuming responsibility for a broader policy of energy security. Some EU governments also believe that discussion of energy security at NATO sends the wrong signal to other governments, which might assume that the allies are contemplating military action to ensure the flow of oil and gas. Some of these governments propose instead that there first be a high-level "seminar" that includes the United States, representatives of key EU countries, Russia, and such countries as Uzbekistan, Kazakhstan, and Azerbaijan. There, some participants would reiterate the importance of market forces and the interdependence of producers and suppliers, and the need to protect and maintain energy infrastructure.

In addition, some NATO partner governments in Central Asia and the Middle East might be reluctant to accept allied assistance in securing the resource that is central to their survival. The belief is widespread in the Middle East that the United States invaded Iraq in part to secure access to its oil. There might be popular opposition to any NATO effort to secure energy infrastructure in some of these countries. Moreover, the United States has been unable to provide full security to pipelines in Iraq, and NATO might have similar difficulties in partnership countries. Russia is also a factor. Turkmenistan and Kazakhstan depend upon Russia as a transit country for their pipeline shipments to the west, and could be subject to Moscow's pressure to spurn NATO proposals of assistance.

The World Energy Council (WEC) Safeguarding Energy Security

The World Energy Council (WEC, 2007) is the foremost multi-energy organization in the world today. WEC has Member Committees in over 90 countries, including most of the largest energy-producing and energy consuming countries. Established in 1923; the organization covers all types of energy, including coal, oil, natural gas, nuclear, hydro, and renewables, and is UN-accredited, nongovernmental, non-commercial and non-aligned. WEC is a UK-registered charity headquartered in London. WEC's Mission is "to promote the sustainable supply and use of energy for the greatest benefit of all people." WEC's objectives as they exist today are to promote the sustainable supply and use of energy for the greatest benefit of all people, by:

a. Collating data about and undertaking and promoting research into the means of supplying and using energy having, short and long-term, the greatest social benefit and the least harmful impact on the natural environment, and publishing or otherwise disseminating the useful results of such research;

b. Undertaking actions, including but not limited to the holding of congresses, workshops and seminars, to facilitate such supply and use of energy; this includes the Triennial World Energy congress, a major energy industry event with 5,000+ delegates, comprehensive technical programmes, meetings, networking sessions and a major energy exhibition. The next Congress is taking place in November this year in Rome;

c. Collaborating with other organizations in the energy sector with compatible goals. WEC's projects look at how current energy challenges can be tackled today, tomorrow and in the future. **Global Studies**: In depth studies highlighting the longer-term global implications of energy issues.

- Scenarios 2050: Policies to achieve sustainable energy supply and use;
- Energy & Climate Change: How effective climate change policies can shape sustainable energy development;
- Survey of Energy Resources—21st Edition: Comprehensive collection of global energy statistics.

Strengthening Global Alliances—Oil imports and Global Reserves

The U.S. influence on overall world markets is substantial in terms of production and consumption. The United States is the world's second largest natural gas producer and its third largest oil producer. The United States consumes over 25 percent of the oil produced worldwide, slightly more than half of which it imports. Nevertheless, because the price of our domestic and imported oil is determined by a world market, our energy security interests transcend the source of our physical energy supplies.

Larger Question of Improving Market Transparency: The United States must work with oil producers to improve the transparency, timeliness, and accuracy of the data that guide global oil markets. A lack of timely and accurate data relating to both oil production and inventory levels has contributed to the price volatility witnessed in 2000. Discussions among the major oil producers and consumer countries should be designed to improve the transparency, accuracy, and timeliness of data that guide the market. In turn, enhanced data quality and increased data transparency will improve market efficiency. Refocusing that dialogue beyond short-term market developments to long-term issues of world economic growth, improving data quality, and addressing energy infrastructure is needed to maintain a smooth flow of energy from the wellhead to the consumer.

The Role of Fossil Fuels in the Future Energy Mix

Likely fossil fuels will be the main energy driver at least for the next three decades to fulfill energy demand growth and support economic growth particularly in emerging economies. Strategy, required long-term policy, and appropriate policy instruments including its associated mechanisms to support the national program on decarburization need further to be established, otherwise within the next three decades fossil fuels will remain the dominant source of energy.

The goals of national energy security and environmental protection need to be reconciled, which requires strong and coordinated government action and public support. It needs firm action to steer the national energy system onto sustainable energy path while supporting national economic growth, with aims to enhance national energy security and mitigating CO_2 emissions. To render low carbon emissions in energy path more firm efforts mainly on deployments and diffusions of environmentally sound technologies are really required (including development & transfer of technologies) in order to drive the energy system toward low carbon energy sources, low-carbon & carbon-free energy technologies, greater efficiency in energy production & distribution and in energy use.

Salient Items on Development and Transfer of Environmentally Sound Technologies (EST)

At least there are three salient items on development and transfer of Environmentally Sound Technologies (EST) that need to be pondered as a reference for our policy makers with a view towards covering important aspects such as: (i) strategy, mechanisms and required long-term policy for successful development and transfer of EST, (ii) proposed policy instruments to support the national program on decarbonization, iii) innovative financing mechanisms for development & transfer of technology.

So far, there have been 2 proposed mechanisms that had been raised under development & transfer of technology issues: under the convention and market-based. It seems difficult to reconcile these 2 mechanisms since each comes from fundamentally different approaches and perspectives. It can be noted further that there is a concern particularly from developing countries that implementation of development and transfer of technologies has not been realized as expected. The process has been slow even though in the beginning there has been option available pass through CDM project activities which has been expected as a viable mechanism. Financing and appropriate technology transfer mechanisms to support the development and transfer of technology are the main issues.

Thrust Areas of EST Applications

The need to curb the growth in fossil-energy demand, to improve national energy mix by geographic and fuel supply diversity and to reduce emissions in mitigating climate change is more urgent than before this linkages to energy security versus climate change.

The energy trajectory for reaching the national energy mix target needs to be strongly managed. Indonesia must maintain its economic growth rate of at least 7% a year to eradicate poverty and meets its economic and human development goals, accordingly sustainable growth of primary energy requirements must be maintained to deliver such economic growth.

The goals of national energy security and environmental protection need to be reconciled, which requires strong and coordinated government action and public support. It needs firm action to steer the national energy system onto sustainable energy path while supporting national economic growth, with aims to enhance national energy security and mitigating CO_2 emissions.

Drive the energy system toward low carbon energy sources, low-carbon and carbon-free energy technologies, greater efficiency in energy production and distribution and in energy use and proposed long-term policy and its policy instruments to support national energy policy and national program on decarbonization.

At least 2 important issues that need to be addressed for development and transfer of environmentally sound technologies to developing countries: (i) the need for long-term technology policy which includes associated strategic policy instruments and appropriate technology transfer mechanism to support the development and transfer of technology, and (ii) the need for innovative financing mechanisms.

Some Selected Policies such as: Power sector: enhancing the role of renewable energy, the role of nuclear power, carbon capture & storage; shifting towards new/other low-carbon & carbon-free energy technologies, improving energy efficiency (upstream to downstream activities); Industry and Manufacturing sector; Building sector; Transport (Mobility) sector; Customer Choices; Overcoming Hurdles to Government Action, etc., which need to be enhanced and established.

Emerging Energy Security Issues

The traditional energy security elements—supply sources, demand centers, geopolitics and market structures—have been joined by additional considerations. These include the interconnectedness of world economies and energy infrastructure systems, climate change concerns, technological innovation and increased pressure from a broader array of stakeholders. Oil has been a global commodity for many decades, delivered across borders via pipeline, by rail and by tanker trucks and ships. As mentioned above, natural gas is also increasingly becoming a global commodity. International pipelines already transport natural gas from North Africa to Europe, from Russia to Europe, from Canada to the United States, from Bolivia to Brazil and eventually from Russia to Asian markets, while natural gas movements by LNG tankers also continue to grow. These emerging transport links offer opportunities for cooperation during energy emergencies, but also provide additional risks to economies that are so interdependent.

Supply Disruptions

During the North American supply disruptions caused by Hurricanes Katrina and Rita, the interconnectedness of the energy infrastructure became crystal clear. Oil product and natural gas pipelines were not able to move product because the electric power that operated compressor stations was shut down. Refineries that depended on power from the grid were not able to resume operations until the electric power lines were reconnected. In some instances, neither telephone land lines nor cell phones were operable because the electronic connections were out of service. The energy industry is integrated and tied to physical and communication infrastructures in ways that influence how energy security concerns, including the risk of terrorism, need to be reassessed. Geopolitical alliances continue to shift along with supply sources and demand centres. The Russian oil and gas sector is increasingly linked to both Europe in the west and potentially to Asia in the east. The traditional East-West and North-South structures have become far more complex with the development of multiple international trading agreements and the rise of the World Trade Organization. The opening up of Russia, the Caspian Sea region and Eastern Europe is leading to new economic and political connections that need to be integrated into any conversations about energy security.

Climate Change

Climate change concerns also affect the perceptions of energy security. The objective of diversification of oil supplies has been replaced by the desire for diversification of *all* energy sources to meet energy security and environmental and reliability concerns. Although natural gas is referred to as "the fuel of choice," in fact, the emphasis should be on "choice." Many more fuel options are available today, compared to the 1970s. Wind power is competitive in some markets and subsidized in others. Photovoltaic cells have experienced an annual average growth rate of 43% over the past five years, resulting in total shipments of 1,195 megawatts in 2004. And nuclear power appears to be experiencing a renaissance.

Globally, four gigawatts (GW) of new nuclear plants have come online since January 1, 2005, and an additional 19 GW, representing 24 new nuclear power plants, are currently under construction. A number of US power companies and partners have taken initial steps to develop new nuclear reactors. These would be the first nuclear plant orders in the US for more than 25 years.

Bio-fuels Gaining Momentum

The transportation sector, the primary market for oil, is expanding its choices of fuels as well. The growth in hybrid vehicle sales and the push by several major automobile manufacturers to shift to hydrogen, indicate that the transport sector may well join the power sector with a broader selection of fuel options.

In many large cities in Asia, Europe and North America, public transport systems are fuelling buses with compressed natural gas and bio-fuels are gaining in popularity as well. Government incentives and regulations promoting ethanol and biodiesel are being stepped up around the world, as is research into biology and energy. A renewed interest in energy efficiency supports both energy security and climate change objectives. The tightness of energy markets can be relieved by reducing demand—through conservation and energy efficiency, or through the undesirable method of lower economic growth rates—or by increasing supplies. A combination of greater efficiency and additional supplies is required. However, the political will to focus on conservation has been lacking. Price signals may assist with energy efficiency. However, successful efforts will be short-lived unless consumers either believe that higher price levels will be sustained or there is a stronger market/political/knowledge matrix to support conservation. The strong interest in carbon capture and storage (CCS) technology can also be linked to both energy security and climate change. Although the oil industry has led the way in CCS technology, it is of growing interest to the power sector. Building new coal-fired power plants that are based on integrated gas combined-cycle technology allows the operators to separate, capture and store streams of carbon dioxide. Because coal is both the most carbon-intensive and the most abundant fossil fuel, carbon capture and storage offers an attractive opportunity to keep coal in the fuel mix for energy security without releasing greenhouse gas emissions into the atmosphere.

Energy and Environment

The usage of energy resources in industry leads to environmental damages by polluting the atmosphere. Few of examples of air pollution are sulphur-dioxide (SO_2), nitrous oxide (NO_X) and carbon monoxide (CO) emissions from boilers and furnaces, chloro-fluro carbons (CFC) emissions from refrigerants use, etc. In chemical and fertilizers industries, toxic gases are released. Cement plants and power plants spew out particulate matter.

Air Pollution

A variety of air pollutants have known or suspected harmful effects on human health and the environment. These air pollutants are basically the products of combustion from fossil fuel use. Air pollutants from these sources may not only create problems near to these sources but also can cause problems far away. Air pollutants can travel long distances, chemically react in the atmosphere to produce secondary pollutants such as acid rain or ozone.

Evolutionary Trends in Pollution Problems

In both developed and rapidly industrializing countries, the major historic air pollution problem has typically been high levels of smoke and SO_2 arising from the combustion of sulphur-containing fossil fuels such as coal for domestic and industrial purposes.

Smogs resulting from the combined effects of black smoke, sulphate/acid aerosol and fog have been seen in European cities until few decades ago and still occur in many cities in developing world. In developed countries, this problem has significantly reduced over recent decades as a result of changing fuel-use patterns; the increasing use of cleaner fuels such as natural gas, and the implementation of effective smoke and emission control policies.

In both developed and developing countries, the major threat to clean air is now posed by traffic emissions. Petrol- and diesel-engine motor vehicles emit a wide variety of pollutants, principally carbon monoxide (CO), oxides of nitrogen (NO_x), volatile organic compounds (VOCs) and particulates, which have an increasing impact on urban air quality.

In addition, photochemical reactions resulting from the action of sunlight on NO_2 and VOCs from vehicles lead to the formation of ozone, a secondary long-range pollutant, which impacts in rural

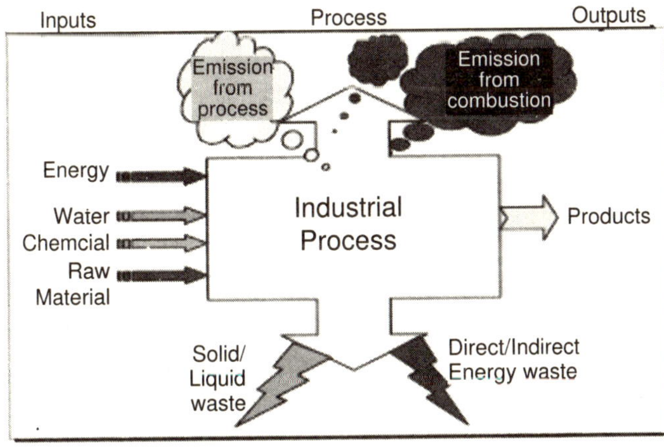

Fig. 8.1: Inputs and outputs of process

areas often far from the original emission site. Acid rain is another long-range pollutant influenced by vehicle NOx emissions.

Industrial and domestic pollutant sources, together with their impact on air quality, tend to be steady-state or improving over time. However, traffic pollution problems are worsening world-wide. The problem may be particularly severe in developing countries with dramatically increasing vehicle population, infrastructural limitations, poor engine/emission control technologies and limited provision for maintenance or vehicle regulation.

The principle pollutants produced by industrial, domestic and traffic sources are sulphur dioxide, nitrogen oxides, particulate matter, carbon monoxide, ozone, hydrocarbons, benzene, 1,3-butadiene, toxic organic micro pollutants, lead and heavy metals.

Brief introduction to the principal pollutants are as follows:

Sulphur dioxide is a corrosive acid gas, which combines with water vapour in the atmosphere to produce acid rain. Both wet and dry depositions have been implicated in the damage and destruction of vegetation and in the degradation of soils, building materials and watercourses. SO_2 in ambient air is also associated with asthma and chronic bronchitis. The principal source of this gas is power stations and industries burning fossil fuels, which contain sulphur.

Nitrogen oxides are formed during high temperature combustion processes from the oxidation of nitrogen in the air or fuel. The principal source of nitrogen oxides-nitric oxide (NO) and nitrogen dioxide (NO_2), collectively known as NO_x—is road traffic. NO and NO_2 concentrations are greatest in urban areas where traffic is heaviest. Other important sources are power stations and industrial processes.

Nitrogen oxides are released into the atmosphere mainly in the form of NO, which is then readily oxidized to NO_2 by reaction with ozone. Elevated levels of NO_x occur in urban environments under stable meteorological conditions, when the air mass is unable to disperse.

Nitrogen dioxide has a variety of environmental and health impacts. It irritates the respiratory system and may worsen asthma and increase susceptibility to infections. In the presence of sunlight, it reacts with hydrocarbons to produce photochemical pollutants such as ozone. Nitrogen oxides combine with water vapour to form nitric acid. This nitric acid is in turn removed from the atmosphere by direct deposition to the ground, or transfer to aqueous droplets (e.g. cloud or rainwater), thereby contributing to acid deposition.

Acidification from SO_2 and NOx

Acidification of water bodies and soils, and the consequent impact on agriculture, forestry and fisheries are the result of the re-deposition of acidifying compounds resulting principally from the oxidation of primary SO_2 and NO_2 emissions from fossil fuel combustion. Deposition may be by either wet or dry processes, and acid deposition studies often need to examine both of these acidification routes.

Airborne particulate matter varies widely in its physical and chemical composition, source and particle size. PM_{10} particles (the fraction of particulates in air of very small size (<10 ìm)) are of major current concern, as they are small enough to penetrate deep into the lungs and so potentially pose significant health risks. In addition, they may carry surface-absorbed carcinogenic compounds into the lungs. Larger particles, meanwhile, are not readily inhaled, and are removed relatively efficiently from the air by settling.

A major source of fine primary particles are combustion processes, in particular diesel combustion, where transport of hot exhaust vapour into a cooler exhaust pipe can lead to spontaneous nucleation of "carbon" particles before emission. Secondary particles are typically formed when low volatility products are generated in the atmosphere, for example the oxidation of sulphur-di-oxide to sulphuric acid. The atmospheric lifetime of particulate matter is strongly related to particle size, but may be as long as 10 days for particles of about 1mm in diameter.

Concern about the potential health impacts of PM_{10} has increased very rapidly over recent years. Increasingly, attention has been turning towards monitoring of the smaller particle fraction $PM_{2.5}$ capable of penetrating deepest into the lungs, or to even smaller size fractions or total particle numbers.

Carbon monoxide (CO) is a toxic gas, which is emitted into the atmosphere as a result of combustion processes, and from oxidation of hydrocarbons and other organic compounds. In urban areas, CO is produced almost entirely (90%) from road traffic emissions. CO at levels found in ambient air may reduce the oxygen-carrying capacity of the blood. It survives in the atmosphere for a period of approximately 1 month and finally gets oxidized to carbon dioxide (CO_2).

Ground-level Ozone (O_3), unlike other primary pollutants mentioned above, is not emitted directly into the atmosphere, but is a secondary pollutant produced by reaction between nitrogen dioxide (NO_2), hydrocarbons and sunlight. Ozone can irritate the eyes and air passages causing breathing difficulties and may increase susceptibility to infection. It is a highly reactive chemical, capable of attacking surfaces, fabrics and rubber materials. Ozone is also toxic to some crops, vegetation and trees.

Whereas nitrogen dioxide (NO_2) participates in the formation of ozone, nitrogen oxide (NO) destroys ozone to form oxygen (O_2) and nitrogen dioxide (NO_2). For this reason, ozone levels are not as high in urban areas (where high levels of NO are emitted from vehicles) as in rural areas. As the nitrogen oxides and hydrocarbons are transported out of urban areas, the ozone-destroying NO is oxidized to NO_2, which participates in ozone formation.

Hydrocarbons

There are two main groups of hydrocarbons of concern: volatile organic compounds (VOCs) and polycyclic aromatic hydrocarbons (PAHs). VOCs are released in vehicle exhaust gases either as unburned fuels or as combustion products, and are also emitted by the evaporation of solvents and motor fuels. Benzene and 1, 3-butadiene are of particular concern, as they are known carcinogens. Other VOCs are important because of the role they play in the photochemical formation of ozone in the atmosphere.

Benzene is an aromatic VOC, which is a minor constituent of petrol (about 2% by volume). The main sources of benzene in the atmosphere are the distribution and combustion of petrol. Of these, combustion by petrol vehicles is the single biggest source (70% of total emissions) whilst the refining, distribution and evaporation of petrol from vehicles accounts for approximately a further 10% of total emissions. Benzene is emitted in vehicle exhaust not only as unburnt fuel but also as a product of the decomposition of other aromatic compounds. Benzene is a known human carcinogen.

1, 3-butadiene, like benzene, is a VOC emitted into the atmosphere principally from fuel combustion of petrol and diesel vehicles. Unlike benzene, however, it is not a constituent of the fuel but is produced by the combustion of olefins. 1,3-butadiene is also an important chemical in certain industrial processes, particularly the manufacture of synthetic rubber. It is handled in bulk at a small number of industrial locations. Other than in the vicinity of such locations, the dominant source of 1, 3-butadiene in the atmosphere are the motor vehicles. 1, 3 Butadiene is also a known, potent, human carcinogen.

TOMPs (Toxic Organic Micro pollutants) are produced by the incomplete combustion of fuels. They comprise a complex range of chemicals some of which, although they are emitted in very small quantities, are highly toxic or and carcinogenic. Compounds in this category include:

- PAHs (PolyAromatic Hydrocarbons)
- PCBs (Polychlorinated Biphenyls)
- Dioxins
- Furans

Heavy Metals and Lead

Particulate metals in air result from activities such as fossil fuel combustion (including vehicles), metal processing industries and waste incineration. There are currently no emission standards for metals other than lead. Lead is a cumulative poison to the central nervous system, particularly detrimental to the mental development of children.

Lead is the most widely used non-ferrous metal and has a large number of industrial applications. Its single largest industrial use worldwide is in the manufacture of batteries and it is also used in paints, glazes, alloys, radiation shielding, tank lining and piping.

As tetraethyl lead, it has been used for many years as an additive in petrol; with the increasing use of unleaded petrol, however, emissions and concentrations in air have reduced steadily in recent years.

Climatic Change

Human activities, particularly the combustion of fossil fuels, have made the blanket of greenhouse gases (water vapour, carbon dioxide, methane, ozone etc.) around the earth thicker. The resulting increase in global temperature is altering the complex web of systems that allow life to thrive on earth such as rainfall, wind patterns, ocean currents and distribution of plant and animal species.

Greenhouse Effect and the Carbon Cycle

Life on earth is made possible by energy from the sun, which arrives mainly in the form of visible light. About 30 percent of the sunlight is scattered back into space by outer atmosphere and the balance 70 percent reaches the earth's surface, which reflects it in form of infrared radiation. The escape of slow moving infrared radiation is delayed by the green house gases. A thicker blanket of greenhouse gases traps more infrared radiation and increase the earth's temperature (Fig. 5)

Greenhouse gases makeup only 1 percent of the atmosphere, but they act as a blanket around the earth, or like a glass roof of a greenhouse and keep the earth 30 degrees warmer than it would be otherwise—without greenhouse gases, earth would be too cold to live. Human activities that are responsible for making the greenhouse layer thicker are emissions of carbon dioxide from the combustion of coal, oil and natural gas; by additional methane and nitrous oxide from farming activities and changes in land use; and by several man made gases that have a long life in the atmosphere. The increase in greenhouse gases is happening at an alarming rate. If greenhouse gases emissions continue to grow at current rates, it is almost certain that the atmospheric levels of carbon dioxide will increase twice or thrice from pre-industrial levels during the 21st century. Even a small increase in earth's temperature will be accompanied by changes in climate—such as cloud cover, precipitation, wind patterns and duration of seasons. In an already highly crowded and stressed earth, millions of people depend on weather patterns, such as monsoon rains, to continue as they have in the past. Even minimum changes will be disruptive and difficult.

Carbon dioxide is responsible for 60 percent of the "enhanced greenhouse effect". Humans are burning coal, oil and natural gas at a rate that is much faster than the rate at which these fossil fuels were created. This is releasing the carbon stored in the fuels into the atmosphere and upsetting the carbon cycle (a precise balanced system by which carbon is exchanged between the air, the oceans and land vegetation taking place over millions of years). Currently, carbon dioxide levels in the atmospheric are rising by over 10 percent every 20 years.

Current Evidence of Climatic Change

Cyclones, storm, hurricanes are occurring more frequently and floods and draughts are more intense than before. This increase in extreme weather events cannot be explained away as random events.

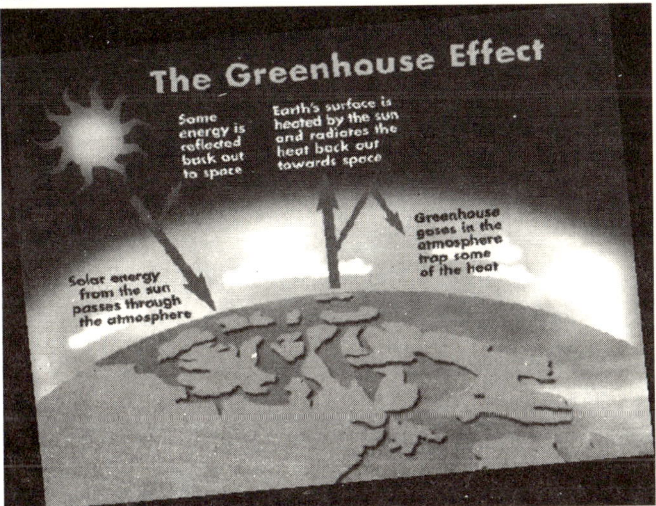

Fig. 8.2: The Greenhouse Effect

This trend toward more powerful storms and hotter, longer dry periods is predicted by computer models. Warmer temperatures mean greater evaporation, and a warmer atmosphere is able to hold more moisture and hence there is more water aloft that can fall as precipitation. Similarly, dry regions are prone to lose still more moisture if the weather is hotter and hence this leads to more severe droughts and desertification.

Chapter 9

Nuclear Energy

NUCLEAR POWER

Introduction

Nuclear power is any nuclear technology designed to extract usable energy from atomic nuclei via controlled nuclear reactions. The most common method today is through nuclear fission, though other methods include nuclear fusion and radioactive decay. All utility-scale reactors heat water to produce steam, which is then converted into mechanical work for the purpose of generating electricity or propulsion. Today, more than 15% of the world's electricity comes from nuclear power, more than 150 nuclear-powered naval vessels have been built, and a few radioisotope rockets have been produced.

The Status of Nuclear Power Globally

As of 2007, nuclear power provided 6.3% of the world's energy and 15% of the world's electricity, with the U.S., France, and Japan together accounting for 56.5% of nuclear generated electricity. IAEA reported there are 439 nuclear power reactors in operation in the world operating in 31 countries. The United States produces the most nuclear energy, with nuclear power providing 19% of the electricity it consumes, while France produces the highest percentage of its electrical energy from nuclear reactors—78% as of 2006. In the European Union as a whole, nuclear energy provides 30% of the electricity. Nuclear energy policy differs between European Union countries, and some, such as Austria and Ireland, have no active nuclear power stations. In comparison, France has a large number of these plants, with 16 multi-unit stations in current use. Many military and some civilian (such as some icebreaker) ships use nuclear marine propulsion, a form of nuclear propulsion. A few space vehicles have been launched using full-fledged nuclear reactors: the Soviet RORSAT series and the American SNAP-10A.

International research is continuing into safety improvements such as passively safe plants, the use of nuclear fusion, and additional uses of process heat such as hydrogen production (in support of a hydrogen economy), for desalinating sea water, and for use in district heating systems.

History of Nuclear Power

Nuclear fission was first experimentally achieved by Enrico Fermi in 1934 when his team bombarded uranium with neutrons. In 1938, German chemists Otto Hahn and Fritz Strassmann, along with Austrian physicists Lise Meitner and Meitner's nephew, Otto Robert Frisch, conducted experiments with the products of neutron-bombarded uranium. They determined that the relatively tiny neutron split the nucleus of the massive uranium atoms into two roughly equal pieces, which was a surprising result. Numerous scientists, including Leo Szilard who was one of the first, recognized that if fission reactions released additional neutrons, a self-sustaining nuclear chain reaction could result. This spurred scientists in many countries (including the United States, the United Kingdom, France, Germany, and the Soviet Union) to petition their government for support of nuclear fission research.

In United States, where Fermi and Szilard had both emigrated, this led to the creation of the first man-made reactor, known as Chicago Pile-1, which achieved criticality on December 2, 1942. This work became part of the Manhattan Project, which built large reactors at the Hanford Site (formerly the town of Hanford, Washington) to breed plutonium for use in the first nuclear weapons. A parallel uranium enrichment effort also was pursued. After World War II, the fear that reactor research would encourage the rapid spread of nuclear weapons and technology, combined with what many scientists thought would be a long road of development, created a situation in which reactor research was kept under strict government control and classification. In addition, most reactor research centered on purely military purposes. Electricity was generated for the first time by a nuclear reactor on December 20, 1951 at the EBR-I experimental station near Arco, Idaho, which initially produced about 100 kW (the Arco Reactor was also the first to experience partial meltdown, in 1955). In 1952, a report by the Paley Commission (The President's Materials Policy Commission) for President Harry Truman made a "relatively pessimistic" assessment of nuclear power, and called for "aggressive research in the whole field of solar energy." A December 1953 speech by President Dwight Eisenhower, "Atoms for Peace," emphasized the useful harnessing of the atom and set the U.S. on a course of strong government support for international use of nuclear power.

Calder Hall nuclear power station in England was the world's first nuclear power station to produce electricity in commercial quantities. The Shippingport Atomic Power Station in Shippingport, Pennsylvania was the first commercial reactor in the USA and was opened in 1957. In 1954, Lewis Strauss, then chairman of the United States Atomic Energy Commission (forerunner of the U.S. Nuclear Regulatory Commission and the United States Department of Energy) spoke of electricity in the future being "too cheap to meter." While few doubt he was thinking of atomic energy when he made the statement, he may have been referring to hydrogen fusion, rather than uranium fission. Actually, the consensus of government and business at the time was that nuclear (fission) power might eventually become merely economically competitive with conventional power sources. On June 27, 1954, the USSRs Obninsk Nuclear Power Plant became the world's first nuclear power plant to generate electricity for a power grid, and produced around 5 megawatts electric power. In 1955 the United Nations' "First Geneva Conference", then the world's largest gathering of scientists and engineers, met to explore the technology. In 1957 EURATOM was launched alongside the European Economic Community (the latter is now the European Union). The same year also saw the launch of the International Atomic Energy Agency (IAEA). The world's first commercial nuclear power station, Calder Hall in

Sellafield, England was opened in 1956 with an initial capacity of 50 MW (later 200 MW). The first commercial nuclear generator to become operational in the United States was the Shippingport Reactor (Pennsylvania, December, 1957). One of the first organizations to develop nuclear power was the U.S. Navy, for the purpose of propelling submarines and aircraft carriers. It has a good record in nuclear safety, perhaps because of the stringent demands of Admiral Hyman G. Rickover, who was the driving force behind nuclear marine propulsion as well as the Shippingport Reactor. The U.S. Navy has operated more nuclear reactors than any other entity, including the Soviet Navy with no publicly known major incidents. The first nuclear-powered submarine, USS Nautilus (SSN-571), was put to sea in December 1954. Two U.S. nuclear submarines, USS Scorpion and USS Thresher, have been lost at sea. These vessels were both lost due to malfunctions in systems not related to the reactor plants. Also, the sites are monitored and no known leakage has occurred from the onboard reactors. Enrico Fermi and Leó Szilárd in 1955 shared U.S. Patent 2,708,656 for the nuclear reactor, belatedly granted for the work they had done during the Manhattan Project.

Installed nuclear capacity initially rose relatively quickly, rising from less than 1 gigawatt (GW) in 1960 to 100 GW in the late 1970s, and 300 GW in the late 1980s. Since the late 1980s worldwide capacity has risen much more slowly, reaching 366 GW in 2005. Between around 1970 and 1990, more than 50 GW of capacity was under construction (peaking at over 150 GW in the late 70s and early 80s)—in 2005, around 25 GW of new capacity was planned. More than two-thirds of all nuclear plants ordered after January 1970 were eventually cancelled. Washington Public Power Supply System Nuclear Power Plants 3 and 5 were never completed. During the 1970s and 1980s rising economic costs (related to extended construction times largely due to regulatory changes and pressure-group litigation) and falling fossil fuel prices made nuclear power plants then under construction less attractive. In the 1980s (U.S.) and 1990s (Europe), flat load growth and electricity liberalization also made the addition of large new baseload capacity unattractive. The 1973 oil crisis had a significant effect on countries, such as France and Japan, which had relied more heavily on oil for electric generation (39% and 73%

respectively) to invest in nuclear power. Today, nuclear power supplies about 80% and 30% of the electricity in those countries, respectively. A general movement against nuclear power arose during the last third of the 20th century, based on the fear of a possible nuclear accident, fears of radiation, nuclear proliferation, and on the opposition to nuclear waste production, transport and final storage. Perceived risks on the citizens' health and safety, the 1979 accident at Three Mile Island and the 1986 Chernobyl disaster played a part in stopping new plant construction in many countries, although the public policy organization Brookings Institution suggests that new nuclear units have not been ordered in the U.S. because the Institution's research concludes they cost 15–30% more over their lifetime than conventional coal and natural gas fired plants. Unlike the Three Mile Island accident, the much more serious Chernobyl accident did not increase regulations affecting Western reactors since the Chernobyl reactors were of the problematic RBMK design only used in the Soviet Union, for example lacking "robust" containment buildings. Many of these reactors are still in use today. However, changes were made in both the reactors themselves (use of low enriched uranium) and in the control system (prevention of disabling safety systems) to prevent the possibility of a duplicate accident. An international organization to promote safety awareness and professional development on operators in nuclear facilities was created: WANO; World Association of Nuclear Operators. Opposition in Ireland, New Zealand and Poland prevented nuclear programs there, while Austria (1978), Sweden (1980) and Italy (1987) (influenced by Chernobyl) voted in referendums to oppose or phase out nuclear power.

Future of Nuclear Power

As of 2007, Watts Bar 1, which came on-line in 7 February 1996, was the last U.S. commercial nuclear reactor to go on-line. This is often quoted as evidence of a successful worldwide campaign for nuclear power phase-out. However, political resistance to nuclear power has only ever been successful in New Zealand, and parts of Europe and the Philippines. Even in the U.S. and throughout Europe, investment in research and in the nuclear fuel cycle has continued, and some experts predict that electricity shortages, fossil fuel price increases, global warming and heavy metal emissions from fossil fuel use, new technology such as passively safe plants, and national energy security will renew the demand for nuclear power plants. According to the World Nuclear Association, globally during the 1980s one new nuclear reactor started up every 17 days on average, and by the year 2015 this rate could increase to one every 5 days.

Many countries remain active in developing nuclear power, including Japan, China and India, all actively developing both fast and thermal technology, South Korea and the United States, developing thermal technology only, and South Africa and China, developing versions of the Pebble Bed Modular Reactor (PBMR). Several EU member states actively pursue nuclear programs, while some other member states continue to have a ban for the nuclear energy use. Japan has an active nuclear construction program with new units brought on-line in 2005. In the U.S., three consortia responded in 2004 to the U.S. Department of Energy's solicitation under the Nuclear Power 2010 Program and were awarded matching funds—the Energy Policy Act of 2005 authorized loan guarantees for up to six new reactors, and authorized the Department of Energy to build a reactor based on the Generation IV Very-High-Temperature Reactor concept to produce both electricity and hydrogen. As of the early 21st century, nuclear power is of particular interest to both China and India to serve their rapidly growing economies—both are developing fast breeder reactors. See also energy development. In the energy policy of the United Kingdom it is recognized that there is a likely future energy supply shortfall, which may have to be filled by either new nuclear plant construction or maintaining existing plants beyond their programmed lifetime.

There is a possible impediment to production of nuclear power plants, due to a backlog at Japan Steel Works, the only factory in the world able to manufacture the central part of a nuclear reactor's containment vessel in a single piece, which reduces the risk of a radiation leak. The company can only make four per year of the steel forgings. It will double its capacity in the next two years, but still will not be able to meet current global demand alone. Utilities across the world are submitting orders years in advance of any actual need. Other manufacturers are examining various options, including making the component themselves, or finding ways to make a similar item using alternate methods. Other solutions include using designs that do not require single piece forged pressure vessles such as Canada's Advanced CANDU Reactors or Sodium-cooled Fast Reactors. Other companies able to make the large forgings required for reactor pressure vessels include: Russia's OMZ, which is upgrading to be able to manufacture three or four pressure vessels per year; South Korea's Doosan Heavy Industries; and Mitsubishi Heavy Industries, which is doubling capacity for reactor pressure vessels and other large nuclear components. The UK's Sheffield Forgemasters is evaluating the benefit of tooling-up for nuclear forging work.

A 2007 status report from the anti-nuclear European Greens claimed that, "even if Finland and France build a European Pressurized water Reactor (EPR), China started an additional 20 plants and Japan, Korea or Eastern Europe added one or the other plant, the overall global trend for nuclear power capacity will most likely be downwards over the next two or three decades. With extremely long lead times of 10 years and more, it is practically impossible to maintain or even increase the number of operating nuclear power plants over the next 20 years, unless operating lifetimes would be substantially increased beyond 40 years on average." In fact, China plans to build more than 100 plants, while in the US the licenses of almost half its reactors have already been extended to 60 years, and plans to build more than 30 new ones are under consideration.

Nuclear Reactor Technology

Conventional thermal power plants all have a fuel source to provide heat. Examples are gas, coal, or oil. For a nuclear power plant, this heat is provided by nuclear fission inside the nuclear reactor's core. When a relatively large fissile atomic nucleus is struck by a neutron it forms two or more smaller nuclei as fission products, releasing energy and neutrons in a process called nuclear fission. The neutrons then trigger further fission, and so on. When this nuclear chain reaction is controlled, the energy released can be used to heat water, produce steam and drive a turbine that generates electricity. While a nuclear power plant uses the same fuel, uranium-235 or plutonium-239, a nuclear explosive involves an uncontrolled chain reaction, and the rate of fission in a reactor is not capable of reaching sufficient levels to trigger a nuclear explosion because commercial reactor grade nuclear fuel is not enriched to a high enough level. Naturally found uranium contains 0.711% U-235 by mass, the rest being U-238 and trace amounts of other isotopes. Most reactor fuel is enriched to only 3–4%, but some designs use natural uranium or highly enriched uranium. Reactors for nuclear submarines and large naval surface ships, such as aircraft carriers, commonly use highly enriched uranium. Although highly enriched uranium is more expensive, it reduces the frequency of refueling, which is very useful for military vessels. CANDU reactors are able to use unenriched uranium because the heavy water they use as a moderator and coolant does not absorb neutrons like light water does. The chain reaction is controlled through the use of materials that absorb and moderate neutrons. In uranium-fueled reactors, neutrons must be moderated (slowed down) because slow neutrons are more likely to cause fission when colliding with a uranium-235 nucleus. Light water reactors use ordinary water to moderate and cool the reactors. When at operating temperatures if the temperature of the water increases, its density drops, and fewer neutrons passing through it are slowed enough to trigger further reactions. That negative feedback stabilizes the reaction rate.

A number of other designs for nuclear power generation, the Generation IV reactors, are the subject of active research and may be used for practical power generation in the future. A number of the advanced nuclear reactor designs could also make critical fission reactors much cleaner, much safer and/or much less of a risk to the proliferation of nuclear weapons. It should be noted that such Generation IV reactors are not necessarily fuel by uranium but by thorium, a more abundant fertile material that decays into U233 after being exposed to neutrons. Such reactors use about 1/300 the amount of fuel to power them. The Liquid Fluoride Reactor is one such example of this.

For the future, design changes are being pursued to lessen the risks of fission reactors; in particular, passively safe plants (such as the ESBWR) are available to be built and inherently safe designs are being pursued. Fusion reactors, which may be viable in the future, have no risk of explosive radiation-releasing accidents, and even smaller risks than the already extremely small risks associated with nuclear fission. Whilst fusion power reactors will produce a very small amount of reasonably short lived, intermediate-level radioactive waste at decommissioning time, as a result of neutron activation of the reactor vessel, they will not produce any high-level, long-lived materials comparable to those produced in a fission reactor. Even this small radioactive waste aspect can be mitigated through the use of low-activation steel alloys for the tokamak vessel.

Life Cycle

The Nuclear Fuel Cycle begins when uranium is mined, enriched, and manufactured into nuclear fuel, (1) which is delivered to a nuclear power plant. After usage in the power plant, the spent fuel is delivered to a reprocessing plant (2) or to a final repository (3) for geological disposition. In reprocessing 95% of spent fuel can be recycled to be returned to usage in a power plant. A nuclear reactor is only part of the life-cycle for nuclear power. The process starts with mining (see Uranium mining). Uranium mines are underground, open-pit, or in-situ leach mines. In any case, the uranium ore is extracted, usually converted into a stable and compact form such as yellowcake, and then transported to a processing facility. Here, the yellowcake is converted to uranium hexafluoride, which is then enriched using various techniques. At this point, the enriched uranium, containing more than the natural 0.7% U-235, is used to make rods of the proper composition and geometry for the particular reactor that the fuel is destined for. The fuel rods will spend about 3 operational cycles (typically 6 years total now) inside the reactor, generally until about 3% of their uranium has been fissioned, then they will be moved to a spent fuel pool where the short lived isotopes generated by fission can decay away. After about 5 years in a cooling pond, the spent fuel is radioactively and thermally cool enough to handle, and it can be moved to dry storage casks or reprocessed.

Conventional Fuel Resources

Uranium is a fairly common element in the Earth's crust. Uranium is approximately as common as tin or germanium in

Earth's crust, and is about 35 times more common than silver. Uranium is a constituent of most rocks, dirt, and of the oceans. The world's present measured resources of uranium, economically recoverable at a price of 130 USD/kg, are enough to last for "at least a century" at current consumption rates. This represents a higher level of assured resources than is normal for most minerals. On the basis of analogies with other metallic minerals, a doubling of price from present levels could be expected to create about a tenfold increase in measured resources, over time. The fuel's contribution to the overall cost of the electricity produced is relatively small, so even a large fuel price escalation will have relatively little effect on final price. For instance, typically a doubling of the uranium market price would increase the fuel cost for a light water reactor by 26% and the electricity cost about 7%, whereas doubling the price of natural gas would typically add 70% to the price of electricity from that source. At high enough prices, eventually extraction from sources such as granite and seawater become economically feasible. Current light water reactors make relatively inefficient use of nuclear fuel, fissioning only the very rare uranium-235 isotope. Nuclear reprocessing can make this waste reusable and more efficient reactor designs allow better use of the available resources.

Breeding

As opposed to current light water reactors which use uranium-235 (0.7% of all natural uranium), fast breeder reactors use uranium-238 (99.3% of all natural uranium). It has been estimated that there is up to five billion years' worth of uranium-238 for use in these power plants. Breeder technology has been used in several reactors, but the high cost of reprocessing fuel safely requires uranium prices of more than 200 USD/kg before becoming justified economically. As of December 2005, the only breeder reactor producing power is BN-600 in Beloyarsk, Russia. The electricity output of BN-600 is 600 MW—Russia has planned to build another unit, BN-800, at Beloyarsk nuclear power plant. Also, Japan's Monju reactor is planned for restart (having been shut down since 1995), and both China and India intend to build breeder reactors. Another alternative would be to use uranium-233 bred from thorium as fission fuel in the thorium fuel cycle.

Thorium is about 3.5 times as common as uranium in the Earth's crust, and has different geographic characteristics. This would extend the total practical fissionable resource base by 450%. Unlike the breeding of U-238 into plutonium, fast breeder reactors are not necessary—it can be performed satisfactorily in more conventional plants. India has looked into this technology, as it has abundant thorium reserves but little uranium.

Fusion

Fusion power commonly propose the use of deuterium, an isotope of hydrogen, as fuel and in many current designs also lithium. Assuming a fusion energy output equal to the current global output and that this does not increase in the future, then the known current lithium reserves would last 3000 years, lithium from sea water would last 60 million years, and a more complicated fusion process using only deuterium from sea water would have fuel for 150 billion years.

Solid Waste

The safe storage and disposal of nuclear waste is a significant challenge. The most important waste stream from nuclear power plants is spent fuel. A large nuclear reactor produces 3 cubic metres (25–30 tonnes) of spent fuel each year. It is primarily composed of unconverted uranium as well as significant quantities of transuranic actinides (plutonium and curium, mostly). In addition, about 3% of it is made of fission products. The actinides (uranium, plutonium, and curium) are responsible for the bulk of the long-term radioactivity, whereas the fission products are responsible for the bulk of the short-term radioactivity.

High Level Radioactive Waste

Spent fuel is highly radioactive and needs to be handled with great care and forethought. However, spent nuclear fuel becomes less radioactive over time. After 40 years, the radiation flux is 99.9% lower than it was the moment the spent fuel was removed, although still dangerously radioactive. Spent fuel rods are stored in shielded basins of water (spent fuel pools), usually located on-site. The water provides both cooling for the still-decaying fission products, and shielding from the continuing radioactivity. After a few decades some on-site storage involves moving the now cooler, less radioactive fuel to a dry-storage facility or dry cask storage, where the fuel is stored in steel and concrete containers until its radioactivity decreases naturally ("decays") to levels safe enough for other processing. This interim stage spans years or decades, depending on the type of fuel. Most U.S. waste is currently stored in temporary storage sites requiring oversight, while suitable permanent disposal methods are discussed.

As of 2007, the United States had accumulated more than 50,000 metric tons of spent nuclear fuel from nuclear reactors. Underground storage at Yucca Mountain in U.S. has been proposed as permanent storage. After 10,000 years of radioactive decay, according to United States Environmental Protection Agency standards, the spent nuclear fuel will no longer pose a threat to public health and safety.

The amount of waste can be reduced in several ways, particularly reprocessing. Even so, the remaining waste will be substantially radioactive for at least 300 years even if the actinides are removed, and for up to thousands of years if the actinides are left in. Even with separation of all actinides, and using fast breeder reactors to destroy by transmutation some of the longer-lived non-actinides as well, the waste must be segregated from the environment for one to a few hundred years, and therefore this is properly categorized as a long-term problem. Subcritical reactors or fusion reactors could also reduce the time the waste has to be stored. It has been argued that the best solution for the nuclear waste is above ground temporary storage since technology is rapidly changing. The current waste may well become a valuable resource in the future.

France is one of the world's most densely populated countries. According to a 2007 story broadcast on 60 Minutes, nuclear power gives France the cleanest air of any industrialized country, and the cheapest electricity in all of Europe. France reprocesses its nuclear waste to reduce its mass and make more energy. However, the article continues, "Today we stock containers of waste because currently scientists don't know how to reduce or eliminate the toxicity, but maybe in 100 years perhaps scientists will ... Nuclear waste is an enormously difficult political problem which to date no country has solved. It is, in a sense, the Achilles heel of the nuclear industry ... If France is unable to solve this issue, says Mandil, then 'I do not see how we can continue our nuclear program.' Further, reprocessing itself has its critics, such as the Union of Concerned Scientists.

Low-level Radioactive Waste

The nuclear industry also produces a volume of low-level radioactive waste in the form of contaminated items like clothing, hand tools, water purifier resins, and (upon decommissioning) the materials of which the reactor itself is built. In the United States, the Nuclear Regulatory Commission has repeatedly attempted to allow low-level materials to be handled as normal waste: landfilled, recycled into consumer items, et cetera. Most low-level waste releases very low levels of radioactivity and is only considered radioactive waste because of its history. For example, according to the standards of the NRC, the radiation released by coffee is enough to treat it as low level waste.

Comparing Radioactive Waste to Industrial Toxic Waste

In countries with nuclear power, radioactive wastes comprise less than 1% of total industrial toxic wastes, which remain hazardous indefinitely unless they decompose or are treated so that they are less toxic or, ideally, completely non-toxic. Overall, nuclear power produces far less waste material than fossil-fuel based power plants. Coal-burning plants are particularly noted for producing large amounts of toxic and mildly radioactive ash due to concentrating naturally occurring metals and radioactive material from the coal. Contrary to popular belief, coal power actually results in more radioactive waste being released into the environment than nuclear power. The population effective dose equivalent from radiation from coal plants is 100 times as much as nuclear plants.

Reprocessing

Reprocessing can potentially recover up to 95% of the remaining uranium and plutonium in spent nuclear fuel, putting it into new mixed oxide fuel. This produces a reduction in long-term radioactivity within the remaining waste, since this is largely short-lived fission products, and reduces its volume by over 90%. Reprocessing of civilian fuel from power reactors is currently done on large scale in Britain, France and (formerly) Russia, soon will be done in China and perhaps India, and is being done on an expanding scale in Japan. The full potential of reprocessing has not been achieved because it requires breeder reactors, which are not yet commercially available. France is generally cited as the most successful reprocessor, but it presently only recycles 28% (by mass) of the yearly fuel use, 7% within France and another 21% in Russia. Unlike other countries, the US stopped civilian reprocessing from 1976 to 1981 as one part of US non-proliferation policy, since reprocessed material such as plutonium could be used in nuclear weapons: however, reprocessing is now allowed in the U.S. Even so, in the U.S. spent nuclear fuel is currently all treated as waste. In February, 2006, a new U.S. initiative, the Global Nuclear Energy Partnership was announced. It would be an international effort to reprocess fuel in a manner making nuclear proliferation unfeasible, while making nuclear power available to developing countries.

Depleted Uranium

Uranium enrichment produces many tons of depleted uranium (DU) which consists of U-238 with most of the easily fissile U-235 isotope removed. U-238 is a tough metal with several commercial uses—for example, aircraft production, radiation shielding, and armor—as it has a higher density than lead. Depleted uranium is also useful in munitions as DU penetrators (bullets or APFSDS tips) 'self sharpen', due to uranium's tendency to fracture along adiabatic shear bands. There are concerns that U-238 may lead to health problems in groups exposed to this material excessively, like tank crews and civilians living in areas where large quantities of DU ammunition have been used. In January 2003 the World Health Organization released a report finding that contamination from DU munitions were localized to a few tens of meters from the impact sites and contamination of local vegetation and water was 'extremely low'. The report also states that approximately 70% of ingested DU will leave the body after twenty four hours and 90% after a few days.

Debate on Nuclear Power

Proponents of nuclear energy aver that nuclear power is a sustainable energy source that reduces carbon emissions and increases energy security by decreasing dependence on foreign oil. Proponents also claim that the risks of storing waste are small and can be further reduced by the technology in the new reactors and the operational safety record is already good when compared to the other major kinds of power plants. Critics believe that nuclear power is a potentially dangerous and declining energy source, with decreasing proportion of nuclear energy in power production, and dispute whether the risks can be reduced through new technology. Critics also point to the problem of storing radioactive waste, the potential for possibly severe radioactive contamination by accident or sabotage, the possibility of nuclear proliferation and the disadvantages of centralized electrical production. Arguments of economics and safety are used by both sides of the debate.

Energy Security

For some countries, nuclear power affords energy independence. Nuclear power has been relatively unaffected by embargoes, and uranium is mined in "reliable" countries, including Australia and Canada.

Reliability

Nuclear power plants are some of the more complex mechanical systems ever devised, although much of that complexity is due to redundancy of systems, extensive backups, and the defense in depth strategy of the designs. In 2005, out of all nuclear power plants in the world, the average capacity factor was 86.8%, the number of SCRAMs per 7,000 hours critical was 0.6, and the unplanned capacity loss factor was 1.6%. Capacity factor is the net power produced over the maximum amount possible running at 100% all the time, thus this includes all scheduled maintenance/refueling outages as well as unplanned losses. The 7,000 hours is roughly representative of how long any given reactor will remain critical in a year, meaning that the scram rates translates into a sudden and unplanned shutdown about 0.6 times per year for any given reactor in the world. The unplanned capacity loss factor represents amount of power not produced due to unplanned scrams and postponed restarts. The World Nuclear Association states that "Sun, wind, tides and waves cannot be controlled to provide directly either continuous base-load power, or peak-load power when it is needed. In practical terms they are therefore limited to some 10–20% of the capacity of an electricity grid, and cannot directly be applied as economic substitutes for coal or nuclear power, however important they may become in particular areas with favourable conditions." "The fundamental problem, especially for electricity supply, is their variable and diffuse nature. This means either that there must be reliable duplicate sources of electricity, or some means of electricity storage on a large scale. Apart from pumped-storage hydro systems, no such means exist at present and nor are any in sight." "Relatively few places have scope for pumped storage dams close to where the power is needed, and overall efficiency is low. Means of storing large amounts of electricity as such in giant batteries or by other means have not been developed."

In 2006, several European nations were forced to take some plants offline and reduce operations at others and France, normally an electricity exporter, had to buy electricity on European spot market to meet demand. Also in Western Europe, nuclear plants also had to secure exemptions from regulations in order to discharge overheated water into the environment.

Economics

This is a controversial subject, since multi-billion dollar investments ride on the choice of an energy source. Which power source (generally coal, natural gas, nuclear or wind) is most cost-effective depends on the assumptions used in a particular study—several are quoted in the main article. Nuclear plants generally have very high capital costs with operating costs just under those of coal-fired generation, but very low fuel costs. In 2008 World Nuclear Association gave a 2005 comparison table and said "Nuclear energy is, in many places, competitive with fossil fuel for electricity generation, despite relatively high capital costs and the need to internalize all waste disposal and decommissioning costs. If the social, health and environmental costs of fossil fuels are also taken into account, nuclear is outstanding."

Subsidies

Critics of nuclear power claim that it is the beneficiary of inappropriately large economic subsidies—mainly taking the forms of taxpayer-funded research and development and limitations on disaster liability—and that these subsidies, being subtle and indirect, are often overlooked when comparing the economics of nuclear against other forms of power generation. However, competing energy sources also receive subsidies. Fossil fuels receive large direct and indirect subsidies, such as tax benefits and not having to pay for the greenhouse gases they emit. Renewables receive large direct production subsidies and tax breaks in many nations. Energy research and development (R&D) for nuclear power alone has and continues to receive much larger state subsidies than R&D for all renewable energy sources put together or for fossil fuels. In Europe, the FP7 research program has more subsidies for nuclear than for renewable and energy efficiency together. Part of this research money goes into ITER. However, today most of this takes places in Japan and France: in most other nations renewable R&D as a whole get more money. In the US, public research money for nuclear fission declined from 2,179 to 35 million dollars between 1980 and 2000. However, in order to restart the industry, the next six US reactors will receive subsidies equal to those of renewables and, in the event of cost overruns due to delays, at least partial compensation for the overruns. A May 12, 2008 editorial in the Wall St. Journal stated, "For electricity generation, the EIA concludes that solar energy is subsidized to the tune of $24.34 per megawatt hour, wind $23.37 and 'clean coal' $29.81. By contrast, normal coal receives 44 cents, natural gas a mere quarter, hydroelectric about 67 cents and nuclear power $1.59."

Environmental Effects

The primary environmental impacts of nuclear power come from uranium mining, radioactive effluent emissions, and waste heat, as under normal generating conditions nuclear power does not produce greenhouse gas emissions [CO_2, NO_2] directly (although the nuclear fuel cycle produces them indirectly, though at much smaller rates than fossil fuels). Nuclear generation does not directly produce sulfur dioxide, nitrogen oxides, mercury or other pollutants associated with the combustion of fossil fuels. In 2008, The Economist stated that "nuclear reactors are the one proven way to make carbon-dioxide-free electricity in large and reliable quantities that does not depend (as hydroelectric and geothermal energy do) on the luck of the geographical draw."

Nuclear plants require more, but not significantly more, cooling water than fossil-fuel power plants due to their slightly lower generation efficiencies. Uranium mining can use large amounts of water—for example, the Roxby Downs mine in South Australia uses 35 million litres of water each day and plans to increase this to 150 million litres per day. The effect on prices of uranium should be considered. Other issues include disposal of nuclear waste and nuclear decommissioning. Most countries with nuclear power agree that sequestering spent fuel in Deep geological repositories is the best option for waste disposal, but no such long-term waste repositories yet exist.

Safety: The topic of nuclear safety covers:

- The research and testing of the possible incidents/events at a nuclear power plant,
- What equipment and actions are designed to prevent those incidents/events from having serious consequences,
- The calculation of the probabilities of multiple systems and/or actions failing thus allowing serious consequences,
- The evaluation of the worst-possible timing and scope of those serious consequences (the worst-possible in extreme cases being a release of radiation),
- The actions taken to protect the public during a release of radiation,
- The training and rehearsals performed to ensure readiness in case an incident/event occurs.

Numerous different and usually redundantly duplicated safety features have been designed into (and in some cases backfitted to) nuclear power plants.

Accidents

The International Nuclear Event Scale (INES), developed by the International Atomic Energy Agency (IAEA), is used to communicate the severity of nuclear accidents on a scale of 0 to 7. The two most significant events were the Three Mile Island accident (1979) and the Chernobyl disaster (1986).

The Chernobyl disaster at the Chernobyl Nuclear Power Plant in the Ukrainian Soviet Socialist Republic (now Ukraine) remains the worst nuclear accident in history and is the only event to receive an INES score of 7. The power excursion and resulting steam explosion and fire spread radioactive contamination across large portions of Europe. The UN report 'CHERNOBYL : THE TRUE SCALE OF THE ACCIDENT' published 2005 concluded that the death toll includes the 50 workers who died of acute radiation syndrome, nine children who died from thyroid cancer, and an estimated 4000 excess cancer deaths in the future.This accident occurred due to both the flawed operation of the reactors and critical design flaws in the Soviet RBMK reactors, such as lack of a containment building. This disaster however has led to some "lessons learned" for Western power plants, large improvements in safety at Soviet-designed nuclear power plants and major improvements to the remaining RBMK reactors (with the shutdown of some). The accident at Three Mile Island Unit 2 was the worst civilian nuclear accident outside the Soviet Union (INES score of 5). The reactor experienced a partial core meltdown. However, according to the NRC, the reactor vessel and containment building were not breached and little radiation was released to the environment, with no significant impact on health or the environment. Several studies have found no increase in cancer rates. Greenpeace has produced a report titled An American Chernobyl: Nuclear "Near Misses" at U.S. Reactors Since 1986 which "reveals that nearly two hundred "near misses" to nuclear meltdowns have occurred in the United States". At almost 450 nuclear plants in the world that risk is greatly magnified, they say. This is not to mention numerous incidents, many supposedly unreported, that have occurred. Another report produced by Greenpeace called Nuclear Reactor Hazards: Ongoing Dangers of Operating Nuclear Technology in the 21st Century claims that risk of a major accident has increased in the past years.

Cases where governments have misinformed or underinformed the public underlies much of the distrust. Incidents such as Brookhaven National Laboratory (a military-purpose reactor not regulated by the Nuclear Regulatory Commission) leaking tritium into community groundwater for up to 12 years and classified accidents at the Rocky Flats Nuclear Weapons Plant, along with the extreme nuclear secrecy of East Bloc governments during the Cold War, may create the impression that the health and safety of communities surrounding nuclear facilities is of secondary importance. However such mistrust is often misdirected—while the industrial sites that were built to support the Manhattan Project and the Cold War's nuclear arms race display many cases of significant environmental contamination and other safety concerns, in the United States such facilities are operated and regulated completely separately from commercial nuclear power plants.

Contrasting Radioactive Accident Emissions with Industrial Emissions

Proponents aver that the problems of nuclear waste do not come anywhere close to approaching the problems of fossil fuel waste. A 2004 article from the BBC states: "The World Health Organization (WHO) says 3 million people are killed worldwide by outdoor air pollution annually from vehicles and industrial emissions, and 1.6 million indoors through using solid fuel." In the U.S. alone, fossil fuel waste kills 20,000 people each year. A coal power plant releases 100 times as much radiation as a nuclear power plant of the same wattage. It is estimated that during 1982, US coal burning released 155 times as much radioactivity into the atmosphere as the Three Mile Island incident. The World Nuclear Association provides a comparison of deaths due to accidents among different forms of energy production. In their comparison, deaths per TW-yr of electricity produced from 1970 to 1992 are quoted as 885 for hydropower, 342 for coal, 85 for natural gas, and 8 for nuclear.

Health Effect on Population near Nuclear Plants and Workers

Most human exposure to radiation comes from natural

background radiation. Most of the remaining exposure comes from medical procedures. Several large studies in the US, Canada, and Europe have found no evidence of any increase in cancer mortality among people living near nuclear facilities. For example, in 1991, the National Cancer Institute (NCI) of the National Institutes of Health announced that a large-scale study, which evaluated mortality from 16 types of cancer, found no increased incidence of cancer mortality for people living near 62 nuclear installations in the United States. The study showed no increase in the incidence of childhood leukemia mortality in the study of surrounding counties after start-up of the nuclear facilities. The NCI study, the broadest of its kind ever conducted, surveyed 900,000 cancer deaths in counties near nuclear facilities. Some areas of Britain near industrial facilities, particularly near Sellafield (a nuclear reprocessing plant), have displayed elevated childhood leukemia levels, in which children living locally are 10 times more likely to contract the cancer. One study of those near Sellafield has ruled out any contribution from nuclear sources, and the reasons for these increases, or clusters, are unclear. Apart from anything else, the levels of radiation at these sites are orders of magnitude too low to account for the excess incidences reported. One possible explanation is viruses or other infectious agents being introduced into a local community by the mass movement of migrant workers. Likewise, studies have found an increased incidence of childhood leukaemia near nuclear power plants has been found in Germany and France. Nonetheless, the results of larger multi-site studies in these countries invalidate the hypothesis of an increased risk of leukaemia related to nuclear discharge. The methodology and very small samples in the studies finding an increased incidence has been criticized.

In December 2007, it was reported that a study showed that German children who lived near nuclear power plants had a higher rate of cancer than those who did not. However, the study also stated that there was no extra radiation near the nuclear power plants, and scientists were puzzled as to what was causing the higher rate of cancer. Workers in the nuclear industry from the 1980s were found to be slightly more likely (2 extra deaths per year in the group of 65,000) to die from heart disease if they were exposed to high levels of radiation. It is unclear if radiation, or other issues such as stress, level of education, etc. are the cause of this increased mortality. However, the report also said "the study of nearly 65,000 nuclear workers shows that they are healthier overall than the general population, even after taking into account the extra health risks resulting from exposure to radiation in the workplace."

Alternative Reactor Designs

The US Government is leading a plan to develop small "disposable" nuclear reactors (SSTAR) for deployment in developing countries. However, there has been considerable debate about the security and nuclear proliferation risks of such a proposal. Russia has constructed on the first of seven nuclear power station ships which each will carry a 70-megawatt nuclear reactor. The ships will provide power to remote coastal towns, or be sold abroad, and 12 countries, including Algeria and Indonesia, have expressed interest. There is considerable debate about the safety of such "floating" nuclear reactors, especially since they may lack a containment building around them. The Estonian Maritime Academy has developed a project to construct an underwater nuclear reactor off the Baltic Sea coast. The project, submitted to the Estonian Eesti Energia company, proposes the construction of a 1,000-MWt nuclear power plant on a granite shelf in the Muuga Bay. The Head of the Academy has said that the construction of a nuclear reactor on the seabed is completely safe. However, an underwater nuclear power plant would be more costly than a similar land-based project. Local environmentalists have also expressed doubts about the ecological safety of such a giant undertaking on the sea shelf.

Nuclear Proliferation and Terrorism Concerns

Nuclear proliferation is the spread of nuclear weapons and related technology to nations not recognized as "Nuclear Weapon States" by the Nuclear Nonproliferation Treaty (NNPT). Since the days of the Manhattan Project it has been known that reactors could be used for weapons-development purposes—the first nuclear reactors were developed for exactly this reason—as the operation of a nuclear reactor converts U-238 into plutonium. As a consequence, since the 1950s there have been concerns about the possibility of using reactors as a dual-use technology, whereby apparently peaceful technological development could serve as an approach to nuclear weapons capability. For that reason, the United Nation's International Atomic Energy Agency (IAEA) closely monitors all reactors of nations who have joined.

Vulnerability of Plants to Attack

Each nuclear power plant's reactor (except those in Russia) are surrounded by a thick containment building. In the U.S. the plants are surrounded by a double row of tall fences which are electronically monitored, and the plant grounds are patrolled by a sizeable force of armed guards. The NRC's "Design Basis Threat" criteria for plants is a secret, and so what size attacking force the plants are able to protect against is unknown. However, to scram a plant takes less than 5 seconds while unimpeded restart takes hours, severely hampering a terrorist force in a goal to release radioactivity.

Use of Waste Byproduct as a Weapon

An additional concern with nuclear power plants is that if the by-products of nuclear fission (the nuclear waste generated by the plant) were to be left unprotected it could be stolen and used as a radiological weapon, colloquially known as a "dirty bomb". There were incidents in post-Soviet Russia of nuclear plant workers attempting to sell nuclear materials for this purpose (for example, there was such an incident in Russia in 1999 where plant workers attempted to sell 5 grams of radioactive material on the open market, and an incident in 1993 where Russian workers were caught attempting to sell 4.5 kilograms of enriched uranium.), and there are additional concerns that the transportation of nuclear waste along roadways or railways opens it up for potential theft. The United Nations has since called upon world leaders to improve security in order to prevent radioactive material falling into the hands of terrorists, and such fears have been used as justifications for centralized, permanent, and secure waste repositories and increased security along transportation routes.

Public Confidence

Polls consistently show that populations continue to fear

nuclear, but desire the energy security. A comprehensive public opinion survey, performed in May and June 2006 in the European Union member countries, concluded that EU citizens perceive great future promise in the use of renewable energies, but despite majority opposition, nuclear energy also has its place in the future energy mix.

Safety Culture in Host Nations

Nuclear's safety also depends strongly on building, maintaining and operating the reactors as designed. The Chernobyl disaster was directly caused by a poor safety culture in the former Soviet Union. Some developing countries which plan to go nuclear have very poor industrial safety records and problems with political corruption.

Indo-US Civilian Nuclear Agreement

The Indo-U.S. civilian nuclear agreement is the name commonly attributed to a bilateral agreement on nuclear cooperation between the United States of America and the Republic of India. The framework for this agreement was a Joint Statement by Indian Prime Minister Manmohan Singh and U.S. President George W. Bush, under which India agreed to separate its civil and military nuclear facilities and place civil facilities under International Atomic Energy Agency (IAEA) safeguards and, in exchange, the United States agreed to work toward full civil nuclear cooperation with India. On August 1, 2008, the IAEA approved the safeguards agreement with India, after which the United States approached the Nuclear Suppliers Group (NSG) to grant a waiver to India to commence civilian nuclear trade. The 45-nation NSG granted the waiver to India on September 6, 2008 allowing it to access civilian nuclear technology and fuel from other countries. However, India can commence nuclear trade with the United States only after the deal is passed by the US Congress and is likely to be the main focus of its last session which starts on September 8, 2008.

The Henry J. Hyde United States-India Peaceful Atomic Energy Cooperation Act of 2006, also known as the Hyde Act, is the U.S. domestic law that modifies the requirements of Section 123 of the U.S. Atomic Energy Act to permit nuclear cooperation with India and in particular to negotiate a 123 agreement to operationalize the 2005 Joint Statement. As a domestic U.S. law, the Hyde Act is binding on the United States. The Hyde Act cannot be binding on India's sovereign decisions although it can be construed as prescriptive for future U.S. reactions. As per the Vienna convention, an international treaty such as the 123 agreement cannot be superseded by an internal law such as the Hyde Act. The 123 agreement defines the terms and conditions for bilateral civilian nuclear cooperation, and requires separate approvals by the U.S. Congress and by Indian cabinet ministers. According to the Nuclear Power Corporation of India, the agreement will help India meet its goal of adding 25,000 MW of nuclear power capacity through imports of nuclear reactors and fuel by 2020. After the terms of the 123 agreement were concluded on July 27, 2007, it ran into trouble because of stiff opposition in India from the communist allies of the ruling United Progressive Alliance. The government survived a confidence vote in the parliament on July 22, 2008 by 275–256 votes in the backdrop of defections from both camps to the opposite camps. The deal also had faced opposition from non-proliferation activists, anti-nuclear organizations, and some states within the Nuclear Suppliers Group. A deal which is inconsistent with the Hyde Act and does not place restrictions on India has also faced opposition in the U.S. House and may not receive a vote until 2009. In February 2008 U.S. Secretary of State Condoleezza Rice said that any agreement would be "consistent with the obligations of the Hyde Act".

Parties tc the Non Proliferation Treaty (NPT) have a recognized right of access to peaceful uses of nuclear energy and an obligation to cooperate on civilian nuclear technology. Separately, the Nuclear Suppliers Group has agreed on guidelines for nuclear exports, including reactors and fuel. Those guidelines condition such exports on comprehensive safeguards by the International Atomic Energy Agency, which are designed to verify that nuclear energy is not diverted from peaceful use to weapons programs. Though neither India, Israel, nor Pakistan have signed the NPT, India argues that instead of addressing the central objective of universal and comprehensive non-proliferation, the treaty creates a club of "nuclear haves" and a larger group of "nuclear have-nots" by restricting the legal possession of nuclear weapons to those states that tested them before 1967, who alone are free to possess and multiply their nuclear stockpiles. India insists on a comprehensive action plan for a nuclear-free world within a specific time-frame and has also adopted a voluntary "no first use policy".

In response to a growing Chinese nuclear arsenal, India conducted a nuclear test in 1974 (called "peaceful nuclear explosion" and explicitly not for "offensive" first strike military purposes but which could be used as a "peaceful deterrence"). Led by the US, other states have set up an informal group, the Nuclear Suppliers Group (NSG), to control exports of nuclear materials, equipment and technology. Consequently, India was left outside the international nuclear order, which forced India to develop it own resources for each stage of the nuclear fuel cycle and power generation, including fast breeder reactors and thorium-fueled thermal breeder reactors. This sanctions regime also provided India with the impetus to continue developing its own nuclear weapons technology with a specific goal of achieving self-sufficiency for all key components for weapons design, testing and production. Despite success in developing these new technologies, India continued to face shortfalls in nuclear fuel supply, particularly uranium for its current installed based of heavy water and light water nuclear power plants.

Consequently, India's nuclear isolation constrained its civil nuclear program, but left India relatively immune to foreign reactions to a prospective nuclear test. Partly for this reason, but mainly due to continued unchecked covert nuclear and missile proliferation activities between Pakistan, China and North Korea, India conducted five more nuclear tests in May, 1998 at Pokhran. The strategic objectives of these tests were:

(i) To validate Indian nuclear weapons design, including miniaturization.

(ii) To create strategic pressure on Pakistan to match the Indian tests; deterring further nuclear cooperation between Pakistan and its partners, China, Iran and North Korea

(iii) To demonstrate India's Nuclear Deterrent capability as part of implementing an open transparent nuclear weapons program and doctrine commensurate with

India's status as an emerging economic and military power.

India was subject to international sanctions after its May 1998 nuclear tests. However, due to the size of the Indian economy and its relatively large domestic sector, these sanctions had little impact on India, with Indian GDP growth increasing from 4.8% in 1997-1998 (prior to sanctions) to 6.6% (during sanctions) in 1998-1999. Consequently, at the end of 2001, the Bush Administration decided to drop all sanctions on India. Although India achieved its strategic objectives from the Pokhran nuclear weapons tests in 1998, it continued to find its civil nuclear program isolated internationally.

The growing energy demands of the Indian and Chinese economies have raised questions on the impact of global availability to conventional energy. The Bush Administration has concluded that an Indian shift toward nuclear energy is in the best interest for America to secure its energy needs of coal, crude oil, and natural gas. While India still harbors aspirations of being recognized as a nuclear power before considering signing the NPT as a nuclear weapons state (which would be possible if the current 1967 cutoff in the definition of a "nuclear weapon state" were pushed to 1975), other parties to the NPT are not likely to support such an amendment. As a compromise, the proposed civil nuclear agreement implicitly recognizes India's "de facto" status even without signing the NPT. The Bush administration justifies a nuclear pact with India because it is important in helping to advance the non-proliferation framework by formally recognizing India's strong non-proliferation record even though it has not signed the NPT. The former Under Secretary of State of Political Affairs, Nicholas Burns, one of the architects of the Indo-U.S. nuclear deal said "India's trust, its credibility, the fact that it has promised to create a state-of-the-art facility, monitored by the IAEA, to begin a new export control regime in place, because it has not proliferated the nuclear technology, we can't say that about Pakistan." when asked whether the U.S. would offer a nuclear deal with Pakistan on the lines of the Indo-U.S. deal. Mohammed ElBaradei, head of the International Atomic Energy Agency, which would be in charge of inspecting India's civilian reactors has praised the deal as "it would also bring India closer as an important partner in the nonproliferation regime". However, members of the IAEA safeguards staff have made it clear that Indian demands that New Delhi be allowed to determine when Indian reactors might be inspected could undermine the IAEA safeguards system.

Financially, the U.S. also expects that such a deal could spur India's economic growth and bring in $150 billion in the next decade for nuclear power plants, of which the US wants a share. It is India's stated objective to increase the production of nuclear power generation from its present capacity of 4,000 MWe to 20,000 MWe in the next decade. However, the developmental economic advising firm Dalberg, which advises the IMF and the World Bank, moreover, has done its own analysis of the economic value of investing in nuclear power development in India. Their conclusion is that for the next 20 years such investments are likely to be far less valuable economically or environmentally than a variety of other measures to increase electricity production in India. They have noted that U.S. nuclear vendors cannot sell any reactors to India unless and until India caps third party liabilities or establishes a credible liability pool to protect U.S. firms from being sued in the case of an accident or a terrorist act of sabotage against nuclear plants.

Since the end of the Cold War, The Pentagon, along with certain U.S. ambassadors such as Robert Blackwill, have requested increased strategic ties with India and a de-hyphenization of Pakistan with India. The United States also sees India as a viable counter-weight to the growing influence of China. While India is self-sufficient in thorium, possessing 25% of the world's known and economically viable thorium, it possesses a meager 1% of the similarly calculated global uranium reserves. Indian support for cooperation with the U.S. centers around the issue of obtaining a steady supply of sufficient energy for the economy to grow. Indian opposition to the pact centers around the concessions that would need to be made, as well as the likely de-prioritization of research into a thorium fuel-cycle if uranium becomes highly available given the well understood utilization of uranium in a nuclear fuel cycle.

On March 2, 2006 in New Delhi, George W. Bush and Manmohan Singh signed a Civil Nuclear Cooperation Agreement, following an initiation during the July 2005 summit in Washington between the two leaders over civilian nuclear cooperation. Heavily endorsed by the White House, the agreement is thought to be a major victory to George W. Bush's foreign policy initiative and was described by many lawmakers as a cornerstone of the new strategic partnership between the two countries. The agreement is widely considered to help India fulfill its soaring energy demands and boost U.S. and India into a strategic partnership. The Pentagon speculates this will help ease global demand for crude oil and natural gas. On August 3, 2007, both the countries released the full text of the 123 agreement. Nicholas Burns, the chief negotiator of the India-United States nuclear deal, said the U.S. has the right to terminate the deal if India tests a nuclear weapon and that no part of the agreement recognizes India as a nuclear weapons state.

On December 18, 2006 President George W. Bush signed the Hyde Act into law. The Act was passed by an overwhelming 359–68 in the United States House of Representatives on July 26 and by 85–12 in the United States Senate on November 16 in a strong show of bipartisan support. The House version (H.R. 5682) and Senate version (S. 3709) of the bill differed due to amendments each had added before approving, but the versions were reconciled with a House vote of 330–59 on December 8 and a Senate voice-vote on December 9 before being passed on to President G.W. Bush for final approval. The White House had urged Congress to expedite the reconciliation process during the end-2006 lame duck session, and recommended removing certain amendments which would be deemed deal-killers by India. Nonetheless, while softened, several clauses restricting India's strategic nuclear program and conditions on having India align with U.S. views over Iran were incorporated in the Hyde Act.

In response to the language Congress used in the Act to define U.S. policy toward India, President Bush, stated "Given the Constitution's commitment to the authority of the presidency to conduct the nation's foreign affairs, the executive branch shall construe such policy statements as advisory," going on to cite sections 103 and 104 (d) (2) of the bill. To assure Congress that its work would not be totally discarded, Bush continued by saying that the executive would give "the due weight that comity between the legislative and executive branches should require, to the extent consistent with U.S. foreign policy."

On July 9, 2008, India formally submitted the safeguards agreement to the IAEA. This development came after the Prime Minister of India Manmohan Singh returned from the 34th G8 summit meeting in Tokyo where he met with U.S. President George W. Bush. On June 19, 2008, news media reported that Indian Prime Minister Dr. Manmohan Singh threatened to resign his position if the Left Front, whose support was crucial for the ruling United Progressive Alliance to prove its majority in the Indian parliament, continued to oppose the nuclear deal and he described their stance as irrational and reactionary. According to the Hindu, External Affairs Minister's Pranab Mukherjee's earlier statement said "I cannot bind the government if we lose our majority," implying that United Progressive Alliance government would not put its signature on any deal with IAEA if it lost the majority in either a 'opposition-initiated no-confidence motion' or if failing to muster a vote of confidence in Indian parliament after being told to prove its majority by the president. On July 08, 2008, Prakash Karat announced that the Left Front is withdrawing its support to the government over the decision by the government to go ahead on the United States-India Peaceful Atomic Energy Cooperation Act. The left front had been a staunch advocate of not proceeding with this deal citing national interests. On 22 July 2008 the UPA faced its first confidence vote in the Lok Sabha after the Communist Party of India (Marxist) led Left Front withdrew support over India approaching the IAEA for Indo-US nuclear deal. The UPA won the confidence vote with 275 votes to the opposition's 256, (10 members abstained from the vote) to record a 19-vote victory. The IAEA Board of Governors approved the safeguards agreement on August 1, 2008, and the 45-state Nuclear Suppliers Group next had to approve a policy allowing nuclear cooperation with India. U.S. President Bush can then make the necessary certifications and seek final approval by the U.S. Congress. There were objections from Pakistan, Iran, Ireland, Norway, Switzerland and Austria at the IAEA meeting.

On September 6, 2008 India was granted the waiver at the NSG meeting held in Vienna, Austria. The consensus was arrived at after overcoming misgivings expressed by Austria, Ireland and

New Zealand and is an unprecedented step in giving exemption to a country which has not signed the NPT and the Comprehensive Test Ban Treaty (CTBT). The Indian team who worked on the deal includes Manmohan Singh, Pranab Mukherjee, Shiv Shankar Menon, Shyam Saran, MK Narayanan, Anil Kakodkar, RB Grover, and DB Venkatesh Varma. An August 2008 U.S. draft exemption would have granted India a waiver based on the "steps that India has taken voluntarily as a contributing partner in the non-proliferation regime". Based on these steps, and without further conditions, the draft waiver would have allowed for the transfer to India of both trigger list and dual-use items (including technology), waiving the full-scope safeguards requirements of the NSG guidelines. A September 2008 waiver would have recognized additional "steps that India has voluntarily taken". The waiver called for notifying the NSG of bilateral agreements and for regular consultations; however, it also would have waived the full-scope safeguards requirements of the NSG guidelines without further conditions. The U.S. draft underwent further changes in an effort to make the language more acceptable to the NSG. The deal had initial support from the United States, the United Kingdom, France, Japan, Russia, and Germany. After some initial opposition, there were reports of Australia, Switzerland, and Canada expressing their support for the deal. Selig S. Harrison, a former South Asia bureau chief of The Washington Post, has said the deal may represent a tacit recognition of India as a nuclear weapon state, while former U.S. Undersecretary of State for Arms Control and International Security Robert Joseph says the U.S. State Department made it "very clear that we will not recognize India as a nuclear-weapon state".

Norway, Austria, Brazil, and Japan all warned that their support for India at the IAEA did not mean that they would not express reservations at the NSG. New Zealand, which is a member of the NSG but not of the IAEA Board of Governors, cautioned that its support should not be taken for granted. Ireland, which launched the non-proliferation treaty process in 1958 and signed it first in 1968, doubted India's nuclear trade agreement with the U.S. Russia, a potentially large nuclear supplier to India, expressed reservations about transferring enrichment and reprocessing technology to India. China argued the agreement constituted "a major blow to the international non-proliferation regime". New Zealand said it would like to see a few conditions written in to the waiver: the exemption ceasing if India conducts nuclear tests, India signing the International Atomic Energy Agency's (IAEA) additional protocol, and placing limits on the scope of the technology that can be given to India and which could relate to nuclear weapons. Austria, Ireland, the Netherlands, Switzerland and Scandinavian countries proposed similar amendments.

After the first NSG meeting in August 2008, diplomats noted that up to 20 of the 45 NSG states tabled conditions similar to the Hyde Act for India's waiver to do business with the NSG. "There were proposals on practically every paragraph," a European diplomat said. A group of seven NSG members suggested including some of the provisions of the U.S. Hyde Act in the final waiver. Daryll Kimball, executive director of the Washington-based Arms Control Association, said the NSG should at a minimum "make clear that nuclear trade with India shall be terminated if it resumes testing for any reason. If India cannot agree to such terms, it suggests that India is not serious about its nuclear test moratorium pledge."[80] It is believed that the U.S. will return with a new draft. After India was granted the waiver on September 6, the United Kingdom said that the NSG's decision would make a "significant contribution" to global energy and climate security. U.S. National Security Council spokesman Gordon Johndroe said, "this is a historic achievement that strengthens global non-proliferation principles while assisting India to meet its energy requirements in an environmentally friendly manner. The United States thanks the participating governments in the NSG for their outstanding efforts and cooperation to welcome India into the global non-proliferation community. We especially appreciate the role Germany played as chair to move this process forward." New Zealand praised the NSG consensus and said that it got the best possible deal with India. One of India's strongest allies Russia said in a statement, "We are convinced that the exemption made for India reflects Delhi's impeccable record in the non-proliferation sphere and will guarantee the peaceful uses of nuclear exports to India."

Initially, there were reports of People's Republic of China

analyzing the extent of the opposition against the waiver at the NSG and then revealing its position over the issue. On September 1, 2008, prominent Chinese newspaper People's Daily expressed its strong disapproval of the civilian agreement with India. India's National Security Advisor remarked that one of the major opponents of the waiver was China and said that he would express Indian government's displeasure over the issue. It was also revealed that China had abstained during the final voting process, indicating its non-approval of the nuclear agreement. In a statement, Chinese delegation to the NSG said the group should address the aspirations of other countries too, an implicit reference to Pakistan. There were also unconfirmed reports of India considering the cancellation of a state visit by Chinese Foreign Minister Yang Jiechi. However, External Affairs Minister Pranab Mukherjee said the Chinese Foreign Minister will be welcomed "as an honored guest". The Times of India noted that China's stance could have a long-term implication on Sino-Indian relations. There were some other conflicting reports on China's stance, however. The Hindu reported that though China had expressed its desire to include more stern language in the final draft, they had informed India about their intention to back the agreement. In an interview to the Hindustan Times, Chinese Assistant Foreign Minister Hu Zhengyue said that "China understands India's needs for civil nuclear energy and related international cooperation." Chinese Foreign Minister Yang Jiechi told India's CNN-IBN, "We didn't do anything to block it. We played a constructive role. We also adopted a positive and responsible attitude and a safeguards agreement was reached, so facts speak louder ... than some reports". Indian PM Manmohan Singh is expected to visit Washington D.C. on September 26, 2008 to celebrate the conclusion of the agreement with US President George W. Bush. He will also be visiting France to convey his appreciation for the country's stance. India's External Affairs Minister Pranab Mukherjee expressed his deep appreciation for India's allies in the NSG, especially the United States, United Kingdom, France, Russia, Germany, South Africa and Brazil for helping India achieve NSG's consensus on the nuclear deal. India also said that it would convey its special thanks to New Zealand's Governor General Anand Satyanand during his scheduled visit to New Delhi. Bhartiya Janata Party's Yashwant Sinha, who also formerly held the post of India's External Affairs Minister, criticized the Indian government's decision to seek NSG's consensus and remarked that "India has walked into the non-proliferation trap set by the US, we have given up our right to test nuclear weapons forever, it has been surrendered by the government". However, another prominent member of the same party and India's former National Security Advisor Brajesh Mishra supported the development at the NSG and said that the waiver granted made "no prohibition" on India to conduct nuclear tests in the future. Former President of India and noted Indian scientist, APJ Abdul Kalam, also supported the agreement and remarked that New Delhi may break its "voluntary moratorium" on further nuclear tests in "supreme national interest". However, analyst M K Bhadrakumar deferred. He said that the consensus at NSG was achieved on the "basis" of Pranab Mukherjee's commitment on India's voluntary moratorium on nuclear testing and by doing so, India has entered into a "multilateral commitment" bringing it within "the ambit of the CTBT and NPT". The NSG consensus was welcomed by several major Indian companies. Major Indian corporations like Videocon Group, Tata Power and Jindal Power saw a US$40 billion nuclear energy market in India in the next 10-15 years. On a more optimistic note, some of India's largest and most well-respected corporations like Bharat Heavy Electricals Limited, National Thermal Power Corporation and Larsen & Toubro were eyeing a US$100 billion business in this sector over the same time period. More than 150 non-proliferation activists and anti-nuclear organizations called for tightening the initial NSG agreement to prevent harming the current global non-proliferation regime. Among the steps called for were:

- ceasing cooperation if India conducts nuclear tests or withdraws from safeguards
- supplying only an amount of fuel which is commensurate with ordinary reactor operating requirements
- expressly prohibiting the transfer of enrichment, reprocessing and heavy water production items to India
  opposing any special safeguards exemptions for India
  conditioning the waiver on India stopping fissile production and legally binding itself not to conduct nuclear tests

- not allowing India to reprocess nuclear fuel supplied by a member state in a facility that is not under permanent and unconditional IAEA safeguards
- agreeing that all bilateral nuclear cooperation agreements between an NSG member-state and India explicitly prohibit the replication or use of such technology in any unsafeguarded Indian facilities

The call said that the draft Indian nuclear "deal would be a nonproliferation disaster and a serious setback to the prospects of global nuclear disarmament" and also pushed for all world leaders who are serious about ending the arms race to "to stand up and be counted."

Dr. Kaveh L Afrasiabi, who has taught political science at Tehran University, has argued the agreement will set a new precedent for other states, adding that the agreement represents a diplomatic boon for Tehran. Ali Ashgar Soltanieh, the Iranian Deputy Director General for International and Political Affairs, has complained the agreement may undermine the credibility, integrity and universality of the Nuclear Nonproliferation Treaty. Pakistan argues the safeguards agreement "threatens to increase the chances of a nuclear arms race in the subcontinent." Pakistani Foreign Minister Shah Mahmood Qureshi has suggested his country should be considered for such an accord, and Pakistan has also said the same process "should be available as a model for other non-NPT states". Israel is citing the Indo-U.S. civil nuclear deal as a precedent to alter Nuclear Suppliers Group (NSG) rules to construct its first nuclear power plant in the Negev desert, and is also pushing for its own trade exemptions.

Brahma Chellaney, a Professor of Strategic Studies at the New Delhi-based Centre for Policy Research, argued that the wording of the U.S. exemption sought to irrevocably tether New Delhi to the nuclear non-proliferation regime. He argued India would be brought under a wider non-proliferation net, with India being tied to compliance with the entire set of NSG rules. India would acquiesce to its unilateral test moratorium being turned into a multilateral legality. He concluded that instead of the "full" civil nuclear cooperation that the original July 18, 2005, deal promised, India's access to civil nuclear enrichment and reprocessing technologies would be restricted through the initial NSG waiver.

The Bush Administration told Congress in January 2008 that the United States may cease all cooperation with India if India detonates a nuclear explosive device. The Administration further said it was not its intention to assist India in the design, construction or operation of sensitive nuclear technologies through the transfer of dual-use items. The statements were considered sensitive in India because debate over the agreement in India could have toppled the government of Prime Minister Manmohan Singh. The State Department had requested they remain secret even though they were not classified. Secretary of State Condoleezza Rice also previously told the House Foreign Affairs Panel in public testimony that any agreement "will have to be completely consistent with the obligations of the Hyde Act". Both the Assistant Secretary of State for South and Central Asian Affairs Richard Boucher and the Former Assistant Secretary of State for Legislative Affairs Jeffrey Bergner have also said the agreement would be in conformity with the Hyde Act.

Howard Berman, chair of the U.S. House Foreign Affairs Committee, in a letter to US Secretary of State Condoleezza Rice has warned that an NSG waiver "inconsistent" with the 2006 Hyde Act will "jeopardise" the Indo-US nuclear deal in US Congress. Speaker of the House of Representatives Nancy Pelosi and Senate Majority leader Harry Reid have set September 26, 2008 as the adjournment date for Congress. Congressional officials have said the White House may be able to work with lawmakers to expedite a vote before Congress goes in to recess, while a hurdle for the White House is that a Democratic congress might not be inclined to give President Bush a significant victory during his waning days in office.

Representative Berman has said he will push for more information about the negotiations in Vienna before expediting a vote. Berman further said the Administration would have to show how the NSG decision is consistent with the Hyde Act, including which technologies can be sent to India and what impact a nuclear test by India would have. Edward J. Markey, co-chairman of the House Bipartisan Task Force on Non-proliferation, said there need to be clear consequences if India breaks its commitments or resumes nuclear testing.

Chapter 10

Overview of Alternative Energy Resources

RENEWABLE ENERGY

Introduction

Renewable energy is the energy generated from natural resources which are naturally replenished. Renewable Energy Technologies (RETs) include solar power, biomass, wind power, hydroelectricity, micro hydro, geothermal, bio-fuels, OTEC.

In 2006, 18% of global energy consumption came from renewables, with about 13% delivered by traditional biomass. Hydro was the next largest renewable source, providing 3%, followed by hot water/heating, which contributed 1.3%. Modern technologies, such as geothermal, wind, solar, and ocean energy together provided some 0.8% of final energy consumption. The technical potential for their use is very large, exceeding all other readily available sources.

Renewable energy technologies, though being dependent on nature and being intermittent, yet its importance is being realized and it is penetrating the market. Wind power, the most popular on commercial scale, is growing at the rate of 30 percent annually, with a worldwide installed capacity of over 100 GW. The manufacturing output of the photovoltaics industry reached more than 2,000 MW in 2006 and photovoltaic (PV) power stations are getting very popular in Germany. Solar thermal power stations operate in the USA and Spain, and the largest of these is the 354 MW SEGS power plant in the Mojave Desert. The world's largest geothermal power installation is The Geysers in California, with a rated capacity of 750 MW. Brazil has been aggressively involved in the production of ethanol fuel from sugar cane, and ethanol now provides 18 percent of the country's automotive fuel. Ethanol producing plants are also cultivated and used for fuel production very widely in the USA.

While there are many large-scale renewable energy projects and production, renewable technologies also suits small off-grid applications, sometimes in rural and remote areas, where energy is often crucial in human development. The higher initial cost of RETs is offset by the huge cost and difficulties involved in providing energy via conventional technologies to the far flung rural areas. Kenya has the world's highest household solar ownership rate with roughly 30,000 small (20–100 watt) solar power systems sold per year.

Climate change concerns coupled with energy security, high oil prices, and increasing government support are driving renewable energy legislation, incentives and commercialization. European Union leaders reached an agreement in principle in March 2007 that 20 percent of their nations' energy should be produced from renewable fuels by 2020, as part of its drive to cut emissions of carbon dioxide, blamed in part for global warming. Investment capital flowing into renewable energy climbed from $80 billion in 2005 to a record $100 billion in 2006. This level of investment combined with continuing double digit percentage increases each year has moved what once was considered alternative energy to mainstream. Wind was the first to provide 1% of electricity, but solar is not far behind. Some very large corporations such as BP, General Electric, Sharp, and Royal Dutch Shell are investing in the renewable energy sector.

Main Renewable Energy Technologies

The majority of renewable energy technologies are directly or indirectly powered by the sun. The Earth-Atmosphere system is in equilibrium such that heat radiation into space is equal to incoming solar radiation, the resulting level of energy within the Earth-Atmosphere system can roughly be described as the Earth's "climate." The hydrosphere (water) absorbs a major fraction of the incoming radiation. Most radiation is absorbed at low latitudes around the equator, but this energy is dissipated around the globe in the form of winds and ocean currents. Wave motion may play a role in the process of transferring mechanical energy between the atmosphere and the ocean through wind stress. Solar energy is also responsible for the distribution of precipitation which is tapped by hydroelectric projects, and for the growth of plants used to create bio-fuels.

Renewable energy is derived from natural processes that are replenished constantly. In its various forms, it derives directly from the sun, or from heat generated deep within the earth. Included in the definition is electricity and heat generated from solar, wind, ocean, hydropower, biomass, geothermal resources, and bio-fuels and hydrogen derived from renewable resources. Each of these sources has unique characteristics which influence how and where they are used.

Wind Power

Wind power is the conversion of wind energy into a useful form, such as electricity, using wind turbines. At the end of 2007, worldwide capacity of wind-powered generators was 94.1 gigawatts. Although wind produces about 1% of world-wide electricity use, it accounts for approximately 19% of electricity production in Denmark, 9% in Spain and Portugal, and 6% in Germany and the Republic of Ireland. Globally, wind power generation increased more than fivefold between 2000 and 2007.

The principle application of wind power is to generate electricity. Large scale wind farms are connected to electrical grids. Individual turbines can provide electricity to isolated locations. In the case of windmills, wind energy is used directly as mechanical energy for pumping water or grinding grain.

Wind energy is plentiful, renewable, widely distributed, clean, and reduces greenhouse gas emissions when it displaces fossil-fuel-derived electricity. Therefore, it is considered by experts to be more environmentally friendly than many other energy sources. The intermittency of wind seldom creates problems when using wind power to supply a low proportion of total demand. Where wind is to be used for a moderate fraction of demand, additional costs for compensation of intermittency are considered to be modest.

History of Wind Power

Humans have been using wind power for at least 5,500 years, and architects have used wind-driven natural ventilation in buildings since similarly ancient times. The use of wind to provide mechanical power came somewhat later in antiquity.

The Babylonian emperor Hammurabi planned to use wind power for his ambitious irrigation project in the 17th century BC. An early historical reference to a rudimentary windmill was used to power an organ in the 1st century AD. The first practical windmills were later built in Sistan, Afghanistan, from the 7th century. These were vertical-axle windmills, which had long vertical driveshafts with rectangle shaped blades. Made of six to twelve sails covered in reed matting or cloth material, these windmills were used to grind corn and draw up water, and were used in the gristmilling and sugarcane industries. Horizontal-axle windmills were later used extensively in Northwestern Europe to grind flour beginning in the 1180s, and many Dutch windmills still exist. In the United States, the development of the "water-pumping windmill" was the major factor in allowing the farming and ranching of vast areas of North America, which were otherwise devoid of readily accessible water. They contributed to the expansion of rail transport systems throughout the world, by pumping water from wells to supply the needs of the steam locomotives of those early times.

The multi-bladed wind turbine atop a lattice tower made of wood or steel was, for many years, a fixture of the landscape throughout rural America. The modern wind turbine was developed beginning in the 1980s, although designs are still under development.

Wind Energy

The origin of wind is complex. The Earth is unevenly heated by the sun resulting in the poles receiving less energy from the sun than the equator does. Also, the dry land heats up (and cools down) more quickly than the seas do. The differential heating drives a global atmospheric convection system reaching from the

Earth's surface to the stratosphere which acts as a virtual ceiling. Most of the energy stored in these wind movements can be found at high altitudes where continuous wind speeds of over 160 km/h (100 mph) occur. Eventually, the wind energy is converted through friction into diffuse heat throughout the Earth's surface and the atmosphere. There is an estimated 72 TW of wind energy on the Earth that potentially can be commercially viable. Not all the energy of the wind flowing past a given point can be recovered.

Distribution of Wind Speed

Distribution of wind speed (red) and energy (blue) for all of 2002 at the Lee Ranch facility in Colorado. The histogram shows measured data, while the curve is the Rayleigh model distribution for the same average wind speed. Energy is the Betz limit through a 100 meter diameter circle facing directly into the wind. Total energy for the year through that circle was 15.4 gigawatt-hours.The strength of wind varies, and an average value for a given location does not alone indicate the amount of energy a wind turbine could produce there. To assess the frequency of wind speeds at a particular location, a probability distribution function is often fit to the observed data. Different locations will have different wind speed distributions. The Rayleigh model closely mirrors the actual distribution of hourly wind speeds at many locations. Because so much power is generated by higher windspeed, much of the energy comes in short bursts. The 2002 Lee Ranch sample is telling; half of the energy available arrived in just 15% of the operating time. The consequence is that wind energy does not have as consistent an output as fuel-fired power plants; utilities that use wind power must provide backup generation for times that the wind is weak. Making wind power more consistent requires that storage technologies must be used to retain the large amount of power generated in the bursts for later use.

Grid Management System

Induction generators often used for wind power projects require reactive power for excitation, so substations used in wind-power collection systems include substantial capacitor banks for power factor correction. Different types of wind turbine generators behave differently during transmission grid disturbances, so extensive modelling of the dynamic electromechanical characteristics of a new wind farm is required by transmission system operators to ensure predictable stable behaviour during system faults In particular, induction generators cannot support the system voltage during faults, unlike steam or hydro turbine-driven synchronous generators (however properly matched power factor correction capacitors along with electronic control of resonance can support induction generation without grid). Doubly-fed machines, or wind turbines with solid-state converters between the turbine generator and the collector system, have generally more desirable properties for grid interconnection. Transmission systems operators will supply a wind farm developer with a grid code to specify the requirements for interconnection to the transmission grid. This will include power factor, constancy of frequency and dynamic behaviour of the wind farm turbines during a system fault.

Capacity Factor

Since wind speed is not constant, a wind farm's annual energy production is never as much as the sum of the generator nameplate ratings multiplied by the total hours in a year. The ratio of actual productivity in a year to this theoretical maximum is called the capacity factor. Typical capacity factors are 20-40%, with values at the upper end of the range in particularly favourable sites. For example, a 1 megawatt turbine with a capacity factor of 35% will not produce 8,760 megawatt-hours in a year (1x24x365), but only 0.35x24x365 = 3,066 MWh, averaging to 0.35 MW. Online data is available for some locations and the capacity factor can be calculated from the yearly output. Unlike fueled generating plants, the capacity factor is limited by the inherent properties of wind. Capacity factors of other types of power plant are based mostly on fuel cost, with a small amount of downtime for maintenance. Nuclear plants have low incremental fuel cost, and so are run at full output and achieve a 90% capacity factor. Plants with higher fuel cost are throttled back to follow load. Gas turbine plants using natural gas as fuel may be very expensive to operate and may be run only to meet peak power demand. A gas turbine plant may have an annual capacity factor of 5-25% due to relatively high energy production cost.

According to a 2007 Stanford University study published in the Journal of Applied Meteorology and Climatology, interconnecting ten or more wind farms allows 33 to 47% of the total energy produced to be used as reliable, baseload electric power, as long as minimum criteria are met for wind speed and turbine height.

Intermittency and Penetration Limits

Electricity generated from wind power can be highly variable at several different timescales: from hour to hour, daily, and seasonally. Annual variation also exists, but is not as significant. Because instantaneous electrical generation and consumption must remain in balance to maintain grid stability, this variability can present substantial challenges to incorporating large amounts of wind power into a grid system. Intermittency and the non-dispatchable nature of wind energy production can raise costs for regulation, incremental operating reserve, and (at high penetration levels) could require an increase in the already existing energy demand management, load shedding, or storage solutions or system interconnection with HVDC cables. At low levels of wind penetration, fluctuations in load and allowance for failure of large generating units requires reserve capacity that can also regulate for variability of wind generation. A series of detailed modelling studies which looked at the Europe wide adoption of renewable energy and interlinking power grids using HVDC cables, indicates that the entire power usage could come from renewables, with 70% total energy from wind at the same sort of costs or lower than at present. Intermittency would be dealt with, according to this model, by a combination of geographic dispersion to de-link weather system effects, and the ability of HVDC to shift power from windy areas to non-windy areas. Pumped-storage hydroelectricity or other forms of grid energy storage can store energy developed by high-wind periods and release it when needed. Stored energy increases the economic value of wind energy since it can be shifted to displace higher cost generation during peak demand periods. The potential revenue from this arbitrage can offset the cost and losses of storage; the cost of storage may add 25% to the cost of any wind energy stored, but it is not envisaged that this would apply to a large proportion of wind energy generated. Thus the 2 GW Dinorwig pumped storage plant adds costs to nuclear energy in the UK for which it was built, but not to all the power produced from the 30 or so GW of nuclear plants in the UK. In particular geographic regions, peak wind speeds may not coincide with peak demand for electrical power. In California and Texas, for example, hot days in summer may have low wind speed and high electrical demand due to air conditioning. However as pointed out in the previous paragraph but one, this can be addressed by interconnecting widely dispersed geographic areas with relatively cheap and efficient HVDC inter connectors. In the USA it is estimated that to upgrade the transmission system to take in planned or potential renewables would cost at least $60 billion. Total annual US power consumption in 2006 was 4 thousand billion kilowatt hours. Over an assett life of 40 years and low cost utility investment grade funding, the cost of $60 billion investment would be about 5% p.a. ie $3 billion p.a. Dividing by total power used gives an increased unit cost of around $3,000,000,000 x 100 / 4,000 x 1 exp9 = 0.075 cent / kWh. According to a 2007 Stanford University study published in the Journal of Applied Meteorology and Climatology, interconnecting ten or more wind farms allows 33 to 47% of the total energy produced to be used as reliable, baseload electric power, as long as minimum criteria are met for wind speed and turbine height. In the UK, however, winter demand is higher than summer demand, and so are wind speeds. Solar power tends to be complementary to wind on most days with no wind there is sun and on most days with no sun there is wind. A demonstration project at the Massachusetts Maritime Academy shows the effect. A combined power plant linking solar, wind, bio-gas and hydrostorage is proposed as a way to provide 100% renewable power. A report from Denmark noted that their wind power network was without power for 54 days during 2002. Wind power advocates argue that these periods of low wind can be dealt with by simply restarting existing power stations that have been held in readiness or interlinking with HVDC. The cost of keeping a power station idle is in fact quite low, since the main cost of running a power station is the fuel.

Penetration

Wind energy "penetration" refers to the fraction of energy produced by wind compared with the total available generation capacity. There is no generally accepted "maximum" level of wind penetration. The limit for a particular grid will depend on the existing generating plants, pricing mechanisms, capacity for storage or demand management, and other factors. An interconnected electricity grid will already include reserve generating and transmission capacity to allow for equipment failures; this reserve capacity can also serve to regulate for the varying power generation by wind plants. Studies have indicated that 20% of the total electrical energy consumption may be incorporated with minimal difficulty. These studies have been for locations with geographically dispersed wind farms, some degree of dispatchable energy, or hydropower with storage capacity, demand management, and interconnection to a large grid area export of electricity when needed. Beyond this level, there are few technical limits, but the economic implications become more significant. However In evidence to the House of Lords Economic Affairs Select Committee, the UK System Operator, National Grid have quoted estimates of balancing costs for 40% wind and these lie in the range £500-1000M per annum. "These balancing costs represent an additional £6 to £12 per annum on average consumer electricity bill of around £390." At present, few grid systems have penetration of wind energy above 5%: Denmark (values over 18%), Spain and Portugal (values over 9%), Germany and the Republic of Ireland (values over 6%). The Danish grid is heavily interconnected to the European electrical grid, and it has solved grid management problems by exporting almost half of its wind power to Norway. The correlation between electricity export and wind power production is very strong. Denmark has active plans to increase the percentage of power generated to over 50%. A study commissioned by the state of Minnesota considered penetration of up to 25%, and concluded that integration issues would be manageable and have incremental costs of less than one-half cent ($0.0045) per kWh. ESB National Grid, Ireland's electric utility, in a 2004 study that, concluded that to meet the renewable energy targets set by the EU in 2001 would "increase electricity generation costs by a modest 15%". A recent report by Sinclair

Merz saw no dificulty in accomodating 50% of total power delivered in the UK at modest cost increases.

Wind Power Forecasting

Related to variability is the short-term (hourly or daily) predictability of wind plant output. Like other electricity sources, wind energy must be "scheduled". The nature of this energy source makes it inherently variable. Wind power forecasting methods are used, but predictability of wind plant output remains low for short-term operation.

Wind farm

Good selection of a wind turbine site is critical to economic development of wind power. Aside from the availability of wind itself, other factors include the availability of transmission lines, value of energy to be produced, cost of land acquisition, land use considerations, and environmental impact of construction and operations. Off-shore locations may offset their higher construction cost with higher annual load factors, thereby reducing cost of energy produced. Wind farm designers use specialized wind energy software applications to evaluate the impact of these issues on a given wind farm design. Studies in the UK have shown that if onshore turbines are placed in a straight line then an increased risk of aerodynamic modulation can occur which can result in noise nuisance to nearby residents. The modern wind power industry began in 1979 with the serial production of wind turbines by Danish manufacturers Kuriant, Vestas, Nordtank, and Bonus. These early turbines were small by today's standards, with capacities of 20 to 30 kW each. Since then, they have increased greatly in size, while wind turbine production has expanded to many countries all over the world. There are now many thousands of wind turbines operating, with a total capacity of 73,904 MW of which wind power in Europe accounts for 65% (2006). Wind power was the fastest growing energy source at the end of 2004. World wind generation capacity more than quadrupled between 2000 and 2006. 81% of wind power installations are in the US and Europe, but the share of the top five countries in terms of new installations fell from 71% in 2004 to 62% in 2006. In 2007, the countries with the highest total installed capacity were Germany, the United States, Spain, India, and China. By 2010, the World Wind Energy Association expects 160GW of capacity to be installed worldwide, up from 73.9 GW at the end of 2006, implying an anticipated net growth rate of more than 21% per year. Denmark generates nearly one-fifth of its electricity with wind turbines—the highest percentage of any country—and is fifth in the world in total wind power generation. Denmark is prominent in the manufacturing and use of wind turbines, with a commitment made in the 1970s to eventually produce half of the country's power by wind.

In recent years, the United States has added more wind energy to its grid than any other country; U.S. wind power capacity grew by 45% to 16.8 gigawatts in 2007. Texas has become the largest wind energy producing state, surpassing California. In 2007, the state expects to add 2 gigawatts to its existing capacity of approximately 4.5 gigawatts. Iowa and Minnesota are expected to each produce 1 gigawatt by late-2007. Wind power generation in the U.S. was up 31.8% in February, 2007 from February, 2006. The average output of one megawatt of wind power is equivalent to the average electricity consumption of about 250 American households. According to the American Wind Energy Association, wind will generate enough electricity in 2008 to power just over 1% (4.5 million households) of total electricity in U.S., up from less than 0.1% in 1999. U.S. Department of Energy studies have concluded wind harvested in Texas, Kansas, and North Dakota could provide enough electricity to power the entire nation, and that offshore wind farms could do the same job.

India ranks 4th in the world with a total wind power capacity of 8,000 MW in 2007, or 3% of all electricity produced in India. The World Wind Energy Conference in New Delhi in November 2006 has given additional impetus to the Indian wind industry. Muppandal village in Tamil Nadu state, India, has several wind turbine farms in its vicinity, and is one of the major wind energy harnessing centres in India led by majors like Suzlon, Vestas, Micon among others. In 2005, China announced it would build a 1000-megawatt wind farm in Hebei for completion in 2020. China reportedly has set a generating target of 20,000 MW by 2020 from renewable energy sources—it says indigenous wind power could generate up to 253,000 MW. Following the World Wind Energy

Conference in November 2004, organised by the Chinese and the World Wind Energy Association, a Chinese renewable energy law was adopted. In late 2005, the Chinese government increased the official wind energy target for the year 2020 from 20 GW to 30 GW.

Mexico recently opened La Venta II wind power project as an important step in reducing Mexico's consumption of fossil fuels. The 88 MW project is the first of its kind in Mexico, and will provide 13 percent of the electricity needs of the state of Oaxaca. By 2012 the project will have a capacity of 3500 MW. Another growing market is Brazil, with a wind potential of 143 GW. The federal government has created an incentive program, called Proinfa, to build production capacity of 3300 MW of renewable energy for 2008, of which 1422 MW through wind energy. The program seeks to produce 10% of Brazilian electricity through renewable sources. South Africa has a proposed station situated on the West Coast north of the Olifants River mouth near the town of Koekenaap, east of Vredendal in the Western Cape province. The station is proposed to have a total output of 100MW although there are negotiations to double this capacity. The plant could be operational by 2010. France has announced a target of 12,500 MW installed by 2010. Canada experienced rapid growth of wind capacity between 2000 and 2006, with total installed capacity increasing from 137 MW to 1,451 MW, and showing an annual growth rate of 38%. Particularly rapid growth was seen in 2006, with total capacity doubling from the 684 MW at end-2005. This growth was fed by measures including installation targets, economic incentives and political support. For example, the Ontario government announced that it will introduce a feed-in tariff for wind power, referred to as 'Standard Offer Contracts', which may boost the wind industry across the province. In Quebec, the provincially-owned electric utility plans to purchase an additional 2000 MW by 2013.

Small Scale Wind Power

This wind turbine charges a 12 volt battery to run 12 volt appliances.Small wind generation systems with capacities of 50 kW or, less are usually used to produce power. Isolated communities that otherwise rely on diesel generators may use wind turbines to displace diesel fuel consumption. Individuals purchase these systems to reduce or eliminate their electricity bills, or simply to generate their own clean power. Wind turbines have been used for household electricity generation in conjunction with battery storage over many decades in remote areas. Increasingly, U.S. consumers are choosing to purchase grid-connected turbines in the 1 to 10 kilowatt range to power their whole homes. Household generator units of more than 1 kW are now functioning in several countries, and in every state in the U.S. Grid-connected wind turbines may use grid energy storage, displacing purchased energy with local production when available. Off-grid system users either adapt to intermittent power or use batteries, photovoltaic or diesel systems to supplement the wind turbine. In urban locations, where it is difficult to obtain predictable or large amounts of wind energy (little is known about the actual wind resource of towns and cities), smaller systems may still be used to run low power equipment. Equipment such as parking meters or wireless internet gateways may be powered by a wind turbine that charges a small battery, replacing the need for a connection to the power grid, making the potential carbon savings of small wind turbines difficult to determine. A new Carbon Trust study into the potential of small-scale wind energy has found that small wind turbines could provide up to 1.5 Terawatt Hours (TWh) per year of electricity (0.4% of total UK electricity consumption) and 0.6 million tonnes of carbon dioxide ($MtCO_2$) emission savings. This is based on 10% of households installing turbines at costs competitive with grid electricity, which is currently around 12p per kWh.

Economics and Feasibility

Global Wind Energy Council (GWEC) figures show that 2007 recorded an increase of installed capacity of 20 GW, taking the total installed wind energy capacity to 94 GW, up from 74 GW in 2006. Despite constraints facing supply chains for wind turbines, the annual market for wind continued to increase at an estimated rate of 31% following 32% growth in 2006. In terms of economic value, the wind energy sector has become one of the important players in the energy markets, with the total value of new generating equipment installed in 2007 reaching €25 billion, or

US$36 billion. In 2004, wind energy cost one-fifth of what it did in the 1980s, and some expected that downward trend to continue as larger multi-megawatt turbines are mass-produced. However, installed cost averaged €1,300 per kilowatt in 2007, compared to €1,100 per kilowatt in 2005. Not as many facilities can produce large modern turbines and their towers and foundations, so constraints develop in the supply of turbines resulting in higher costs.

Wind and hydro power have negligible fuel costs and relatively low maintenance costs; in economic terms, wind power has a low marginal cost and a high proportion of capital cost. The estimated average cost per unit incorporates the cost of construction of the turbine and transmission facilities, borrowed funds, return to investors (including cost of risk), estimated annual production, and other components, averaged over the projected useful life of the equipment, which may be in excess of twenty years. Energy cost estimates are highly dependent on these assumptions so published cost figures can differ substantially. A British Wind Energy Association report gives an average generation cost of onshore wind power of around 3.2 pence per kilowatt hour. Cost per unit of energy produced was estimated in 2006 to be comparable to the cost of new generating capacity in the United States for coal and natural gas: wind cost was estimated at $55.80 per MWh, coal at $53.10/MWh and natural gas at $52.50. Other sources in various studies have estimated wind to be more expensive than other sources (see Economics of new nuclear power plants, Clean coal, and Carbon capture and storage). Similar methods apply to other electrical energy sources. Existing generation capacity represents sunk costs, and the decision to continue production will depend on marginal costs going forward, not estimated average costs at project inception. For example, the estimated cost of new wind power capacity may be lower than that for "new coal" (estimated average costs for new generation capacity) but higher than for "old coal" (marginal cost of production for existing capacity). Therefore, the choice to increase wind capacity will depend on factors including the profile of existing generation capacity. Research from a wide variety of sources in various countries shows that support for wind power is consistently between 70 and 80 per cent amongst the general public.

Theoretical Potential

Wind power available in the atmosphere is much greater than current world energy consumption. The most comprehensive study to date found the potential of wind power on land and near-shore to be 72 TW, equivalent to 54,000 MToE (million tons of oil equivalent) per year, or over five times the world's current energy use in all forms. The potential takes into account only locations with mean annual wind speeds = 6.9 m/s at 80 m. It assumes 6 turbines per square km for 77 m diameter, 1.5 MW-turbines on roughly 13% of the total global land area (though that land would also be available for other compatible uses such as farming). The practical limit to exploitation of wind power will be set by economic and environmental factors, since the resource available is far larger than any practical means to develop it.

Many potential sites for wind farms are far from demand centres, requiring substantially more money to construct new transmission lines and substations. Since the primary cost of producing wind energy is construction and there are no fuel costs, the average cost of wind energy per unit of production is dependent on a few key assumptions, such as the cost of capital and years of assumed service. The marginal cost of wind energy once a plant is constructed is usually less than 1 cent per kilowatt-hour. Since the cost of capital plays a large part in projected cost, risk (as perceived by investors) will affect projected costs per unit of electricity. The commercial viability of wind power also depends on the pricing regime for power producers. Electricity prices are highly regulated worldwide, and in many locations may not reflect the full cost of production, let alone indirect subsidies or negative externalities. Customers may enter into long-term pricing contracts for wind to reduce the risk of future pricing changes, thereby ensuring more stable returns for projects at the development stage. These may take the form of standard offer contracts, whereby the system operator undertakes to purchase power from wind at a fixed price for a certain period (perhaps up to a limit); these prices may be different than purchase prices from other sources, and even incorporate an implicit subsidy. In jurisdictions where the price for electricity is based on market mechanisms, revenue for all producers per unit is higher when their production coincides with periods of higher prices. The profitability of wind farms will therefore be higher if their production schedule coincides with these periods. If wind represents a significant portion of supply, average revenue per unit of production may be lower as more expensive and less-efficient forms of generation, which typically set revenue levels, are displaced from economic dispatch. This may be of particular concern if the output of many wind plants in a market have strong temporal correlation. In economic terms, the marginal revenue of the wind sector as penetration increases may diminish.

Most forms of energy production create some form of negative externality: costs that are not paid by the producer or consumer of the good. For electric production, the most significant externality is pollution, which imposes social costs in increased health expenses, reduced agricultural productivity, and other problems. In addition, carbon dioxide, a greenhouse gas produced when fossil fuels are burned, may impose even greater costs in the form of global warming. Few mechanisms currently exist to internalise these costs, and the total cost is highly uncertain. Other significant externalities can include military expenditures to ensure access to fossil fuels, remediation of polluted sites, destruction of wild habitat, loss of scenery/tourism, etc. If the external costs are taken into account, wind energy may be competitive in more cases. Wind energy costs have generally decreased due to technology development and scale enlargement. Wind energy supporters argue that, once external costs and subsidies to other forms of electrical production are accounted for, wind energy is amongst the least costly forms of electrical production. Critics argue that the level of required subsidies, the small amount of energy needs met, the expense of transmission lines to connect the wind farms to population centers, and the uncertain financial returns to wind projects make it inferior to other energy sources. Intermittency and other characteristics of wind energy also have costs that may rise with higher levels of penetration, and may change the cost-benefit ratio.

Incentives

Wind energy benefits from subsidies of various kinds in many jurisdictions, either to increase its attractiveness, or to compensate for subsidies received by other forms of production or which have significant negative externalities. In the United States, wind power receives a tax credit for each kilowatt-hour produced; at 1.9 cents per kilowatt-hour in 2006, the credit has a yearly inflationary adjustment. Another tax benefit is accelerated depreciation. Many American states also provide incentives, such as exemption from property tax, mandated purchases, and additional markets for "green credits." Countries such as Canada and Germany also provide incentives for wind turbine construction, such as tax credits or minimum purchase prices for wind generation, with assured grid access (sometimes referred to as feed-in tariffs). These feed-in tariffs are typically set well above average electricity prices. Secondary market forces also provide incentives for businesses to use wind-generated power, even if there is a premium price for the electricity. For example, socially responsible manufacturers pay utility companies a premium that goes to subsidize and build new wind power infrastructure. Companies like the Borealis Press print millions of greeting cards every year using this wind-generated power, and in return they can claim that they are making a powerful "green" effort, in addition to using recycled, chlorine-free paper, soy inks, and safe press wash.

Environmental Effects

Wind power consumes no fuel for continuing operation, and has no emissions directly related to electricity production. Operation does not produce carbon dioxide, sulfur dioxide, mercury, particulates, or any other type of air pollution, as do fossil fuel power sources. Wind power plants consume resources in manufacturing and construction. During manufacture of the wind turbine, steel, concrete, aluminum and other materials will have to be made and transported using energy-intensive processes, generally using fossil energy sources. The initial carbon dioxide emissions "pay back" is within about 9 months of operation for off shore turbines.

Danger to birds is often the main complaint against the installation of a wind turbine. However, studies show that the number of birds killed by wind turbines is negligible compared to the number that die as a result of other human activities such as traffic, hunting, power lines and high-rise buildings and especially the environmental impacts of using non-clean power sources. For example, in the UK, where there are several hundred turbines, about one bird is killed per turbine per year; 10 million per year are killed by cars alone. Migratory bat species appear to be particularly at risk, especially during key movement periods (spring and more importantly in fall). Lasiurines such as the hoary bat, red bat, and the silver-haired bat appear to be most vulnerable at North American sites. Almost nothing is known about current populations of these species and the impact on bat numbers as a result of mortality at windpower locations. Offshore wind sites 10 km or more from shore do not interact with bat populations. Aesthetics have also been a concern. The Massachusetts Cape Wind project was delayed for years mainly because of aesthetic concerns.

Solar Power

Solar energy refers to the utilization of the radiant energy from the Sun. Solar power is used interchangeably with solar energy, but refers more specifically to the conversion of sunlight into electricity by photovoltaics, concentrating solar thermal devices, or by an experimental technology such as a solar chimney or solar pond.

Solar energy and shading are important considerations in building design. Thermal mass is used to conserve the heat that sunshine delivers to all buildings. Daylighting techniques optimize the use of light in buildings. Solar water heaters heat swimming pools and provide domestic hot water. In agriculture, greenhouses expand growing seasons and pumps powered by solar cells (known as photovoltaics) provide water for grazing animals. Evaporation ponds are used to harvest salt and clean waste streams of contaminants. Solar distillation and disinfection techniques produce potable water for millions of people worldwide. Simple applications include clotheslines and solar cookers which concentrate sunlight for cooking, drying and pasteurization. More sophisticated technologies concentrate sunlight for high-temperature material testing, metal smelting and industrial chemical production. A range of experimental solar vehicles provide ground, air and sea transportation.

Insolation and Solar Radiation

The Earth receives 174 petawatts (PW) of incoming solar radiation (insolation) at the upper atmosphere. Approximately 30% is reflected back to space while the rest is absorbed by clouds, oceans and land masses. The spectrum of solar light at the Earth's surface is mostly spread across the visible and near-infrared ranges with a small part in the near-ultraviolet. The absorbed solar light heats the land surface, oceans and atmosphere. The warm air containing evaporated water from the oceans rises, driving atmospheric circulation or convection. When this air reaches a high altitude, where the temperature is low, water vapor condenses into clouds, which rain onto the earth's surface, completing the water cycle. The latent heat of water condensation amplifies convection, producing atmospheric phenomena such as cyclones and anti-cyclones. Wind is a manifestation of the atmospheric circulation driven by solar energy. Sunlight absorbed by the oceans and land masses keeps the surface at an average temperature of 14°C. The conversion of solar energy into chemical energy via photosynthesis produces food, wood and the biomass from which fossil fuels are derived. Solar radiation along with secondary solar resources such as wind and wave power, hydroelectricity and biomass account for over 99.9% of the available flow of renewable energy on Earth. The total solar energy absorbed by Earth's atmosphere, oceans and land masses is approximately 3,850 zettajoules (ZJ) per year. In 2002, this was more energy in one hour than the world used in one year. Photosynthesis captures approximately 3 ZJ per year in biomass. The amount of solar energy reaching the surface of the planet is so vast that in one year it is about twice as much as will ever be obtained from all of the Earth's non-renewable resources of coal, oil, natural gas, and mined uranium combined.

Applications of Solar Energy Technology

Average insolation showing land area (small black dots) required to replace the total world energy supply with solar electricity. Insolation for most people is from 150 to 300 W/m^2 or 3.5 to 7.0 kWh/m^2/day. Solar energy technologies use solar radiation for practical ends. Technologies that use secondary solar resources such as biomass, wind, waves and ocean thermal gradients can be included in a broader description of solar energy but only primary resource applications are discussed here. Because the performance of solar technologies varies widely between regions, they should be deployed in a way that carefully considers these variations. Solar technologies are broadly characterized as either passive or active depending on the way they capture, convert and distribute sunlight. Active solar techniques use photovoltaic panels, pumps, and fans to convert sunlight into useful outputs. Passive solar techniques include selecting materials with favorable thermal properties, designing spaces that naturally circulate air, and referencing the position of a building to the Sun. Active solar technologies increase the supply of energy and are considered supply side technologies, while passive solar technologies reduce the need for alternate resources and are generally considered demand side technologies.

Architecture and Urban Planning

Darmstadt University of Technology won the 2007 Solar Decathlon in Washington, D.C. with this passive house designed specifically for the humid and hot subtropical climate. Sunlight has influenced building design since the beginning of architectural history. Advanced solar architecture and urban planning methods were first employed by the Greeks and Chinese, who oriented their buildings toward the south to provide light and warmth. The common features of passive solar architecture are orientation relative to the Sun, compact proportion (a low surface area to volume ratio), selective shading (overhangs) and thermal mass. When these features are tailored to the local climate and environment they can produce well-lit spaces that stay in a comfortable temperature range. Socrates' Megaron House is a classic example of passive solar design. The most recent approaches to solar design use computer modeling tying together solar lighting, heating and ventilation systems in an integrated solar design package. Active solar equipment such as pumps, fans and switchable windows can complement passive design and improve system performance. Urban heat islands (UHI) are metropolitan areas with higher temperatures than that of the surrounding environment. The higher temperatures are a result of increased absorption of the Solar light by urban materials such as asphalt and concrete, which have lower albedos and higher heat capacities than those in the natural environment. A straightforward method of counteracting the UHI effect is to paint buildings and roads white and plant trees. Using these methods, a hypothetical "cool communities" program in Los Angeles has projected that urban temperatures could be reduced by approximately 3 ℃ at an estimated cost of US$1 billion, giving estimated total annual benefits of US$530 million from reduced air-conditioning costs and healthcare savings.

Agriculture and Horticulture

Greenhouses like these in the Netherland's Westland municipality grow vegetables, fruits and flowers. Agriculture seeks to optimize the capture of solar energy in order to optimize the productivity of plants. Techniques such as timed planting cycles, tailored row orientation, staggered heights between rows and the mixing of plant varieties can improve crop yields. While sunlight is generally considered a plentiful resource, the exceptions highlight the importance of solar energy to agriculture. During the short growing seasons of the Little Ice Age, French and English farmers employed fruit walls to maximize the collection of solar energy. These walls acted as thermal masses and accelerated ripening by keeping plants warm. Early fruit walls were built perpendicular to the ground and facing south, but over time, sloping walls were developed to make better use of sunlight. In 1699, Nicolas Fatio de Duillier even suggested using a tracking mechanism which could pivot to follow the Sun. Applications of solar energy in agriculture aside from growing crops include pumping water, drying crops, brooding chicks and drying chicken manure. Greenhouses convert solar light to heat, enabling year-round production and the growth (in enclosed environments) of specialty crops and other plants not naturally suited to the local climate. Primitive greenhouses were first used during Roman times to produce cucumbers year-round for the Roman emperor Tiberius. The first modern greenhouses were built in Europe in the 16th century to keep exotic plants brought back from explorations abroad. Greenhouses remain an important part of horticulture today, and plastic transparent materials have also been used to similar effect in polytunnels and row covers.

Solar Lighting

Daylighting features such as this oculus at the top of the Pantheon in Rome have been in use since antiquity. The history of lighting is dominated by the use of natural light. The Romans recognized a right to light as early as the 6th century and English law echoed these judgments with the Prescription Act of 1832. In the 20th century artificial lighting became the main source of interior illumination. Daylighting systems collect and distribute sunlight to provide interior illumination; they are passive systems. They directly offset energy use by replacing artificial lighting, and indirectly offset non-solar energy use by reducing the need for air-conditioning. The use of natural lighting offers physiological and psychological benefits compared to artificial lighting, which is difficult to quantify though. Daylighting design implies careful selection of window types, sizes and orientation; exterior shading devices may be considered as well. Individual features include sawtooth roofs, clerestory windows, light shelves, skylights and light tubes. They may be incorporated into existing structures, but are most effective when integrated into a solar design package that accounts for factors such as glare, heat flux and time-of-use. When daylighting features are properly implemented they can reduce lighting-related energy requirements by 25%. An important active solar lighting method is the hybrid solar lighting (HSL). HSL systems collect sunlight using focusing mirrors that track the Sun and use optical fibers to transmit it into a building's interior to supplement conventional lighting. In single-story applications these systems are able to transmit 50% of the direct sunlight received. Solar lights that charge during the day and light up at dusk are a common sight along walkways. Although daylight saving time is promoted as a way to use sunlight to save energy, recent research has been limited and reports contradictory results: several studies report savings, but just as many suggest no effect or even a net loss, particularly when gasoline consumption is taken into account. Electricity use is greatly affected by geography, climate and economics, making it hard to generalize from single studies.

Solar Thermal

Solar thermal technologies can be used for water heating, space heating, space cooling and process heat generation.

Solar water heaters facing the Sun to maximize gain Solar hot water systems use sunlight to heat water. In low geographical latitudes (below 40 degrees) from 60 to 70% of the domestic hot water use with temperatures up to 60 °C can be provided by solar heating systems. The most common types of solar water heaters are evacuated tube collectors (44%) and glazed flat plate collectors (34%) generally used for domestic hot water; and unglazed plastic collectors (21%) used mainly to heat swimming pools. As of 2007, the total installed capacity of solar hot water systems is approximately 154 GW. China is the world leader in their deployment with 70 GW installed as of 2006 and a long-term goal of 210 GW by 2020. Israel is the per capita leader in the use of solar hot water systems with 90% of homes using them. In the United States, Canada and Australia heating swimming pools is the dominant application of solar hot water with an installed capacity of 18 GW as of 2005.

MIT's Solar House #1, built in 1939, used seasonal thermal storage for year-round heating. In the United States, heating, ventilation and air conditioning (HVAC) systems account for 30% (4.65 EJ) of the energy used in commercial buildings and nearly 50% (10.1 EJ) of the energy used in residential buildings. Solar heating, cooling and ventilation technologies can be used to offset a portion of this energy. Thermal mass is any material that can be used to store heat—heat from the Sun in the case of solar energy. Common thermal mass materials include stone, cement and water. Historically they have been used in arid climates or warm temperate regions to keep buildings cool by absorbing solar energy during the day and radiating stored heat to the cooler atmosphere at night. However they can be used in cold temperate areas to maintain warmth as well. The size and placement of thermal mass depend on several factors such as climate, daylighting and shading conditions. When properly incorporated, thermal mass maintains space temperatures in a comfortable range and reduces the need for auxiliary heating and cooling equipment.

A solar chimney (or thermal chimney, in this context) is a passive solar ventilation system composed of a vertical shaft connecting the interior and exterior of a building. As the chimney warms, the air inside is heated causing an updraft that pulls air through the building. Performance can be improved by using glazing and thermal mass materials in a way that mimics greenhouses. Deciduous trees and plants have been promoted as a means of controlling solar heating and cooling. When planted on the southern side of a building, their leaves provide shade during the summer, while the bare limbs allow light to pass during the winter. Since bare, leafless trees shade 1/3 to 1/2 of incident solar radiation, there is a balance between the benefits of summer shading and the corresponding loss of winter heating. In climates with significant heating loads, deciduous trees should not be planted on the southern side of a building because they will interfere with winter solar availability. They can, however, be used on the east and west sides to provide a degree of summer shading without appreciably affecting winter solar gain.

Desalination and Disinfection

Application of SODIS technology in Indonesia to water disinfection. Solar distillation can be used to make saline or brackish water potable. The first recorded instance of this was by 16th century Arab alchemists. A large-scale solar distillation project was first constructed in 1872 in the Chilean mining town of Las Salinas. The plant, which had solar collection area of 4,700 m^2, could produce up to 22,700 L per day and operated for 40 years. Individual still designs include single-slope, double-slope (or greenhouse type), vertical, conical, inverted absorber, multi-wick, and multiple effect. These stills can operate in passive, active, or hybrid modes. Double-slope stills are the most economical for decentralized domestic purposes, while active multiple effect units are more suitable for large-scale applications. Solar water disinfection (SODIS) involves exposing water-filled plastic polyethylene terephthalate (PET) bottles sunlight for several hours. Exposure times vary depending on weather and climate from a minimum of six hours to two days during fully overcast conditions. SODIS is recommended by the World Health Organization as a viable method for household water treatment and safe storage. Over two million people in developing countries use SODIS for their daily drinking water.

Solar Cooker

The Solar Bowl in Auroville, India, concentrates sunlight on a movable receiver to produce steam for cooking.Solar cookers use sunlight for cooking, drying and pasteurization. They can be grouped into three broad categories: box cookers, panel cookers and reflector cookers. The simplest solar cooker—the box cooker first built by Horace de Saussure in 1767. A basic box cooker consists of an insulated container with a transparent lid. It can be used effectively with partially overcast skies and will typically reach temperatures of 90–150°C. Panel cookers use a reflective panel to direct sunlight onto an insulated container and reach temperatures comparable to box cookers. Reflector cookers use various concentrating geometries (dish, trough, Fresnel mirrors) to focus light on a cooking container. These cookers reach temperatures of 315°C and above but require direct light to function properly and must be repositioned to track the Sun. The solar bowl is a concentrating technology employed by the Solar Kitchen in Auroville, India, where a stationary spherical reflector focuses light along a line perpendicular to the sphere's interior surface, and a computer control system moves the receiver to intersect this line. Steam is produced in the receiver at temperatures reaching 150°C and then used for process heat in the kitchen. A reflector developed by Wolfgang Scheffler in 1986 is used in many solar kitchens. Scheffler reflectors are flexible parabolic dishes that combine aspects of trough and power tower concentrators. Polar tracking is used to follow the Sun's daily course and the curvature of the reflector is adjusted for seasonal variations in the incident angle of sunlight. These reflectors can reach temperatures of 450–650°C and have a fixed focal point, which simplifies cooking. The world's largest Scheffler reflector system in Abu Road, Rajasthan, India is capable of cooking up to 35,000 meals a day. As of 2008, over 2,000 large Scheffler cookers had been built worldwide.

Solar Pond, Salt Evaporation Pond, and Solar Furnace

STEP parabolic dishes used for steam production and electrical generationSolar concentrating technologies such as parabolic dish, trough and Scheffler reflectors can provide process heat for commercial and industrial applications. The first commercial system was the Solar Total Energy Project (STEP) in Shenandoah, Georgia, USA where a field of 114 parabolic dishes provided 50%

of the process heating, air conditioning and electrical requirements for a clothing factory. This grid-connected cogeneration system provided 400 kW of electricity plus thermal energy in the form of 401 kW steam and 468 kW chilled water, and had a one hour peak load thermal storage. Evaporation ponds are shallow pools that concentrate dissolved solids through evaporation. The use of evaporation ponds to obtain salt from sea water is one of the oldest applications of solar energy. Modern uses include concentrating brine solutions used in leach mining and removing dissolved solids from waste streams. Clothes lines, clotheshorses, and clothes racks dry clothes through evaporation. These devices use wind and sunlight instead of electricity or natural gas. Florida legislation specifically protects the 'right to dry' and similar solar rights legislation has been passed in Utah and Hawaii. Unglazed transpired collectors (UTC) are perforated sun-facing walls used for preheating ventilation air. UTCs can raise the incoming air temperature up to 22°C and deliver outlet temperatures of 45–60°C. The short payback period of transpired collectors (3 to 12 years) makes them a more cost-effective alternative than glazed collection systems. As of 2003, over 80 systems with a combined collector area of 35,000 m^2 had been installed worldwide, including an 860 m^2 collector in Costa Rica used for drying coffee beans and a 1,300 m^2 collector in Coimbatore, India used for drying marigolds.

Solar Electricity

Sunlight can be converted into electricity using photovoltaics (PV), concentrating solar power (CSP), and various experimental technologies. PV has mainly been used to power small and medium-sized applications, from the calculator powered by a single solar cell to off-grid homes powered by a photovoltaic array. For large-scale generation, CSP plants like SEGS have been the norm but recently multi-megawatt PV plants are becoming common. Completed in 2007, the 14 MW power station in Clark County, Nevada and the 20 MW site in Beneixama, Spain are characteristic of the trend toward larger photovoltaic power stations in the US and Europe.

Photovoltaics

11 MW Serpa solar power plant in PortugalA solar cell, or photovoltaic cell (PV), is a device that converts light into direct current using the photoelectric effect. The first solar cell was constructed by Charles Fritts in the 1880s. Although the prototype selenium cells converted less than 1% of incident light into electricity, both Ernst Werner von Siemens and James Clerk Maxwell recognized the importance of this discovery. Following the work of Russell Ohl in the 1940s, researchers Gerald Pearson, Calvin Fuller and Daryl Chapin created the silicon solar cell in 1954. These early solar cells cost 286 USD/watt and reached efficiencies of 4.5–6%. The earliest significant application of solar cells was as a back-up power source to the Vanguard I satellite, which allowed it to continue transmitting for over a year after its chemical battery was exhausted. The successful operation of solar cells on this mission was duplicated in many other Soviet and American satellites, and by the late 1960s, PV had become the established source of power for them. Photovoltaics went on to play an essential part in the success of early commercial satellites such as Telstar, and they remain vital to the telecommunications infrastructure today. The high cost of solar cells limited terrestrial uses throughout the 1960s. This changed in the early 1970s when prices reached levels that made PV generation competitive in remote areas without grid access. Early terrestrial uses included powering telecommunication stations, off-shore oil rigs, navigational buoys and railroad crossings. These off-grid applications have proven very successful and accounted for over half of worldwide installed capacity until 2004. Building-integrated photovoltaics cover the roofs of the increasing number of homes. The 1973 oil crisis stimulated a rapid rise in the production of PV during the 1970s and early 1980s. Economies of scale which resulted from increasing production along with improvements in system performance brought the price of PV down from 100 USD/watt in 1971 to 7 USD/watt in 1985. Steadily falling oil prices during the early 1980s led to a reduction in funding for photovoltaic R&D and a discontinuation of the tax credits associated with the Energy Tax Act of 1978. These factors moderated growth to approximately 15% per year from 1984 through 1996. Since the mid-1990s, leadership in the PV sector has

shifted from the US to Japan and Germany. Between 1992 and 1994 Japan increased R&D funding, established net metering guidelines, and introduced a subsidy program to encourage the installation of residential PV systems. As a result, PV installations in the country climbed from 31.2 MW in 1994 to 318 MW in 1999, and worldwide production growth increased to 30% in the late 1990s.

Germany has become the leading PV market worldwide since revising its Feed-in tariff system as part of the Renewable Energy Sources Act. Installed PV capacity has risen from 100 MW in 2000 to approximately 4,150 MW at the end of 2007. Spain has become the third largest PV market after adopting a similar feed-in tariff structure in 2004, while France, Italy, South Korea and the US have seen rapid growth recently due to various incentive programs and local market conditions.

Concentrating Solar Power

Solar troughs are the most widely deployed and the most cost-effective CSP technology. Concentrated sunlight has been used to perform useful tasks since the time of ancient China. A legend claims that Archimedes used polished shields to concentrate sunlight on the invading Roman fleet and repel them from Syracuse. Auguste Mouchout used a parabolic trough to produce steam for the first solar steam engine in 1866, and subsequent developments led to the use of concentrating solar-powered devices for irrigation, refrigeration and locomotion. Concentrating Solar Power (CSP) systems use lenses or mirrors and tracking systems to focus a large area of sunlight into a small beam. The concentrated light is then used as a heat source for a conventional power plant. A wide range of concentrating technologies exist; the most developed are the solar trough, parabolic dish and solar power tower. These methods vary in the way they track the Sun and focus light. In all these systems a working fluid is heated by the concentrated sunlight, and is then used for power generation or energy storage. The PS10 concentrates sunlight from a field of heliostats on a central tower. A solar trough consists of a linear parabolic reflector that concentrates light onto a receiver positioned along the reflector's focal line. The reflector is made to follow the Sun during the daylight hours by tracking along a single axis. Trough systems provide the best land-use factor of any solar technology. The SEGS plants in California and Acciona's Nevada Solar One near Boulder City, Nevada are representatives of this technology. A parabolic dish system consists of a stand-alone parabolic reflector that concentrates light onto a receiver positioned at the reflector's focal point. The reflector tracks the Sun along two axes. Parabolic dish systems give the highest efficiency among CSP technologies. The 50 kW Big Dish in Canberra, Australia is an example of this technology.

A solar power tower uses an array of tracking reflectors (heliostats) to concentrate light on a central receiver atop a tower. Power towers are less advanced than trough systems but offer higher efficiency and better energy storage capability. The Solar Two in Barstow, California and the Planta Solar 10 in Sanlucar la Mayor, Spain are representatives of this technology.

Solar Chemical

Solar radiation stimulated chemical processes use solar energy to drive chemical reactions. They offset energy that would otherwise require an alternate source and can convert solar energy into a storable and transportable fuel. Solar induced chemical reactions can be divided into thermochemical or photochemical. Hydrogen production technologies involving the use of solar light have been a significant area of research since the 1970s. Aside from electrolysis driven by photovoltaic or photochemical cells, several thermochemical processes have been explored. One such route uses concentrators to split water at high temperatures (2300-2600 °C), but this process has been limited by complexity and low solar-to-hydrogen efficiency (1–2%). Another approach uses the heat from solar concentrators to drive the steam reformation of natural gas thereby increasing the overall hydrogen yield. Thermochemical cycles characterized by the decomposition and regeneration of reactants present another avenue for hydrogen production. The Solzinc process under development at the Weizmann Institute uses a 1 MW solar furnace to decompose zinc oxide (ZnO) at temperatures above 1200 °C. This initial reaction produces pure zinc, which can subsequently be reacted with water to produce hydrogen. Sandia's Sunshine to Petrol (S2P) technology uses the high temperatures generated by concentrating sunlight along with a zirconia/ferrite catalyst to break down atmospheric carbon dioxide into oxygen and carbon monoxide (CO). The carbon monoxide can then be used to synthesize methanol, gasoline and jet fuel. Photoelectrochemical cells or PECs consist of a semiconductor, typically titanium dioxide or related titanates, immersed in an electrolyte. When the semiconductor is illuminated an electrical potential develops. There are two types of photoelectrochemical cells: photoelectric cells that convert light into electricity and photochemical cells that use light to drive chemical reactions such as electrolysis. A photogalvanic device is a type of battery in which the cell solution (or equivalent) forms energy-rich chemical intermediates when illuminated. They then can react at the electrodes to produce an electric potential. The ferric-thionine chemical cell is an example of this technology.

Solar Vehicles

Australia hosts the World Solar Challenge where solar cars like the Nuna3 race through a 3,021 km (1,877 mi) course from Darwin to Adelaide. Development of a solar powered car has been an engineering goal since the 1980s. The World Solar Challenge is a biannual solar-powered car race, where teams from universities and enterprises compete over 3,021 kilometres (1,877 mi) across central Australia from Darwin to Adelaide. In 1987, when it was founded, the winner's average speed was 67 kilometres per hour (42 mph) and by 2007 the winner's average speed had improved to 90.87 kilometres per hour (56.46 mph). The North American Solar Challenge and the planned South African Solar Challenge are comparable competitions that reflect an international interest in the engineering and development of solar powered vehicles. In 1975, the first practical solar boat was constructed in England. By 1995, passenger boats incorporating PV panels began appearing and are now used extensively. In 1996, Kenichi Horie made the first solar powered crossing of the Pacific Ocean, and the sun21 catamaran made the first solar powered crossing of the Atlantic Ocean in the winter of 2006–07. There are plans to circumnavigate the globe in 2010. Helios UAV in solar powered flightIn 1974, the unmanned Sunrise II plane made the first solar flight. On 29 April 1979, the Solar Riser made the first flight in a solar powered, fully controlled, man carrying flying machine, reaching an altitude of 40 feet (12 m). In 1980, the Gossamer Penguin made the first piloted flights powered solely by photovoltaics. This was quickly followed by the Solar Challenger which crossed the English Channel in July 1981. In 1990 Eric Raymond in 21 hops flew from California to North Carolina using solar power. Developments then turned back to unmanned aerial vehicles (UAV) with the Pathfinder (1997) and subsequent designs, culminating in the Helios which set the altitude record for a non-rocket-propelled aircraft at 29,524 metres (96,860 ft) in 2001. The Zephyr, developed by BAE Systems, is the latest in a line of record-breaking solar aircraft, making a 54-hour flight in 2007, and month-long flights are envisioned by 2010. A solar balloon is a black balloon that is filled with ordinary air. As sunlight shines on the balloon, the air inside is heated and expands causing an upward buoyancy force, much like an artificially-heated hot air balloon. Some solar balloons are large enough for human flight, but usage is generally limited to the toy market as the surface-area to payload-weight ratio is relatively high. Solar sails are a proposed form of spacecraft propulsion using large membrane mirrors to exploit radiation pressure from the Sun. Unlike rockets, solar sails require no fuel. Although the thrust is small compared to rockets, it continues as long as the Sun shines onto the deployed sail and in the vacuum of space significant speeds can eventually be achieved. The High-altitude airship (HAA) is an unmanned, long-duration, lighter-than-air vehicle using helium gas for lift, and thin-film solar cells for power. The United States Department of Defense Missile Defense Agency has contracted Lockheed Martin to construct it to enhance the Ballistic Missile Defense System (BMDS). Airships have some advantages for solar-powered flight: they do not require power to remain aloft, and an airship's envelope presents a large area to the Sun.

Deployment of Solar Power to Energy Grids

Nellis Solar Power Plant, the largest photovoltaic power plant in North AmericaBeginning with the surge in coal use which accompanied the Industrial Revolution, energy consumption has steadily transitioned from wood and biomass to fossil fuels. The early development of solar technologies starting in the 1860s was driven by an expectation that coal would soon become scarce.

However development of solar technologies stagnated in the early 20th century in the face of the increasing availability, economy, and utility of coal and petroleum. The 1973 oil embargo and 1979 energy crisis caused a reorganization of energy policies around the world and brought renewed attention to developing solar technologies. Deployment strategies focused on incentive programs such as the Federal Photovoltaic Utilization Program in the US and the Sunshine Program in Japan. Other efforts included the formation of research facilities in the US (SERI, now NREL), Japan (NEDO), and Germany (Fraunhofer Institute for Solar Energy Systems ISE). Between 1970 and 1983 photovoltaic installations grew rapidly, but falling oil prices in the early 1980s moderated the growth of PV from 1984 to 1996. Since 1997, PV development has accelerated due to supply issues with oil and natural gas, global warming concerns, and the improving economic position of PV relative to other energy technologies. Photovoltaic production growth has averaged 40% per year since 2000 and installed capacity reached 10.6 GW at the end of 2007. Since 2006 it has been economical for investors to install photovoltaics for free in return for a long-term power purchase agreement. 50% of commercial systems were installed in this manner in 2007 and it is expected that 90% will by 2009. Nellis Air Force Base is receiving photoelectric power for about 2.2 ¢/kWh and grid power for 9 ¢/kWh.

Commercial solar water heaters began appearing in the United States in the 1890s. These systems saw increasing use until the 1920s but were gradually replaced by cheaper and more reliable heating fuels. As with photovoltaics, solar water heating attracted renewed attention as a result of the oil crises in the 1970s but interest subsided in the 1980s due to falling petroleum prices. Development in the solar water heating sector progressed steadily throughout the 1990s and growth rates have averaged 20% per year since 1999. Although generally underestimated, solar water heating is by far the most widely deployed solar technology with an estimated capacity of 154 GW as of 2007. Commercial concentrating solar power (CSP) plants were first developed in the 1980s. CSP plants such as SEGS project in the United States have a LEC of 12–14 ¢/kWh. The 11 MW PS10 power tower in Spain, completed in late 2005, is Europe's first commercial CSP system, and a total capacity of 300 MW is expected to be installed in the same area by 2013. Solar installations in recent years have also largely begun to expand into residential areas, with governments offering incentive programs to make "green" energy a more economically viable option. In Canada the government offers the RESOP (Renewable Energy Standard Offer Program). The program allows residential homeowners with solar panel installations to sell the energy they produce back to the grid (i.e., the government) at 41¢/kWh, while drawing power from the grid at an average rate of 20¢/kWh. The program is designed to help promote the government's green agenda and lower the strain often placed on the energy grid at peak hours. With the incentives offered by the program the average payback period for a residential solar installation (sized between 1.3 kW and 5 kW) is estimated at 18 to 23 years, considering such cost factors as parts, installation and maintenance, as well as the average energy production of a system on an annual basis. Daniel Lincot, the chairman of the 2008 European Photovoltaic Solar Energy Conference and the research director of the Paris-based Photovoltaic Energy Development and Research Institute, said that photovoltaics can cover all the world energy demand. Photovoltaics are 85 times as efficient as growing corn for ethanol. On a 300 feet by 300 feet (1 hectare) plot of land enough ethanol can be produced to drive a car 30,000 miles (48,000 km) per year or 2,500,000 miles (4,020,000 km) by covering the same land with photo cells.

Hydro Power

Hydropower, hydraulic power or water power is power that is derived from the force or energy of moving water, which may be harnessed for useful purposes. Prior to the widespread availability of commercial electric power, hydropower was used for irrigation, and operation of various machines, such as watermills, textile machines, and sawmills. A trompe produces compressed air from falling water, which could then be used to power other machinery at a distance from the water. Saint Anthony Falls Hydropower has been used for hundreds of years. In India, water wheels and watermills were built; in Imperial Rome, water powered mills produced flour from grain, and were also used for sawing timber and stone. The power of a wave of water released from a tank was used for extraction of metal ores in a method known as hushing. Hushing was widely used in Britain in the Medieval and later periods to extract lead and tin ores. It later evolved into hydraulic mining when used during the California gold rush.

In China and the rest of the Far East, hydraulically operated "pot wheel" pumps raised water into irrigation canals. In the 1830s, at the peak of the canal-building era, hydropower was used to transport barge traffic up and down steep hills using inclined plane railroads. Direct mechanical power transmission required that industries using hydropower had to locate near the waterfall. For example, during the last half of the 19th century, many grist mills were built at Saint Anthony Falls, utilizing the 50 foot (15 metre) drop in the Mississippi River. The mills contributed to the growth of Minneapolis. Hydraulic power networks also existed, using pipes carrying pressurized liquid to transmit mechanical power from a power source, such as a pump, to end users. Today the largest use of hydropower is for the creation of hydroelectricity, which allows low cost energy to be used at long distances from the water source.

Hydroelectricity

Hydraulic turbine and electrical generator.Hydroelectric power now supplies about 715,000 MWe or 19% of world electricity (16% in 2003). Large dams are still being designed. The world's largest is the Three Gorges Dam on the third longest river in the world, the Yangtzi River. Apart from a few countries with an abundance of hydro power, this energy source is normally applied to peak load demand, because it is readily stopped and started. It also provides a high-capacity, low-cost means of energy storage, known as "pumped storage". Hydropower produces essentially no carbon dioxide or other harmful emissions, in contrast to burning fossil fuels, and is not a significant contributor to global warming through CO_2. Hydroelectric power can be far less expensive than electricity generated from fossil fuels or nuclear energy. Areas with abundant hydroelectric power attract industry. Environmental concerns about the effects of reservoirs may prohibit development of economic hydropower sources. The chief advantage of hydroelectric dams is their ability to handle seasonal (as well as daily) high peak loads. When the electricity demands drop, the dam simply stores more water (which provides more flow when it releases). Some electricity generators use water dams to store excess energy (often during the night), by using the electricity to pump water up into a basin. Electricity can be generated when demand increases. In practice the utilization of stored water in river dams is sometimes complicated by demands for irrigation which may occur out of phase with peak electrical demands. Not all hydroelectric power requires a dam; a run-of-river project only uses part of the stream flow and is a characteristic of small hydropower projects. A developing technology example is the Gorlov helical turbine.

Small Scale Hydro Power

Small scale hydro or micro-hydro power has been increasingly used as an alternative energy source, especially in remote areas where other power sources are not viable. Small scale hydro power systems can be installed in small rivers or streams with little or no discernible environmental effect on things such as fish migration. Most small scale hydro power systems make no use of a dam or major water diversion, but rather use water wheels. There are some considerations in a micro-hydro system installation. The amount of water flow available on a consistent basis, since lack of rain can affect plant operation. Head, or the amount of drop between the intake and the exit. The more head, the more power that can be generated. There can be legal and regulatory issues, since most countries, cities, and states have regulations about water rights and easements.

Over the last few years, the U.S. Government has increased support for alternative power generation. Many resources such as grants, loans, and tax benefits are available for small scale hydro systems. In poor areas, many remote communities have no electricity. Micro hydro power, with a capacity of 100 kW or less, allows communities to generate electricity. This form of power is supported by various organizations such as the UK's Practical Action. Micro-hydro power can be used directly as "shaft power" for many industrial applications. Alternatively, the preferred option for domestic energy supply is to generate electricity with a generator or a reversed electric motor which, while less efficient, is likely to be available locally and cheaply.

There is a common misconception that economically developed nations have harnessed all of their available hydropower resources. In the United States, according to the US Department of Energy, "previous assessments have focused on potential projects having a capacity of 1 MW and above". This may partly explain the discrepancy. More recently, in 2004, an extensive survey was conducted by the US-DOE which counted sources under 1 MW (mean annual average), and found that only 40% of the total hydropower potential had been developed. A total of 170 GW (mean annual average) remains available for development. Of this, 34% is within the operating envelope of conventional turbines, 50% is within the operating envelope of microhydro technologies (defined as less than 100 kW), and 16% is within the operating envelope of unconventional systems. In 2005, the US generated 1012 kilo-watt hours of electricity. The total undeveloped hydropower resource is equivalent to about one-third of total US electricity generation in 2005. Developed hydropower accounted for 6.4% of total US electricity generated in 2005.

Tidal Power

Harnessing the tides in a bay or estuary has been achieved in France (since 1966), Canada and Russia, and could be achieved in other areas with a large tidal range. The trapped water turns turbines as it is released through the tidal barrage in either direction. A possible fault is that the system would generate electricity most efficiently in bursts every six hours (once every tide). This limits the applications of tidal energy; tidal power is highly predictable but not able to follow changing electrical demand.

A relatively new technology, tidal stream generators draw energy from currents in much the same way that wind generators do. The higher density of water means that a single generator can provide significant power. This technology is at the early stages of development and will require more research before it becomes a significant contributor. Several prototypes have shown promise.

Wave Power

Harnessing power from ocean surface wave motion might yield much more energy than tides. The feasibility of this has been investigated, particularly in Scotland in the UK. Generators either coupled to floating devices or turned by air displaced by waves in a hollow concrete structure would produce electricity. Numerous technical problems have frustrated progress.

A prototype shore based wave power generator is being constructed at Port Kembla in Australia and is expected to generate up to 500 MWh annually. The Wave Energy Converter has been constructed (as of July 2005) and initial results have exceeded expectations of energy production during times of low wave energy. Wave energy is captured by an air driven generator and converted to electricity. For countries with large coastlines and rough sea conditions, the energy of waves offers the possibility of generating electricity in utility volumes. Excess power during rough seas could be used to produce hydrogen.

Bio-fuel

Plants use photosynthesis to grow and produce biomass. Also known as biomatter, biomass can be used directly as fuel or to produce liquid bio-fuel. Agriculturally produced biomass fuels, such as biodiesel, ethanol and bagasse (often a by-product of sugar cane cultivation) can be burned in internal combustion engines or boilers. Typically bio-fuel is burned to release its stored chemical energy. Research into more efficient methods of converting bio-fuels and other fuels into electricity utilizing fuel cells is an area of very active work.

Liquid bio-fuel

Liquid bio-fuel is usually either a bio-alcohol such as ethanol fuel or a bio-oil such as biodiesel and straight vegetable oil. Biodiesel can be used in modern diesel vehicles with little or no modification to the engine and can be made from waste and virgin vegetable and animal oil and fats (lipids). Virgin vegetable oils can be used in modified diesel engines. In fact the Diesel engine was originally designed to run on vegetable oil rather than fossil fuel. A major benefit of biodiesel is lower emissions. The use of biodiesel reduces emission of carbon monoxide and other hydrocarbons by 20 to 40%.

In some areas corn, cornstalks, sugarbeets, sugar cane, and switchgrasses are grown specifically to produce ethanol (also known as grain alcohol) a liquid which can be used in internal combustion engines and fuel cells. Ethanol is being phased into the current energy infrastructure. E85 is a fuel composed of 85% ethanol and 15% gasoline that is sold to consumers. Bio-butanol is being developed as an alternative to bio-ethanol. There is growing international criticism about bio-fuels from food crops with respect to issues such as food security, environmental impacts (deforestation) and energy balance.

Solid Biomass

Solid biomass is mostly commonly usually used directly as a combustible fuel, producing 10-20 MJ/kg of heat. Its forms and sources include wood fuel, the biogenic portion of municipal solid waste, or the unused portion of field crops. Field crops may or may not be grown intentionally as an energy crop, and the remaining plant byproduct used as a fuel. Most types of biomass contain energy. Even cow manure still contains two-thirds of the original energy consumed by the cow. Energy harvesting via a bioreactor is a cost-effective solution to the waste disposal issues faced by the dairy farmer, and can produce enough biogas to run a farm. With current technology, it is not ideally suited for use as a transportation fuel. Most transportation vehicles require power sources with high power density, such as that provided by internal combustion engines. These engines generally require clean burning fuels, which are generally in liquid form, and to a lesser extent, compressed gaseous phase. Liquids are more portable because they have high energy density, and they can be pumped, which makes handling easier. This is why most transportation fuels are liquids.

Non-transportation applications can usually tolerate the low power-density of external combustion engines, which can run directly on less-expensive solid biomass fuel, for combined heat and power. One type of biomass is wood, which has been used for millennia in varying quantities, and more recently is finding increased use. Two billion people currently cook every day, and heat their homes in the winter by burning biomass, which is a major contributor to man-made climate change global warming.

The black soot that is being carried from Asia to polar ice caps is causing them to melt faster in the summer. In the 19th century, wood-fired steam engines were common, contributing significantly to industrial revolution unhealthy air pollution. Coal is a form of biomass that has been compressed over millennia to produce a non-renewable, highly-polluting fossil fuel.

Wood and its byproducts can now be converted through process such as gasification into bio-fuels such as woodgas, biogas, methanol or ethanol fuel; although further development may be required to make these methods affordable and practical. Sugar cane residue, wheat chaff, corn cobs and other plant matter can be, and are, burned quite successfully. The net carbon dioxide emissions that are added to the atmosphere by this process are only from the fossil fuel that was consumed to plant, fertilize, harvest and transport the biomass. Processes to harvest biomass from short-rotation poplars and willows, and perennial grasses such as switchgrass, phalaris, and miscanthus, require less frequent cultivation and less nitrogen than from typical annual crops. Pelletizing miscanthus and burning it to generate electricity is being studied and may be economically viable.

Biogas

Biogas can easily be produced from current waste streams, such as paper production, sugar production, sewage, animal waste and so forth. These various waste streams have to be slurried together and allowed to naturally ferment, producing methane gas. This can be done by converting current sewage plants into biogas plants. When a biogas plant has extracted all the methane it can, the remains are sometimes better suitable as fertilizer than the original biomass. Alternatively biogas can be produced via advanced waste processing systems such as mechanical biological treatment. These systems recover the recyclable elements of household waste and process the biodegradable fraction in anaerobic digesters. Renewable natural gas is a biogas which has been upgraded to a quality similar to natural gas. By upgrading the quality to that of natural gas, it becomes possible to distribute the gas to the mass market via gas grid.

Geothermal Energy

Geothermal energy is energy obtained by tapping the heat of the earth itself, usually from kilometers deep into the Earth's crust. It is expensive to build a power station but operating costs are low resulting in low energy costs for suitable sites. Ultimately, this energy derives from heat in the Earth's core. The government of Iceland states: "It should be stressed that the geothermal resource is not strictly renewable in the same sense as the hydro resource." It estimates that Iceland's geothermal energy could provide 1700 MW for over 100 years, compared to the current production of 140 MW. The International Energy Agency classifies geothermal power as renewable.

Three types of power plants are used to generate power from geothermal energy: dry steam, flash, and binary. Dry steam plants take steam out of fractures in the ground and use it to directly drive a turbine that spins a generator. Flash plants take hot water, usually at temperatures over 200°C, out of the ground, and allows it to boil as it rises to the surface then separates the steam phase in steam/water separators and then runs the steam through a turbine. In binary plants, the hot water flows through heat exchangers, boiling an organic fluid that spins the turbine. The condensed steam and remaining geothermal fluid from all three types of plants are injected back into the hot rock to pick up more heat.

The geothermal energy from the core of the Earth is closer to the surface in some areas than in others. Where hot underground steam or water can be tapped and brought to the surface it may be used to generate electricity. Such geothermal power sources exist in certain geologically unstable parts of the world such as Chile, Iceland, New Zealand, United States, the Philippines and Italy. The two most prominent areas for this in the United States are in the Yellowstone basin and in northern California. Iceland produced 170 MW geothermal power and heated 86% of all houses in the year 2000 through geothermal energy. Some 8000 MW of capacity is operational in total. There is also the potential to generate geothermal energy from hot dry rocks. Holes at least 3 km deep are drilled into the earth. Some of these holes pump water into the earth, while other holes pump hot water out. The heat resource consists of hot underground radiogenic granite rocks, which heat up when there is enough sediment between the rock and the earths surface. Several companies in Australia are exploring this technology.

Renewable Energy Commercialization

Renewable energy systems encompass a broad, diverse array of technologies, and the current status of these can vary considerably. Some technologies are already mature and economically competitive (e.g. geothermal and hydropower), others need additional development to become competitive without subsidies. This can be helped by improvements to sub-components, such as electric generators.

	2001 energy costs	Potential future energy cost
Electricity		
Wind	4–8 ¢/kWh	3–10 ¢/kWh
Solar PV	25–160 ¢/kWh	5–25 ¢/kWh
Solar Thermal	12–34 ¢/kWh	4–20 ¢/kWh
Large Hydropower	2–10 ¢/kWh	2–10 ¢/kWh
Small Hydropower	2–12 ¢/kWh	2–10 ¢/kWh
Geothermal	2–10 ¢/kWh	1–8 ¢/kWh
Biomass	3–12 ¢/kWh	4–10 ¢/kWh
Coal	4 ¢/kWh	
Heat		
Geothermal	0.5–5 ¢/kWh	0.5–5 ¢/kWh
Bioamss	1–6 ¢/kWh	1–5 ¢/kWh
Solar	2–25 ¢/kWh	2–10 ¢/kWh

The table shows an overview of costs of various renewable energy technologies. For comparison with the prices in the table, electricity production from a conventional coal-fired plant costs about 4¢/kWh. Though in some G8 nations the cost can be significantly higher at 7.88p (~15¢/kWh). Achieving further cost reductions as indicated in the table below requires further technology development, market deployment, an increase in production capacities to mass production levels, and of the establishment of an emissions trading scheme and/or carbon tax which would attribute a cost to each unit of carbon emitted; thus reflecting the true cost of energy production by fossil fuels which then could be used to lower the cost/kWh of these renewable energies.

Index